Visitor's Guide
France
DORDOGNE

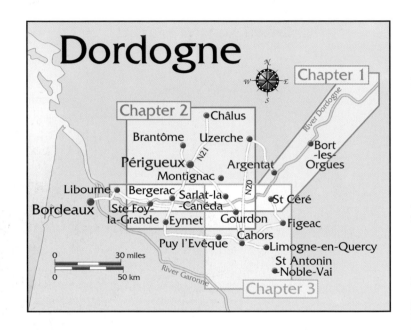

Dordogne

Chapter 1

Chapter 2

Chapter 3

- Châlus
- Brantôme
- Uzerche
- Bort -les- Orgues
- Périgueux
- Argentat
- Montignac
- Libourne
- Bergerac
- Sarlat-la- -Canéda
- St Céré
- Bordeaux
- Ste Foy- la-Grande
- Eymet
- Gourdon
- Figeac
- Puy l'Evêque
- Cahors
- Limogne-en-Quercy
- St Antonin Noble-Vai

River Dordogne

River Garonne

N21

N20

| 0 | 30 miles |
| 0 | 50 km |

Visitor's Guide

FRANCE
DORDOGNE

Barbara Mandell

MPC®
HUNTER

Published by: Moorland Publishing Co Ltd,
Moor Farm Road West, Ashbourne, Derbyshire DE6 1HD England

Published in the USA by: Hunter Publishing Inc,
300 Raritan Center Parkway, CN94, Edison, NJ 08818

ISBN 0 86190 607 1

1st edition 1986, 2nd revised edition 1990
3rd revised edition 1994, 4th revised and redesigned edition 1996

British Library Cataloguing in Publication Data:
A catalogue record for this book is available from the British Library

Colour origination by: Scantrans, Singapore and GA Graphics, Stamford

Printed in Spain by: GraphyCems

Front cover: Château de Milandres *(MPC Picture Collection)*
Title page: Monpazier *(MPC Picture Collection)*

Illustrations have been supplied by: Clermont-Ferrand Regional Tourist Office:
p35 (bottom); Office Départemental de Tourisme de la Dordogne: 123; Martin
Gray: pp35 (top), 38, 39 (top), 50, 51, 59, 62, 66, 67, 70, 74, 78, 114 (top), 134, 143,
146, 151, 159, 171, 174, 179; Limoges Regional Tourist Office: p42; Comité
Départemental du Tourisme du Lot: pp139, 147, 275; P. Whitaker: pp15, 23, 27;
MPC Picture Collection: pp7, 31, 39 (bottom), 43, 54, 83, 95, 99, 103, 106, 110, 111,
114 (bottom), 118, 122.

Acknowledgements
The author would like to thank all those who gave help and advice in both
Périgord and Quercy, particularly Rémi Lassaigne of the Office Départemen-
tal de Tourisme de la Dordogne in Périgueux, Alain Conseil in Brantôme, M.
Audibert in Siorac-en-Périgord and Caroline Fournereau and Christiane
Chassagne, both of the Comité Départemental du Tourisme du Lot in Cahors.

Contents

Key — Symbols

⊓ **Archaeological Site**
🏰 **Castle/Fortification**
🏛 **Museum/Art Gallery**
⛪ **Church**
🦇 **Cave**

🏢 **Building of Interest**
✳ **Other Place of Interest**
🦌 **Nature / Wildlife Reserve**
▲ **Mountain**
🌄 **Beautiful View/Natural Phenomenon**

Topography

Lake
City   Main Road   River   Minor Road   Village
Town   Wooded Areas

How To Use This Guide

This MPC Visitor's Guide has been designed to be as easy to use as possible. Each chapter covers a region or itinerary in a natural progression which gives all the background information to help you enjoy your visit. MPC's distinctive margin symbols, the important places printed in bold, and a comprehensive index enable the reader to find the most interesting places to visit with ease.

At the end of each chapter an Additional Information section gives specific details such as addresses and opening times, making this guide a complete sightseeing companion.

At the back of the guide the Fact File, arranged in alphabetical order, gives practical information and useful tips to help you plan your holiday before you go and while you are there.

The maps of each region show the main towns, villages, roads, and places of interest, but are not designed as route maps and motorists should always use a good recommended road atlas.

Introduction

The name Dordogne means different things to different people. Firstly it is the river, among the most historic waterways in France, which rises high up in the Massif Central and makes its way by easy stages down to the Atlantic north of Bordeaux. Then there is the *département*, created in 1790 and one of the largest in France. It occupies the north-eastern corner of Aquitane, bounded by the provinces of Poitou-Charentes, Limousin and Midi-Pyrénées and its fellow *départements* of Gironde and Lot-et-Garonne. Finally it is the name given these days to an even more extensive, but seldom clearly defined, area. It is not unknown for newcomers to Lot or even Aveyron to stretch the boundary even further by insisting that they live in the Dordogne.

To the indigenous population saying that one lives in the Dordogne means nothing whatsoever — as far as they are concerned this can only apply to the creatures that actually live in the water. The region is still known as Périgord and its inhabitants are Périgourdins. To describe them as Dordognais is totally inaccurate although the uninitiated may occasionally fall into this trap. However the *départements* of Dordogne and Lot have been so closely linked for centuries as Périgord and Quercy that even modern brochures may sometimes treat them as a single entity. As with most areas of France there are very few signs to show where one region ends and the next

Previous page: Puppets at Domme

begins so the traveller can be forgiven for ignoring these borders.

In the days when the world was young the whole of France, with southern England, Italy, south-eastern Europe and parts of North Africa, was beneath the sea. Gradually land masses were thrown up, continents began to take shape and the Mediterranean shrank to more or less its present size. The Atlantic was pushed back from the area between the Pyrénées and the peaks of the Massif Central, leaving behind limestone deposits which slowly emerged as plateaux, now known as the Causses. Heathlands came next and by the time rivers such as the Dordogne, the Vézère and the Lot appeared the whole region was beginning to look a little like it does today.

The volcanoes, which were extremely active in central France some 50 million years ago, subsequently became extinct, although there was a final outburst in northern Auvergne which left craters that are a mere 10 million years old. During the Ice Age there were periods of intense cold with vast glaciers and mountains sheathed in ice which melted during warmer interludes, pouring water, rocks and other debris down onto the lower ground, turning it into a sodden waste.

As the rivers and streams forced their way through faults in the limestone crust they created wider and wider valleys, covering them eventually with fertile soil. The uplands remained rather flat and arid because, despite quite heavy rainfall, the water soaked through the porous surface. This appeared later as springs and rivulets which in turn gouged out new courses for themselves. The result was a series of narrow valleys, sometimes with almost perpendicular sides and overhanging rocks where the water, having failed to make much impression on the granite outcrops, worked its way through softer ground underneath.

Time and the elements combined to create an apparently endless number of caves, indentations and grottoes, usually close to the river banks. They were used initially as shelters by animals such as mammoths, rhinos, bison and bears. Quantities of bones have been discovered of species which either died out or migrated during the last great Ice Age. The herds of reindeer which headed south in search of food and warmer weather brought prehistoric hunters in their wake and it was not long before they turned these shelters into makeshift homes.

About 30,000 years ago they got the idea of drawing on the walls. The first pictures were very primitive, hardly more than a series of lines scratched with a sharp flint. With practice the artists of the time learned to use the contours of the rock to produce a three-dimensional effect, a bump for a haunch or a curve along the line of a back. Natural red and yellow pigments were added and the softer texture of hair or fur was suggested by blowing on the colour through a hollow reed or a reindeer horn.

Over the centuries a damp film spread across the walls which then dried, preserving both the paintings and the original colours in much the same way as varnish does on oils. Even when seen in the glare of a torch or an electric light the animals are amazingly lifelike, but in the flickering light of a candle they appear to move in the same way as they must have done when the artists were working on them in the glow from a fire. Sadly the numbers of visitors who were allowed to see them created unfavourable conditions, the paintings began to deteriorate and Lascaux, generally agreed to be the most magnificent collection so far discovered anywhere in the world, was forced to close.

Other caves and galleries have never been opened to the public. There are nearly fifty known sites of this kind in the vicinity of the Vézère Valley alone, between Tayac in the north-east and Limeuil where the river joins the Dordogne. Only fifteen of them can be visited, apart from Lascaux II. This is a faithful reproduction of part of the original caves down to the very last bump and curve. It took 10 years to create out of an old quarry almost next door and even here the number of visitors allowed in is rigidly controlled. Other caves have been discovered south of the Dordogne and in the valley of the Lot where the most memorable is the Grotte du Pech-Merle near Cabrerets.

The Vézère is only one of a good many rivers that find their way into the Dordogne and the Lot. The Dronne, the Isle and the Cère all help to swell the Dordogne while the

Célé, perhaps the most enchanting of them all, twists and turns between wooded hillsides on its journey through Figeac to join the Lot just to the west of St Cirq-Lapopie.

As the early weather conditions improved so did the vegetation. The Causses still cannot support much more than scrub, juniper bushes, lavender with a few stunted trees, but at slightly lower altitudes there are ancient forests of oak and chestnuts interspersed with walnuts and newly-planted pines. Poplars line the river banks, vineyards march along the hillsides and the farming areas are divided up between a variety of crops, meadows and grazing lands. Cereals, sunflowers, maize and tobacco are grown extensively while orchards provide many different types of fruit to augment the large quantities of melons and strawberries that grow in areas where the soil is ideal for them. Wild flowers in their millions add colour to the countryside and there is no shortage of birds or small animals in the less populated areas.

Industry is something one does not really associate with either Périgord or Quercy. Some of the larger towns have their own factories turning out things like shoes or textiles, cement or even postage stamps, but this is the exception rather than the rule. On the other hand, more and more craftsmen have been opening up small workshops, concentrating on such items as pottery, wrought iron and woodwork which may be either functional or simply decorative.

Foie gras, truffles and walnuts are the three products most closely associated with the region and its traditional recipes. Chestnuts are used for anything from *marron glacé* and stuffing to animal fodder whereas walnuts provide, among other things, oil which is perfect for salads and for cooking. Every homestead seems to have a small flock of geese and these appear regularly on the menu in one form or another quite apart from *foie gras*. Truffles are seasonal and expensive so their place is frequently taken by a variety of delicious mushrooms. Nature has been extremely kind to the region in some respects and the inhabitants have always been quick to appreciate the fact.

Neither Périgord nor Lot could ever be described as over populated, especially on the Causses where life can be hard and not particularly rewarding. Many people have moved into urban areas or into the valleys, leaving semi-deserted hamlets behind them. Nevertheless a cobweb of minor roads and byways covers the whole region, linking small communities, isolated farmsteads and outlying tourist attractions. These are augmented by busy highways and quite a few secondary roads which carry a certain amount of traffic in the high season, but nothing of any real consequence during the rest of the year. Even some scenic roads that keep company with the main rivers are seldom crowded.

The region is hilly rather than mountainous, especially to the east, but levels out as the last vestiges of the Massif Central blend into the plains of Aquitaine. Most of the population congregates in towns like Cahors, Périgueux and Bergerac and, to a lesser extent, Gourdon, Figeac and Sarlat-la-Canéda. However with the slight, though steady, growth in tourism more people are moving into the attractive waterside villages. There is also an ever-increasing demand for second homes, especially in Quercy where it is said that more than half the houses fall into this category. A typical home in Périgord tends to be either square and solid, rather low, or even half timbered, whereas in Lot they are inclined to have somewhat more atmosphere. They are generally built of white limestone with storerooms and perhaps a garage on the ground floor, living quarters above and even a small tower or a turret complete with a pointed roof.

Other features, apart from the dolmens and megaliths, are strange little stone constructions, not unlike outsize beehives, which are sometimes attributed to the Romans. The idea may well have originated in those days but it is hard to believe that they were built so many years ago. Even more eye-catching are the dovecotes which have little or nothing in common with the ones seen in Britain. Some look like small two-storey towers, others are just as solid but stand on sturdy columns well above the ground while a third variety may be attached to a main building or even to the house itself. The idea was to collect the pigeons' droppings which were an extremely valuable source of manure.

Bearing in mind that the whole region served as a battle ground from the Roman invasion onwards it is hardly surprising that it is littered with ancient castles and fortifications. Some are in ruins, others have been carefully restored and yet more were adapted at various times to provide elegant country houses resplendent with painted ceilings, intricate wood carvings and beautiful furniture and tapestries. Many of them are still in private hands, but a fair proportion open to the public, mainly in the high season. During the Hundred Years' War both the English and the French built what are known as *bastides*. These are small fortified villages, all more or less on the same plan, except where they had to be adapted to suit the terrain, and were comparatively easy to defend. They were usually square or rectangular with parallel streets intersected at right angles. The church was located near to the centre, overlooking or adjacent to the market place which was surrounded with arcades and overlooked by houses belonging to wealthy merchants. The whole village was enclosed in high walls and reached through fortified gateways, usually with a watch tower where sentries could be posted in times of trouble. Some have changed very little since the thirteenth or fourteenth centuries, although others have spilled over into the surrounding countryside without changing their character to any great extent. The best examples are Monpazier which was founded by the English, Domme which was built by the French and Eymet which owes its existence to Alphonse de Poitiers, but changed hands with almost monotonous regularity before Louis XIII ordered the ramparts to be pulled down. Villefranche-de-Rouergue and Villeneuve-sur-Lot are two other interesting examples further afield.

The people of Lot and Périgord, the latter in particular, are so used to having foreigners on their doorsteps that they hardly notice them. Indeed there are some unusual little buildings that are known simply as Les Maisons Anglaises because they are not traditional and therefore must have been the work of the English at some time or another! It is also possible to meet a Frenchman who insists that he is partly English because one of his ancestors mixed pleasure with business while following in the steps of the Black Prince.

This neighbourly attitude does not, of course, extend to the language. Even in areas with a good many foreign residents — such as the British around Ribérac or the Dutch in the Périgueux area — it is both necessary and courteous to attempt a few words in French. In outlying districts this can be essential so a dictionary never comes amiss.

HISTORY

Although no single spot on earth can be pinpointed as the birthplace of mankind the Dordogne area comes very high up in the stakes. The French started to take an interest in prehistory at the beginning of the nineteenth century and chose the Vézère Valley as a place which might provide the evidence necessary for their theories. Edouard Lartet, who died in 1871, was among the first scientists to discover traces of human habitation going back more than 150,000 years. Of course similar finds were made elsewhere in the world, as far apart as China and South Africa, but when it came to classifying various stages of development and some of the different types that emerged they were given the names of appropriate sites in the area. The Tayacian period, from Les Eyzies-de-Tayac, and the Mousterian and the Magdalenian periods are three which are easy to identify.

The first inhabitants of Périgord knew how to use fire and make rough tools by chipping flint. Neanderthal man took this a stage further and when Homo-Sapiens eventually replaced him the stage was set for making jewellery and painting the walls of caves. With the onset of warmer weather the tribes which had migrated south to avoid the worst excesses of the last great Ice Age slowly started to move north again and their place was taken by immigrants from Spain and Italy. The practice of living in caves and shelters persisted, and in fact still does today, but the newcomers were inclined to be superstitious and much less gifted artistically. Many of the more inaccessible grottoes with their treasure troves of weapons, tools and bones were abandoned and before long the entrances became blocked with natural debris and overgrown.

In the sixth century BC the Celts invaded Gaul, intermarried, settled down and soon became fully integrated in areas such as the mountainous region to the north-west where they became known as the *Arvernes*. By the time the Romans arrived the local population had re-formed itself into tribes such as the *Petrocorii* and the *Caducci*. They fought valiantly against the invading legions but were no match for Caesar and were finally defeated at *Uxcellodunum* in 51BC.

The Romans immediately began to consolidate their position, building towns and settlements, erecting fortifications and introducing new ideas and customs. Several of the larger towns like Périgueux and Cahors date from this era. In AD16 the Emperor Augustus rationalised the administrative regions under his control. He did this in the south-west by extending Aquitaine northwards from its border on the River Garonne to take in everything south of the Loire which included Berry, most of the Massif Central and even the Cévennes. It might have seemed a good idea at the time but it was to produce endless complications in the centuries that followed. The various regions had their own capitals such as *Vesunna*, now Périgueux, and *Divona Cadurcorum* which was abbreviated first to *Cadurca* and then to Cahors. This was part of the trouble because none of them could see any good reason for kowtowing to the others and made their feelings quite obvious whenever possible.

During the third century AD the Alemans and the Franks invaded the area and, for the moment at least, local rivalries were forgotten. Roman structures were pulled down to reinforce the existing fortifications, but in spite of this a great many towns and villages were destroyed. With the introduction of Christianity conditions became even more chaotic as bishops and archbishops jockeyed for positions of authority and wealth. Things were in a sorry state when the Roman Empire collapsed, leaving behind a number of typical buildings such as temples and baths as well as vineyards and a great many chestnut, walnut and cherry trees. In no time at all the Franks and the Visigoths were at each others' throats, much to the dismay of the local population, who once more hid wherever possible in convenient caves and grottoes. After the Battle of Vouillé, near Poitiers, in 507 Aquitaine found itself with a new overlord — Clovis, the king of the Franks, who included Périgord and Quercy in his spoils of war.

The Saracens made a brief appearance in the early part of the eighth century, when they captured and burned down Bordeaux, but they were unable to sustain their attack and soon returned from whence they came. The main source of trouble was that the Frankish kings, Pepin I and Pepin II, were constantly at odds with the Dukes of Aquitaine, regardless of which local family happened to own the title at the time. Even Charlemagne, the son of Pepin the Short, was unable to find a satisfactory long-term solution before he died in 814. Predictably the remainder of the ninth century was just as unpleasant, especially when the Vikings invaded the French Atlantic seaboard and forced their way up rivers like the Dordogne and the Isle, spreading death and destruction everywhere. By the time the Norsemen had settled down and become more or less law abiding Normans, Périgord and Quercy were in the hands of a number of powerful families who continued to feud and fight amongst themselves. Many can still be recalled by looking at a map, having given their names to towns like Gourdon, Mareuil and Turenne and strongholds such as Bourdeilles, Biron and Castelnau.

When William of Normandy conquered England in 1066 the seeds were sown for a power struggle that was to last, on and off, for more than 300 years. It started with the marriage of his grandson Henry Plantagenet, the Count of Anjou, to Eleanor of Aquitaine. She had inherited the whole region from her father, recovered it intact from the French king, Louis VII after their divorce, and then presented it to her new husband, before he succeeded to the English throne as Henry II.

Not unnaturally, the most powerful and important local families objected strongly to being handed from one king to another and the years that followed were anything but peaceful. Two of Henry and Eleanor's sons, Henri Court-Mantel and Richard Coeur de Lion, were constantly capturing, burning and looting with an occasional break for high-level discussions which ended in agreements that were not worth the parchment they were written on. After Richard's death at Chalus in 1199 it was the turn of Simon de Montfort to indulge in widespread murder and mayhem. For 20 years he led a crusade against the heretics of Albi, a Christian sect who aimed for perfection on earth instead of in heaven and had no time for the Church of Rome or for its teachings. This quite naturally upset the Pope and provided an excellent excuse for attacking anyone who was out of favour on the grounds that they might possibly be helping the Albigeoise.

In 1259 Périgord and Quercy were ceded to the English by the saintly Louis IX under the Treaty of Paris and an uneasy peace ensued. However, when the last of the French Capetain kings died and was succeeded by Philip VI, who was a Valois, England's Edward III decided that he had a better right to the throne and proclaimed himself King of France. The battle for Aquitaine was joined and so began the Hundred Years' War. These turbulant centuries were appropriately known as the Dark Ages.

After one or two early French successes and a resounding English victory at Crécy the Black Death brought a temporary end to hostilities. They were resumed when the people of Bordeaux, mindful of their lucrative wine trade with England, appealed to Edward for help. The Black Prince set sail immediately and took King

A typical village in the Dordogne

Jean II prisoner at the Battle of Poitiers in 1356. This called for fresh negotiations which resulted in the Treaty of Brétigny 5 years later under which Jean II was released; England held on to a sizable chunk of Aquitaine but Edward renounced his right to the French throne. Périgord and Quercy were both in the territory stretching from Poitiers to the Spanish frontier and therefore were part of the deal. With the excep-

tion of a few minor upsets the peace held for about 9 years. Then the French, under Bertrand Du Guesclin, recovered Périgord, the local war-lords came down on one side or the other and fighting resumed.

After the Battle of Agincourt Henry V of England, who had married the French king's daughter, Catherine de Valois, was recognised as the future king of France and the country was parcelled out again —

this time between Henry, the Duke of Burgundy and the Dauphin who was given the central area and Languedoc. Two years later Henry was dead, the Dauphin proclaimed himself king and Joan of Arc, inspired by her voices, put fresh backbone into her countrymen. Even after she was captured and put to death the fighting continued and eventually the Hundred Years' War ended with the French victory at the Battle of Castillon, near Bordeaux, in 1453.

By this time much of Périgord and Quercy lay in ruins. The population was so depleted that reinforcements had to be brought in from surrounding areas to rebuild the towns and villages and to work on the land. It would be logical to suppose that they had learned their lesson, but logic does not come into it. In 1562 it was the turn of the Catholics and Protestants to plunge the country into bloodshed once again, starting with the wholesale massacre of Protestants in Cahors. This religious enmity continued to fester below the surface until 1570 when war was declared. Towns such as Bergerac sided with Henry of Navarre, while Périgueux and Cahors remained staunchly Catholic. Two years later Catherine de Medici and her supporters decided that enough was enough and persuaded Charles IX to strike. A large number of Huguenots had travelled to Paris for the marriage of Henry of Navarre and on St Bartholomew's Day, 24 August 1572, the order was given to exterminate them. The massacre spread quickly to the provinces and contin-

ued unabated until the beginning of October by which time 25,000 to 50,000 had been killed.

With the Wars of Religion under way, fortified castles, towns and villages were captured and recaptured and appalling atrocities committed by both sides. In 1593 Henry of Navarre was converted to Catholicism in order to become King of France but he kept faith with the Huguenots and 5 years later they were given freedom of worship and guaranteed security in centres like Montauban under the Edict of Nantes. However this did not improve matters very much in Périgord and Quercy where the peasants were so impoverished and down-trodden that they twice rose in revolt, burning and lynching without mercy. When the Edict of Nantes was revoked in 1685 the Huguenots left France in their thousands and because they were mainly artisans and labourers this made the whole position considerably worse.

The Revolution, which broke out in 1789, the same year that George Washington became the first President of the United States, brought little respite to the area. The men went off to fight for Napoleon and the rest were left to get on as best they could. Shortly after this Quercy was reorganised to become the *département* of Lot, but that also had a limited life because in 1808 Bonaparte, who was emperor by this time, hived off a good deal of Bas-Quercy to create Tarn-et-Garonne.

After Napoleon was defeated at the Battle of Waterloo, Périgord and

Lot took very little notice as one Bourbon monarch succeeded another in Paris. However Bergerac raised objections, which were dealt with by sending in troops and packing the ringleaders off to the colonies. An outbreak of phylloxera which destroyed many of the vineyards between Bordeaux and Lot resulted in even more widespread unemployment so the return of the House of Bonaparte passed almost unnoticed and so did World War I.

After the defeat of France by Nazi Germany in 1940, Périgord and Lot were in the unoccupied zone, ostensibly controlled by the Petain government from Vichy. This time the region took an extremely active interest in affairs. It became a major centre for the Resistance Movement and at the time of the D-Day invasion vast quantities of arms and equipment were dropped and hidden away in caves and grottoes which had proved equally useful during the Hundred Years' War. Groups such as Bir Hakeim harried the re treating Germans who retaliated by destroying villages, massacring some of the inhabitants and deporting others to the labour camps and gas chambers of the Fatherland.

With the return of peace, men like the author André Malraux, who had been head of the Free French Intelligence and was appointed Minister of Culture, made a determined effort to restore some of the damaged towns and villages. But despite everything that could be done to help them, Périgord and more especially Lot, were faced with a battle against poverty and unemployment. A few small factories were opened in Périgord and craftsmen reappeared in Lot where they set up small workshops in several of the picturesque waterside hamlets. The vineyards are recovering slowly, traditional crops are being harvested and more and more attention is being paid to the needs of tourists, both by way of hotels and sporting facilities. Given time and a certain amount of good luck there is no reason why these regions should not achieve a satisfactory degree of prosperity without losing any of the characteristics that distinguish them from other popular tourist areas in France.

ACCOMMODATION

There is no shortage of accommodation in either Périgord or Lot, except in the most popular tourist resorts at the height of the season when it is advisable to book in advance. Visitors who are touring the area should keep an eye open for likely stopping places towards the end of the afternoon, particularly if they have definite requirements such as a private bath or a room which is accessible to the disabled. Some establishments have lifts or rooms on the ground floor but they are in the minority in smaller towns and villages.

Prices are displayed on the back of the door and are calculated on the basis of two people sharing. In the absence of a single room one person will pay more than half the stated price for a double, but less than half is added if a third member of the party shares the room.

Bolsters, which can be soft or hard and lumpy, are still the norm in France. However the vast majority of hotels and *logis* provide ordinary pillows as well. They are usually tucked away in the cupboard, or are supplied on request, but anyone planning to visit places well off the beaten track, and needing a soft pillow, should take their own.

Guests who book in for the night are not obliged to have dinner on the premises, but if there are a lot of tourists about preference may be given to those who have a meal as well. In the case of restaurants that also have accommodation it is tactful to ask if there is a free table first and then enquire about a room, almost as an afterthought. Many small hotels close for one day a week but this does not affect those already in residence, although they will have to go elsewhere for lunch and dinner. Most, but not all, hotels offer a continental breakfast which is not included in the price of the room except where stated otherwise.

Hotels, like restaurants, furnished accommodation and campsites are divided into different categories according to the amenities on offer, and they charge accordingly. However there is no guarantee that the larger and often more expensive hotels will be preferable to smaller ones. These are frequently owned and run by members of a family who take great pride in making their guests comfortable and serving a wide range of delicious local dishes.

Campsites

There are many campsites ranging from large, well equipped ones with an wide range of facilities to a field allocated by a local farmer for the purpose. Some of these at the top of the market provide bungalows, mobile homes and caravans as well as individual pitches and areas set aside for tents. Even those which have space for several hundred people are usually crowded at the height of the season so do not turn up unannounced in the late afternoon.

Amenities vary considerably, both on the site and in the surrounding area. They may include a swimming pool or bathing in the river, tennis, mini-golf, riding, fishing, canoeing and other sports, plus a small food shop, a bar, a restaurant and take away food. Some sites are open all through the year, while others close at the end of the tourist season. The main information offices in both Périgord and Lot have comprehensive lists with all relevant details.

Gîtes & Meublés

Generally speaking *gîtes* tend to be individual country cottages while *meublés* are more likely to be furnished accommodation in towns and villages. However, whether they are apartments, a self-contained section of a mansion or a farmhouse, or even a bungalow in a holiday village, they all have certain things in common. Each one is furnished and designed for people catering for themselves. Some may have central heating and include such items as a washing machine and a dish washer while others may provide a stove, but not an oven.

Most furnished accommodation is let by the week and provides for about six people. *Gîtes* are extremely popular with holidaymakers and are usually booked up well in advance. Some are even reserved from one year to the next. It is therefore essential to contact the relevant tourist office well in advance.

Hotels

Hotels in France are graded according to their amenities, the general atmosphere and the standard of service they provide. Lot and Périgord have few if any five-star establishments with all the expensive luxuries one would expect to find in Paris or on the Côte d'Azur. Nor are there many of the four-star variety that do not reach quite the same peak of excellence. However there are quite a few very comfortable hotels in centres like Périgueux, Cahors, Brantôme, Bergerac, Figeac and Rocamadour as well as a sprinkling of converted castles and elegant country mansions. These are usually up-market, standing in their own parks and gardens or perched on a rock overlooking one of the main rivers. Next in order come a whole host of two-star establishments which may well have bedrooms en suite, but not necessarily a lift or reception rooms. Finally there are the little places which are quite acceptable, but devoid of frills, and others that are really basic, but usually spotless and occasionally full of atmosphere.

Logis & Auberges

These are the traditional medium sized or small family-run hotels of France. They all belong to their own association, are governed by a quality charter that ensures certain standards, and frequently are noted for their menus based on seasonal produce and traditional recipes. Each one displays a distinctive sign — a yellow chimney piece with a fire burning underneath set in an green shield. There are something like 700 *auberges* and about 4,000 *logis* all over France which are listed in *Logis et Auberges de France*, available from tourist offices. This gives the locations, telephone numbers and current prices. It is possible to book in advance by writing to the owner and enclosing a deposit which will be deducted from the bill, but is not refunded if the visit is postponed or cancelled. Guests are very seldom disappointed in an *auberge* or *logis*.

Other Accommodation

Chambres d'hôtes and *tables d'hôtes* correspond more or less to bed and breakfast establishments elsewhere. They accept guests for the night as well as by the week and will often provide additional meals if requested. They can be easily recognised by their circular medallion showing a bed and a cooking pot under one roof with a smoking chimney, or simply by an ordinary sign-post at the side of the road. They also advertise through the tourist offices, giving addresses, telephone numbers and prices.

Fermes-auberges do not necessarily have rooms to let but they provide a choice of country menus consisting of regional specialities like soup, duck, cheese and fruit accompanied by local wine at reasonable prices. Other farms which reserve special places for tents and caravans can be expected to have fresh produce for sale but should not be relied upon to serve meals as well.

Fermes des séjours accept visitors into their homes as paying guests, sometimes encouraging them to take part in the everyday life of the farm if they feel so inclined. Some organise special courses in such things as producing traditional pottery, prepare local dishes, painting, woodwork, metal work or even music.

Sports enthusiasts can find places which are geared to their own individual requirements. For example, fishermen can book into riverside *logis* and *auberges* where mealtimes are more flexible. Some may provide alternative attractions for other members of the family. There are also overnight stopping places at strategic intervals along the Grandes Randonnées, bridle paths, cycle routes and stretches of river suitable for longer trips in a kayak or a canoe. They are usually small hotels, but in isolated places they may be little more than a mountain refuge.

Other specific types of accommodation include youth hostels for young people on a budget, and special centres where children can be left safely while their parents are away on expeditions such as potholing. Details of these different options are available from tourist offices, but only the Loisirs-Accueil will handle bookings. There is usually someone on the staff who speaks English and they seldom make any charge except occasionally for telephone calls.

FAIRS, FÊTES & FESTIVALS

These vary as much in Périgord and Lot as elsewhere. The most atmospheric is the traditional Félibrée, held each July in a different town in Périgord. The centre whose turn it is decorates all the streets and houses with paper flowers of every imaginable colour. The trees are festooned with them, shrubs blossom in a way nature never intended and floral arches appear in unlikely places. The crowds who gather from all over the *département* are often dressed in traditional costumes. The men wear mainly black velvet jerkins, white shirts and large black hats, while the women wear long skirts, beautifully embroidered shawls and extremely becoming lace veils and headdresses. The queen of the day, surrounded by her retinue, accepts the keys of the town before a procession sets off to the sound of music to attend mass at the local church. The banquet that follows is an even more boisterous affair at which traditional soup is served in special plates that are treasured afterwards as souvenirs.

Nearly every small town and village celebrates its own saint's day with almost as much enthusiasm, but fewer decorations, whereas the larger centres hold festivals ranging from drama to classical concerts, folk music and jazz. The first of these annual events is the Fair of Kings in Brive-la-Gaillarde in early January, held ostensibly in honour of the Magi although it is actually more concerned with truffles. Figeac has its May Fair while St Emilion has a New Wine Festival in June. July and August are crammed with events such as a Blues Festival in Cahors and concerts of various descriptions in Souillac, Brantôme, Turenne, Cénevières, Beaulieu-en-Rouergue and St-Céré among others. Sarlat and Gourdon stage drama festivals, Montignac makes a feature of its International Folklore gatherings towards the end of July and Rocamadour is the focal point of a pilgrimage in early September. It would be impossible to list all the events such as the August Craft Festival in Bonaguil and Gourdon's September Village Music Festival, or even Carjac which is in festive mood almost continuously from June until September. However the tourist offices have comprehensive lists with precise dates for all the celebrations, both large and small, including the *foie gras* and walnut festivals that take place in the winter.

FOOD & DRINK

Every region of France has its own specialities, particularly of food, drink and souvenirs, and Périgord and Quercy are no exceptions.

Food

Périgord and Lot are considered to be among the leading gastronomic areas of France. Local *pâtés* were literally food for kings from the fifteenth century onwards and even at the time of the Revolution the new regime saw no reason to guillotine this admirable delicacy. However the famous *foie gras*, made with goose liver and truffles, was only perfected at the beginning of the eighteenth century. It is very rich and tastes delicious, but some people object to the practice of force-feeding geese, which is a necessary part of the process, and refuse to eat it for this reason. Luckily there are other similar alternatives to *foie gras* such as duck or partridge *pâté*.

Truffles are almost as famous as *foie gras* and are expensive. This unattractive looking fungus is found growing among the roots of trees such as hazel and lime, but most especially oaks. It is shaped something like a potato and is blackish-brown on the outside and covered with hard warts. Because nothing shows above the ground pigs and dogs are trained to smell them out, both in wooded areas and in groves of oaks specially planted to augment the natural supply. Périgord truffles are considered to be the most delicious of about thirty different varieties and are used to flavour everything from *pâtés* and omelettes to poultry dishes. Truffles can also be eaten on their own provided the chef has a sufficient quantity on hand and the diner is prepared to pay an extremely high price for them. Mushrooms of various descriptions are also used in many traditional dishes.

Chestnuts, which were a valuable source of food before potatoes were introduced from Peru by the Spaniards in the early sixteenth century, are grown quite extensively. However they take second place to walnuts. These are harvested in large quantities throughout the region and are used for making both cooking oil and *eau de vie*. They also appear in other dishes, are added to cakes and salads, are combined with cheese or may be served separately.

All kinds of fruit are grown in orchards along the river valleys but the strawberries are particularly memorable. Large quantities find their way to Paris and other main cities throughout France. They may be eaten on their own, with wine, orange juice or soured cream or used for ices, tarts and pastries.

There are several dishes that should be tried by anyone anxious to discover the full flavour of the region. *Tourain* is a thick white garlic soup made with eggs while *sobronade*, a concoction of pork and vegetable, is more like a stew. Goose appears in many different forms such as *cou d'oie farci* which is the neck, stuffed and served either hot or cold, when it is cut into slices. *Confits* are another speciality dating back to the time when there were no refrigerators. Pieces of goose, duck, turkey or even pork are cooked in fat for several hours and then preserved in earthenware containers to be taken out when needed and fried in their own juices. These days they can also be bought in tins and prepared in the same way. Lamb which has grazed on the lavender-covered Causses is delicious and so is *bresolles*, consisting of veal baked with ham, herbs and wine, but beef is less predictable and can be good, tough or merely indifferent. Some of the best local cheeses are made from sheep's or goats' milk and may prove a bit too strong for those who prefers the milder commercial varieties.

Drinks

The local wines can be anything from the so-called 'black' wine of Cahors, much favoured by the Popes of Avignon, to the sweet white varieties produced around Bergerac. The lighter reds from the Bordeaux area, which the British still insist on calling claret, have also been famous for centuries. Connoisseurs argue for hours about the relative claims of various *châteaux*, using terms that mean nothing to the layman, and will invariably pay high prices for them. On the other hand some very pleasant new wines have appeared recently and are not outlandishly expensive. Anyone who is anxious to learn something about the subject can improve their knowledge at one of the wine museums and then visit

Shuttered windows in a side street

the growers and co-operatives advertising wine tastings. Visitors with less demanding palates will often be quite happy with the reasonably priced house wines suggested by hotels and restaurants.

Coffee can be delicious or rather nasty, depending partly on one's own preference and partly on the way it is made. This is usually served black in small cups, so visitors who like it large and white should make a point of saying so. Most hotels nowadays offer a choice of tea or coffee for breakfast and although the general preference is for tea with lemon it is interesting to know that the habit of adding milk is thought to have originated in France. There are many different kinds of tea such as camomile, orange, mint, rosehip and so on which were known as *tisanes* and have been around for centuries. Pasteurised milk is readily available in France and it is quite safe to drink the fresh water served in hotels and restaurants but certainly not from a tap labelled *eau non potable*.

Restaurants & Cafés

Restaurants are graded similarly to hotels. There are few really sophisticated and exotic examples, but this is of no consequence because the whole area is regarded as a haven for gourmets. Small establishments can produce some superb dishes, beautifully prepared and cooked and attractively presented. They are accompanied by local wines, some of which are widely known and appreciated throughout France.

Each restaurant and hotel dining room posts up its menus outside with the prices of set meals as well as *à la carte*. As long as one is prepared to try unfamiliar dishes it is a good plan to choose a busy establishment in preference to an almost empty one, because the French are very particular about food and how much it costs and a place which is popular is almost certain to be good.

Set menus are usually the best value for money and more often than not there are three to choose from, starting with one of three courses, probably with a choice in each one. The most expensive can run to six or seven courses and quite frequently have more costly items or ingredients. Wine, soft drinks and coffee are all extra unless stated otherwise.

Lunch is generally served at 12.30pm and may be over by 2pm when everyone has either returned to work or gone shopping. Dinner starts at around 7pm and lasts for 1½ hours, 2 hours or even longer depending on the type of restaurant and the location. In country areas it is often essential to be on time. Sunday is different. Many places are crowded at lunch time, when French housewives take a rest from the kitchen, but may be closed in the evening. Apart from first grade and commercial hotels and restaurants most of them close for one day a week but not all of them advertise the fact on their notice boards.

Cafés do not keep such rigid hours, so it is usually possible to find something to eat in the main towns and tourist centres, even if it is only a light snack. Some country hotels may be willing to rustle up a sandwich, wine and coffee after the chef has left, but it will not be particularly cheap, so it should not be considered a good way of saving money. Under these circumstances it is better to buy such things as bread, *pâté*, cheese and fruit before the shops close and opt for an alfresco lunch.

SPORTS & PASTIMES

By their very nature Périgord and Lot are excellent places for sports and outdoor activities. The choice is wide and varied with no shortage of facilities or organisations ready to give help and advice.

Ballooning

Those interested in hot air ballooning can spend a night at the historic Château de Veyrignac in the region of Villefranche-du-Périgord in July or August. The visit includes one flight and a morning free to play tennis, walk, cycle or relax. Make arrangements through the Service de Réservation Loisirs Accueil in Périgueux.

Alternatively, balloon trips are advertised at Siorac-en-Périgord on the Dordogne. They can be arranged quite easily by telephone provided the weather conditions are suitable.

Climbing & Caving

Visitors are not actively encouraged to go rock climbing or caving on their own but with so many enticing opportunities many cannot resist taking advantage of them. It is wiser to contact an appropriate organisation and join a party or be accompanied by a guide. These can be found in Le Liauzu, Carjac and Orniac in Lot while the Loisirs-Accueil office in Perigueux organises special local holidays for those interested. The reservations are made subject to conditions such as age and physical fitness. For details contact the Loisirs-Accueil in Périgueux or the Comité Départemental de Spéléologie, M. Lafaurie, 46150, Catus.

Cycling

Cycling probably attracts more people than any other single activity in France, whether they are visitors or locals. Bicycles can be hired at most large railway stations and from well publicised centres in about twenty towns and villages throughout Lot and Périgord. There are as many, if not more, cycle clubs, some of which will accept temporary members. The rules which apply to cyclists are the same as those in Britain, but remember to ride on the right and to use a cycle path whenever possible.

Special tours have been worked out for cyclists, incorporating minor roads and *randonnées* where they are available. Some of the larger towns and tourist centres suggest local circuits of 25km to 100km (15 miles to 62 miles) which offer a variety of scenery and an opportunity to visit historic *châteaux* and other places of interest in the vicinity. Where longer trips are involved lists of *gîtes d'étape* are available for overnight stops, along with alternative hotels and campsites. It is possible to book all-in tours which include accommodation, provide transport for any surplus luggage and a guide. Maps and brochures can be obtained from the Comité Départemental de Cyclotourisme, Avenue de la Dordogne, 46000 Martel ☎ 65 37 30 82 in the case of Lot, or from the Office Départemental de Tourisme de la Dordogne in Périgueux. Anyone wanting to book an all-in holiday should do it through the Service de Réservation Loisirs Accueil in Périgueux or Cahors, whichever is applicable.

Fishing

Fishermen are well catered for in both *départements*. Although Lot provides rather more information about its lakes and rivers, the general rules apply equally to both. It is necessary to have a licence and to observe the regulations regarding the permitted size of the catch, the dates of various open and closed seasons and any particular type of fishing which may be forbidden in a given area. There are several local associations which will provide all the necessary help and advice. The most common species which may not be caught at certain times of the year include trout, pike, gudgeon and crayfish while salmon may be prohibited altogether. Details are available from the main tourist office in Périgueux or from the Fédération Départementalé de Peche, 182 Quai Cavaignac, 46000 Cahors ☎ 65 35 50 22.

Golf

Golf is not played to a great extent in Lot or Périgord although a number of resorts are beginning to offer facilities for mini-golf. However there is a 9-hole course at Périgueux and another at Lachapelle-Auzac near Souillac. It is worth knowing that there is a hotel devoted almost exclusively to golf just across the border in Lot-et-Garonne. It has two courses, one 18-hole and the other 9-hole, a driving range with forty places, eight of them under cover, as well as an instructor and an appropriate shop. In addition there may be be individual apartments available overlooking the course. Full details can be obtained from the Hotel du Golf de Castelnaud, Castelnaud-de-Gratecambe, Lot-et-Garonne ☎ 53 01 60 19 (hotel) and 53 01 74 64 (golf).

Parachuting

There is parachuting at the aerodrome near Bergerac from February to September. An all-in holiday can be organised through the Loisirs Accueil which includes a week at a two-star *logis*. Permission to jump must be obtained from the doctor.

Flights only are available from the aero clubs at Bergerac ☎ 53 57 31 36 and at the Périgueux-Bassillac aerodrome ☎ 53 54 41 19.

Riding

Périgord has more than a dozen main equestrian centres as far apart as Jumilhac-le-Grand, Montaigne

Lazing in the shade by a street café

and Monpazier, with many other affiliated stables throughout the *département*. Some of them specialise in teaching riding at all levels and preparing students for competitions and examinations. Others are more concerned with making sure that everyone can handle a horse before taking small groups for short outings or on longer expeditions. The latter can last for anything from three to twelve days, stopping at night at selected *gîtes* or *logis*. One or two centres add a touch of variety with facilities for such things as tennis, swimming, canoeing and sightseeing. Several will provide full details of their programmes on request. Lists of these centres are obtainable from the Association Départementale de Tourisme Equestre de la Dordogne, Chambre d'Agriculture de la Dordogne, 4-6 Place Francheville, 24000 Périgueux ☎ 53 09 26 26.

Those who prefer to drive a horse rather than ride it may be interested in a day out in an old-world rustic carriage supplied by Le Périgord en Calèche at Mazeyrolles ☎ 53 29 98 99. Each vehicle has enough space for four-five people and picnic lunches are provided if required. Another alternative is to hire a horse-drawn caravan. These are fully equipped for four people, are available in the Bergerac area and can be reserved through the Service Loisirs-Accueil in Périgueux.

Lot has just as many equestrian centres and 'Poneys [sic] Clubs' with an equally wide choice of outings and expeditions. The bridle paths cover some 1,200km (744 miles), call in at all the places of outstanding interest and have special *gîtes d'étape* which will provide overnight accommodation for both the riders and their horses. Several round trips are suggested, lasting 3 days on the Causse de Limogne, in the Gramat area or along the Dordogne Valley but twice as long for anyone who wants to explore the area west of Cahors or make a round trip from the capital up as far as Rocamadour.

There are also centres providing well-equipped horse-drawn caravans or little carriages for jaunts into the surrounding countryside. The

Château d'Aynac also offers accommodation and is one of two run by Tourisme Attelé Diffusion, 58 Rue Dulong, 75017 Paris ☎ 47 66 17 75. All the other information is available from the Association Départementale de Tourisme Equestre, BP 103, 46002 Cahors ☎ 65 35 07 09.

Shooting

Weekend shooting trips can also be arranged through the Loisirs Accueil in Périgueux. They include hotel accommodation in Ribérac and restaurant lunches beside the Grand Etang de la Jemaye. The season only lasts from early December to the beginning of January and anyone going out with a gun must have an official permit.

Special Interest Holidays

Opportunities for pre-arranged holidays on a given theme are to be had in both Lot and Périgord. They can last for anything from a weekend to a week or more and cover an unexpectedly wide range of subjects. There are classes in traditional cookery at selected farms and *logis* while other establishments specialise in such things as painting, making pottery or jewellery, wood carving, metal work and weaving. The all-in prices usually cover full pension and may occasionally include wine and coffee as well. Where special materials are involved these will almost certainly be charged for separately. Other suggestions are for specialised holidays with no tuition involved and may or may not call for pre-arranged accommodation.

Squash

At the moment there are hardly any courts available to visitors but games can be arranged in Cahors by contacting Squash-Loisirs, Regourd, 46000 Cahors ☎ 65 22 13 18.

Swimming

There are a great many swimming pools throughout the region, from public baths to the private variety owned by some hotels and campsites. Bathing is also possible in some lakes and rivers, particularly at campsites located along the water's edge. Care should be taken because the currents can be strong in places.

Tennis

Nearly every town and village has at least one tennis court which can be used by visitors. They are part of every leisure park and are frequently one of the attractions offered by hotels which have enough space in the garden. A large proportion of *gîtes* and campsites include tennis in their lists of sports activities but in some cases the court, or courts, may be a few kilometres away. Additional details can be obtained from the main tourist office in Périgueux or from the Comité Départemental de Tennis, Avenue Henri-Martin, 46000 Cahors ☎ 65 35 26 60.

Walking

Walking is another extremely popular pastime in both Périgord and Lot. Visitors can go for a short ramble almost anywhere or set out on a determined long distance trek by using the Sentiers de Grandes Randonnées that cover practically the whole of France. There are also any number of marked footpaths known as Les Sentiers de Promenade, most of which end up exactly where they started and can be completed in as little as 30 minutes or take a good many hours, depending on personal preference.

The two *départements* share some of the Grandes Randonnées, especially the ones such as the GR6, the GR36 and the GR64 which wander about a good deal but nevertheless tend to run across the regions concerned rather than up and down. These official trails are designed to call at, or pass close to, places of particular interest such as prehistoric caves and ancient towns and villages, to follow the river courses or search out memorable views. Each one is clearly marked with signs indicating the way ahead, anticipating a change of direction or warning hikers that they have taken the wrong path. Some also include the number of the route and the distance to the next town.

All along the Grandes Randonnées there are overnight stopping places at reasonable intervals which may be small inns, *gîtes*, *chambres d'hôtes* or even campsites with tents and sometimes a small shop and the possibility of a hot meal. Some of these little hotels have formed themselves into groups and will pass on their visitors from hand to hand according to what they want to see and how much time is at their disposal.

Some may feel like becoming a latter day Robert Louis Stevenson and starting out on their journey with a donkey to carry the bags. Special tours can be arranged which include dinner, bed and breakfast in addition to a picnic lunch. They can be unaccompanied, or with a guide, and usually last about a week. There are centres in Périgord Noir which can be contacted through the Service de Reservation Loisirs Accueil in Périgueux, or in Cours and Duravel in which case contact the Comité Départemental de la Randonnée Pedestre, BP 79, 46002 Cahors Cedex ☎ 65 35 07 09. Any enquiries about other walking tours should be addressed to the same *départements* which will supply illustrated maps and any other relevant information.

Watersports

Although there is some boating and sailing, water skiing and windsurfing, mainly on the larger lakes, most of the activity involves kayaks and canoes on rivers such as the Célé, Cère, Dordogne, Dronne, Isle, Lot and Vézère. Various stretches are classified from 1 to 5. Class 1 is very easy and particularly suitable for beginners whereas Class 4 is difficult and Class 5 should only be attempted by people with the necessary skill and experience. The conditions also vary with the seasons and while some sections are navigable throughout the year others can only be negotiated over short periods.

Kayaks and canoes are available for hire at several places along the river banks, either with or without tuition. They can be taken out for an hour or two or used for much longer trips, in which case there are both hotels and campsites beside the water which provide meals and overnight accommodation. Organised expeditions are also arranged under the eye of an experienced instructor when the overall price includes such things as buoyancy aids, watertight holdalls and transport back to the point of departure. These trips are commonplace at the height of the season but may have to be arranged in advance at other times of the year.

Rafting is available in certain places on the main rivers where the conditions are suitable. Meanwhile, those with neither the energy nor the inclination to handle craft on their own can still enjoy a river trip. Pleasure boats operate from centres such as Bergerac, Beynac, Bouziès and Trémolat. Trips last for an average of 1½ to 2 hours with frequent services during the season, when it is advisable to reserve seats in advance.

The Dordogne *1*

The Dordogne is not only one of the longest rivers in France, it is also one of the most beautiful and certainly amongst the most historic. From its source on the slopes of the Puy-de-Sancy, the highest point of the Massif Central where the Dore and the Dogne meet, it rushes headlong through Le Monts Dore, past the giant but fortunately extinct volcano of Cantal to the granite outcrops of Limousin. At one time it carved out deep ravines for itself where melting snow and heavy rains built up vicious torrents that surged down towards the plains of Aquitaine leaving a trail of death and destruction in their wake. Today the river has been partly tamed. Barrages and their attendant lakes and reservoirs control the floodwaters at several points while at the same time providing an efficient hydro-electric system for the area.

After leaving the Lac de Bort the river snakes its way along the border between Auvergne and Limousin, through some attractively wooded but not very spectacular gorges, en route for Argentat. Once clear of this town it heads south to Beaulieu-sur-Dordogne, an enchanting little place founded by the Benedictine Order more than 1,000 years ago. Thereafter the river crosses into Lot and wanders across the plain to its meeting point with the River Cère which has also come down from Cantal but by a very different route. Refreshed and replenished the Dordogne picks

up speed again, etching its way through the limestone plateau in a series of loops and hairpin bends, past ancient castles, prehistoric caves and photogenic towns and villages.

Castles come thick and fast once the Dordogne has reached Périgord Noir. Some are grim and forbidding, steeped in the tragedies of the Hundred Years' War and the Wars of Religion, while others have an almost benign air about them. Along the river attractive little hamlets nestle at the foot of the cliffs, poplars and willows line the banks and wherever the ground is fertile it is assiduously cultivated. The meadows beyond are full of flowers, narcissus in the spring followed by wild roses, honeysuckle, scarlet poppies and a rainbow selection of other varieties, some almost hidden in the multi-coloured grasses. At one time the Dordogne was a busy waterway. The Vikings made use of it during their forays into the interior, boat-building flourished at several of the little medieval ports and bandits were a constant source of irritation to both the sailors and the fishermen. Most of these have now disappeared, leaving the way clear for holidaymakers in kayaks and canoes, small waterside resorts, swimmers, anglers, walkers, rafts and pleasure boats.

A number of lesser streams and rivers find their way into the Dordogne, the most important at this stage being the Vézère, lined with prehistoric caves and grottoes. It makes contact at Limeuil just below an attractive elbow bridge called Pont Coude. Downstream the valley becomes much wider, the lands on either side are sown with wheat, maize and tobacco and, apart from a few rapids, the river heads sedately for Bergerac. This is where the vineyards start to make their presence felt. Whole battalions of them march in perfect formation across the Guyenne plains, past Castillon-la-Bataille to the walled city of St Emilion. The last place of any consequence is the inland port of Libourne which has been kept busy exporting wine for several hundred years. The river here is tidal and has lost most of its charm although it still has a short course to run through unspectacular country to the Bec d'Ambès, 500km (310 miles) from its source. At this point the Dordogne joins forces with the Garonne, a river of comparable size but greater depth that has already left Bordeaux behind. Together they form the Gironde for the last part of their journey to the sea.

Whereas the Loire begins life by gushing out of a pipe in Ardèche the Dordogne makes its debut in the form of a waterfall surrounded by pastures some 1,883m (6,000ft) up in the Massif Central. Above it towers the **Puy-de-Sancy** where energetic visitors climb laboriously up to the summit while the rest make the trip by cable car from a hotel on the slopes below. There is also a restaurant and plenty of parking space where motorists can leave their cars alongside the dozens of coaches that have come out loaded with tourists determined to see the magnificent views. The stream has grown into a small river by the time it reaches **Le Mont-Dore** which combines all the advantages of a spa, a summer resort and a winter sports centre. The baths, which were fully developed during the 1890s, contain a few reminders of the time when the Romans took the waters there, but apart from these and the sparse remains of a temple, all trace of their occupation has disappeared. The resort grew in popularity during the eighteenth century and now has a casino looking out towards the mountains, a 9-hole golf course on the outskirts, tennis, riding and walking and a dozen or more hotels and restaurants, although nothing in the luxury class.

By the time the river reaches **La Bourboule** it has dropped about 950m (3,000ft) and splashes its way swiftly and cheerfully through the town, spanned by a number of small but colourful bridges. This is another thermal centre, short on ancient history but well endowed with gardens, modest hotels, a casino and a whole range of entertainments from tennis and riding to mini-golf, swimming and *boules*. The baths, which were attracting clients with health problems as long ago as 1463, were updated in the nineteenth century and again in 1976 along lines suggested by Le Corbusier, the famous French architect who had been drowned in the Mediterranean off Cap Martin 12 years before. Children as well as adults appear to thrive on the waters despite the fact that they are said to have the highest

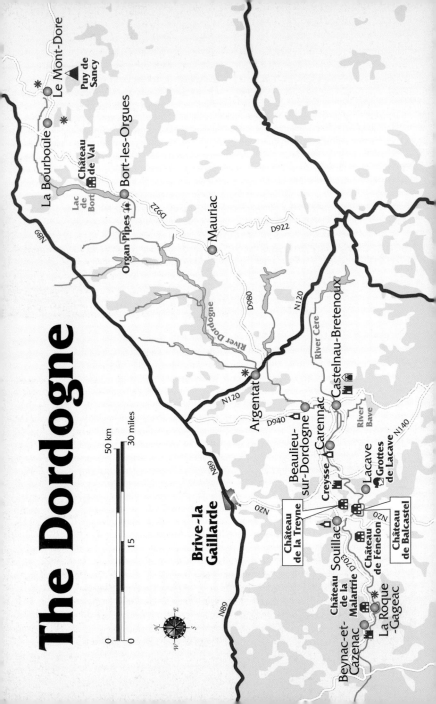

Horse riding on the Puy-de-Sancy

Skiing at Le Mont-Dore

arsenic content of any spa in Europe. Everyone tries it for themselves and the general opinion is that it is much the same as spa water anywhere else! The Fenêstre Park, with its sequoia trees, shaded paths and mini-train for anyone who feels disinclined to walk, has a cable car up to the Plâteau de Charlannes, although people with no head for heights can also get up there by car.

The Dordogne takes life a bit more easily beyond La Bourboule, leaving the Avèze to supply an odd gorge or two, until it reaches the border with Limousin. Here it is confronted by the first of several barrages which control the flow and force it to widen out into the Lac de Bort, a 17km (11 mile) long stretch of water that only ends at Bort-les-Orgues. On the way it passes the **Château de Val**, a medieval fortress built during the Hundred Years' War but now almost completely surrounded by water with a marina where one feels the ramparts ought to be. It is an eye-catching mixture of solid stone walls and functional round towers with tiny windows and pointed roofs, reached by way of a large courtyard guarded by a stone lion. The castle provides space for art exhibitions, invites all and sundry to join conducted tours which take nearly an hour and even lays on motor launches for trips round the lake. There are woods for walking and picnics and a shoreline for sunbathing, windsurfing or sailing. The power house at the **Barrage de Bort** is just as happy to welcome visitors, explain the workings of the hydro-electric system and point them in the direction of the same motor launches for a jaunt in the opposite direction.

Bort-les-Orgues is a fairly ordinary country town without a great deal to recommend it. There is a small fortified church which has kept its original stalls, a statue of Ste Anne and a beautifully enamelled brass reliquary, but the main attraction is a massive natural formation known as the Organ Pipes. This is a high cliff, worn by the elements over many centuries into a series of stark rock pillars 80m to 100m (262ft to 328ft) high. Anyone who wants to inspect them at close quarters will find a parking space under the trees a short walk away, a little stall offering postcards and souvenirs and quite a spectacular view.

Below Bort-les-Orgues the Dordogne and the border continue hand in hand eastward to the Site de St Nazaire and then south through pleasantly wooded gorges to the Pont de Spontour. Here they part company, with the river pressing on into Limousin, passing one barrage after another until it reaches **Argentat**. Few people visiting this rather sleepy waterside town on the busy N120 are aware of its importance in days gone by. Before man in his wisdom decided to improve on nature and, incidentally, provide himself with electricity, large flat-bottomed sailing barges operated constantly along the river with cargoes of wood and passengers bound for places like Limeuil, Bergerac and Bordeaux. Navigating in these waters was not easy, and it was almost impossible to sail upstream again, so a system was developed which suited everybody to perfection. The extensive boat-yards at Argentat were kept fully occupied building the vessels known as *gabariers* or *argentats* which were then taken down fully loaded to Bordeaux where they were broken up and sold as timber. Nowadays the only boats to be seen between the barrages are little pleasure craft like kayaks and canoes and Argentat, with its picturesque houses and a couple of small hotels, has settled down to enjoy a less frenetic old age.

With an attentive road on either side the Dordogne follows an erratic course down to **Beaulieu-sur-Dordogne**, a wholly delightful small town which grew up round a Benedictine abbey founded in 855. Like so many others the monastery came to grief during the Wars of Religion, was revived in the seventeenth century by monks from St-Maur but finally succumbed during the Revolution. All that remains of its past glories is the extremely viewable church of St Pierre with a magnificent south door portraying the Last Judgment carved in 1125. Christ is shown attended by two angels with the blessed and the damned on either side while below them a collection of unearthly monsters appear to be fighting amongst themselves. The interior should also be seen, partly for its intricate carvings and partly for the treasure which includes a twelfth-century statue of the Virgin and a beautiful enamelled reliquary which is younger by some 300 years. Among the lovely old houses sur-

rounding the church and lining the waterfront the most memorable are the Maison d'Adam et Eve, much decorated with statues and medallions, and the Maison de Clarisse with its wooden balcony and matching towers where the local boatmen and fishermen used to live. Constantly admiring its reflection in the river is the ancient Chapelle des Pénitents with a line of blind archways and gable high up on the belfry wall. Beaulieu is by no means averse to tourists. It offers them a selection of small *auberges*, bicycles for hire, blazed trails for hikers, a miniature golf course, tennis, swimming and canoes. The religious highlight of the year is the Feast of Holy Relics, held during the first weekend of September, following an annual exhibition of paintings and regional art.

Once clear of Beaulieu, the Dordogne crosses the border into Lot in time to join forces with the Cère below the massive red stone ramparts of **Castelnau-Bretenoux**. This is a ruin of splendid proportions, partly restored and described by several experts as one of the most perfect examples of medieval military architecture to be found anywhere in France. In the first place, it is enormous with the remains of its encircling walls that covered a distance of 5km (3 miles) enclosing a fortress which could accommodate a garrison numbering 1,500 soldiers and still leave space to stable 100 horses for them. The site was chosen originally by the barons of Castelnau who were both powerful and excessively proud and paid court to no one apart

The bridges at La Bourboule

Opposite: A game of boules in the main park, La Bourboule

Souillac Abbey

from the Counts of Toulouse. When Raymond de Toulouse was insensitive enough to make them subservient to the Vicomtes of Turenne in 1184 the Castelnaus were beside themselves with fury and immediately transferred their allegiance to the French kings. Inevitably this led to war between Turenne and Castelnau. Trouble continued for nearly 40 years until Louis VIII arrived at a solution with something approaching the wisdom of Solomon. Turenne was to remain as overlord but actually this was in name only because the sole tribute he was entitled to receive was one new laid egg each year. The Castelnaus, while not entirely approving of this judgment, decided to fall in gracefully, lodged their tongues firmly in their cheeks and thereafter made a great show of sending a richly-appointed team of four oxen with a large retinue and one small egg to fulfil their annual obligations. The keep in the centre of the castle dates from the eleventh century but the rest of the fortress was added as and when necessary during the Hundred Years' War. The whole complex was abandoned in the eighteenth century, ill-treated during the Revolution and burned out in 1851 by an owner who needed the insurance money.

This might have been the end of the story if Jean Moulierat, an affluent tenor from the Opéra Comique, had not bought it, set about restoring as much of the damage as possible and furnishing a few of the main rooms. He left it to the State in 1932 who carried on the good work adding, amongst other things, a small lapidary museum. A tour of the fortress takes little under an hour and includes the Court of Honour dominated by the keep and the Saracens Tower, the Grand Salon hung with tapestries, the Pewter Hall and the oratory which still has stained glass windows from the fifteenth century. It is also worth casting an eye over the little church below the castle which was built at approximately the same time. Bretenoux village started out as a *bastide* attached to the original castle and still has some elderly houses, an arcaded square, a covered market and a brace of rather basic inns.

The road from Bretenoux follows the south bank of the Dordogne round to **Carennac**, a picturesque little hamlet that was once the home of Francois de Salignac de la Mothe-Fénelon known, for obvious reasons, as Fénelon. He was both a novelist and a priest, a believer in persuasion rather than violence — which was an unpopular stand for any Catholic to take during the Wars of Religion — and eventually tutor to the Duke of Burgundy and Archbishop of Cambrai. Not a great deal remains of the tenth-century priory where he lived for 15 years and is thought to have written *Telemaque*. The Revolution was largely responsible for the destruction of Carennac, including the sale of the deanery by auction in 1791, but there is still a fortified gateway, the prior's house, a tower, a medley of aged houses and the white abbey church of St Pierre. Its beautifully carved twelfth-century doorway shows Christ surrounded by the Apostles above a whole collection of small animals, a theme which is taken up, but with more reliance on mythology, inside the church. The two-storey cloister with a stairway leading down to the terrace has been carefully restored. The adjoining chapterhouse has a *mise au tombeau* in which Joseph and Nicodemus carry the body of Christ, watched by a small group including the Virgin Mary and the everpresent Mary Magdalene. The island in the middle of the river, renamed Calypso after the nymph who captivated Ulysses, and as a gesture to Fénelon, is given over to fishing and water sports. The village has two reasonably well-appointed small hotels, a campsite, bridle paths, easy access to the GR652 and holds summer exhibitions in the *château* next door to the church.

On the far side of Floirac, a village with only a fourteenth-century keep of interest, is the pastel-coloured **Cirque de Montvalent**. Here the road swoops and rises along the cliffs, crossing over to the opposite bank to take in the view from the Belvedere de Copeyre and the delightfully photogenic hamlet of Gluges. Pushing its way forward, sometimes literally through the rock, it calls at **Creysse** where the remains of a castle and its antiquated chapel are reached along a narrow and energy-consuming stone alley that leads to a terrace at the top. For a brief spell after leaving Creysse the road is only separated from the river by a line of weeping willows but

then it changes its mind again, finds a bridge at St Sozy and makes for **Meyronne**, once the home of the bishops of Tulle, where some of the houses are built into the rocks.

The next place of interest along the route is a series of caves called the **Grottes de Lacave** which were discovered in 1902 by Armand Viré who learned his trade from Edouard Martel. About a mile of galleries are open to visitors with both a small underground train and a lift to transport them into the bowels of the earth and cut down slightly on walking time. The first of the caves are full of stalactites and stalagmites worn into a variety of shapes that may look like people, animals or even buildings depending on the imagination of the person concerned. The second group contains underground rivers and limpid pools, a Sal du Lac with formations that glow in the dark and the fascinating Salle de Merveilles. The grottoes were well known in prehistoric times and provided archaeologists with a whole variety of tools and weapons as well as flint implements but so far no wall paintings have come to light. For people who prefer their tourist attractions to be above ground rather than below it an excellent alternative is the **Château de Belcastel**, standing on a perpendicular rock rising up from the Dordogne. It is certainly well named but by no means all of it is original. Part of the east wing and the chapel are left over from the Middle Ages but the rest of the buildings are less than 200 years old. However this hardly matters because only the

La Roque-Gageac on the banks of the River Dordogne

Opposite: Exploring with donkeys in Beaulieu-sur-Dordogne

keep, the chapel and the terraces are open to visitors, many of whom show little interest in anything apart from the view.

This scenic route crosses the river yet again near the **Château de la Treyne** which is now a hotel but allows non-residents to inspect the chapel, the gardens and the park. On the far side of the bridge the road takes a shortcut to **Souillac**, a remarkably busy centre on the N20 which links areas north of Limoges with Toulouse and the Spanish frontier just to the east of Andorra. It is a town with its fingers in several different pies, acting as a market for farmers from the fertile region all round, providing banks, shops and other facilities for the inhabitants as well as the steady stream of people passing through, and catering for holidaymakers staying in the vicinity. There are several hotels which are perfectly acceptable without being in any way luxurious, restaurants with rooms to let, *gîtes* and a campsite beside the river. Visitors can swim, ride and fish, play tennis, explore local potholes, hire canoes or go for long walks by simply following the marked footpaths. On the debit side Souillac has very little in the way of tangible history although it owes a great deal to the Benedictine abbey whose monks drained the marshes all round. The abbey was attacked time after time by the English during the Hundred Years' War, but recovered on each occasion only to be trounced by the Protestants during the Wars of Religion and finally burnt out in 1572. Restoration

work was undertaken in the seventeenth century in plenty of time to attract the attention of the Revolutionaries who destroyed it totally.

Apart from one old and unaccompanied belltower the sole survivor of all these misfortunes is the splendid abbey church, rated second only to the cathedral in Cahors. It is light, airy and dignified with three large domes and not a great many decorations apart from Chassériau's painting *Christ on the Mount of Olives* and a spectacular carved stone doorway that faces inwards instead of out. This was resited in the eighteenth century when the monks decided to replace it with something plainer and more classical; a decision which possibly went a long way towards preserving it. Above the entrance itself is a relief telling the story of Theophilus. Briefly, this monk had a difference of opinion with his superiors and in order to get his own way he signed a pact with the devil, exchanging his soul for his ambitions. Naturally he thought better of it when the time came to keep his side of the bargain and prayed long and earnestly for forgiveness. The Virgin Mary took pity on him, recovered the document and obliterated his signature before showing it to him. Joseph and Isaiah, the latter holding a long scroll, are carved on either side of the door while a richly decorated pillar warns of the dangers inherent in the Seven Deadly Sins, but softens the blow with a promise of redemption. This shows Abraham about to sacrifice Isaac with a heavenly messenger stopping him just in time. After all this the crypt with its elderly sarcophagi is an anticlimax.

From Souillac the Dordogne has a short encounter with the provincal boundary before crossing into Périgord Noir and meandering gently through the fertile countryside. The road twists with the river as far as Rouffillac where motorists have the option of continuing along the D703 or making for St Julien-de-Lampon on the south bank in order to visit the **Château de Fénelon**. This is another medieval pile and the birthplace of the famous priest and writer whose family owned it until the eighteenth century. Like any other castle dating from the Middle Ages it was designed primarily for defence with triple walls, sturdy towers, fortified doorways and a commanding view. The drawbridge has completely disappeared but in its place an attractive staircase in the form of a horseshoe leads up to the courtyard and the cloister. Only the chapel and a small collection of Fénelon memorabilia are on view but to make up for any disappointments the owners have added a small collection of vintage cars.

From the *château* the road continues along beside the river past Veyrignac to make contact with the main route north to Sarlat-la-Canéda. At Carsac-Aillac, on the opposite bank, the D703 heads westwards across the top of the Cingle de Montfort where the Dordogne doubles back on itself in the shadow of **Montfort Castle**. This has been razed and rebuilt so often that very little of the early fortress has sur-

vived. Simon de Montfort was the first offender when he captured and then destroyed it in 1214. The initial replacement was flattened in the Hundred Years' War, the second towards the end of the fifteenth century and the third on the orders of Henry IV when it was a Protestant stronghold during the Wars of Religion. Thereafter all the bits and pieces that remained more or less intact were welded together, to be finally updated about 100 years ago. Since that time the *château* has kept itself very much to itself and has no time at all for visitors.

Of all the little villages that cling tenaciously to perpendicular cliffs along the banks of the Dordogne **La Roque-Gageac** is undoubtedly one of the most spectacular. Its toeholds are so precarious that houses have been known to lose their grip and slide down into the water. However, as with fortresses so with waterside hamlets, and each time La Roque-Gageac has picked itself up, repaired the damage that may also have been caused by falling rocks, and carried on exactly as before. It is a charming mixture of little winding alleys lined with peasant cottages, an old manor house, a twentieth-century *château* built on medieval lines and a small church set into the face of the rock. The village successfully resisted every English attempt to capture it during the Hundred Years' War, kept a weather eye open for sailing barges when the Dordogne was a busy commercial waterway and has now transferred its attention to holidaymakers in kayaks and canoes.

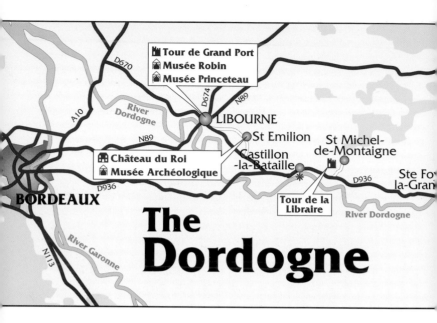

The
Dordogne

The Manor de Tarde, with its pointed gables and conventional tower capped with a witch's hat, was the family home of Jean Tarde, a man of many parts who left behind a wealth of information about the Sarlat area as he knew it in the sixteenth century. The Château de la Malartrie, with no historical connections to boast about, nevertheless invites passers-by to look round the building and sample local delicacies such as *foie gras* before they leave. There are two *auberges* with baths en suite and a third a little way down the road to Vitrac. The countryside hereabouts is pleasant for walking as well as driving and visitors in search of souvenirs should keep a lookout for wayside stalls selling articles made from animal skins. They come in all shapes and sizes and, as the animals in question have all been killed for food, there is no need to feel guilty about buying anything.

Beynac Castle which, among other things, spent the greater part of the Hundred Years' War hurling French insults across the Dordogne at the English-held fortress of Castelnaud opposite, is a most impressive sight. It is a forbidding stronghold rising out of the sheet rock 150m (492ft) above its attendant village which makes a valiant but largely unsuccessful attempt to clamber up the cliff towards it. Beynac was one of the great baronies of Périgord during the Middle Ages. Its nose was put out of joint when Richard Coeur

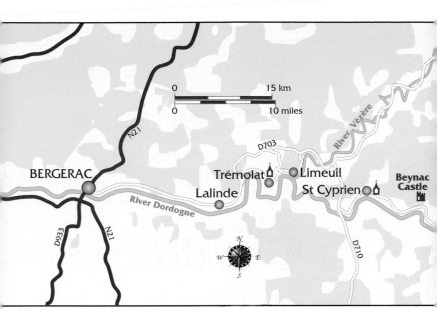

de Lion captured it and installed a master-at-arms called Mercadier who, according to all accounts, was more of a brigand than a soldier. He spent his time looting and destroying everything within reach but it is difficult to tell if this was done in the course of duty or for his own benefit. Nor were conditions much better for Beynac in 1214 when it fell to Simon de Montfort who proceeded to destroy as much of it as possible.

The fortress, rebuilt and strengthened by the Lord of Beynac, started the Hundred Years' War in English hands but was captured by the French in 1368. Thereafter it played a major role in the defence of the Dordogne which was the natural demarkation line between the two sides.

For some reason the castle avoided getting deeply involved in the Wars of Religion and apparently escaped attention during the Revolution, but nevertheless needed considerable restoration and refurbishing to bring it up to twentieth-century standards. It is reached by motorists along the D703 or by determined walkers along a steep footpath from the village. This skirts the towers, finds an arched gateway and calls in at the original chapel which was modernised in the fifteenth century. The keep and part of the main building date from the building work carried out before the Hundred Years' War but the adjoining *château* was added some 200 years later. In addition to the Hall of State, where important personages once met to discuss the weighty matters of their day, there is an oratory decorated with religious frescoes and leading members of the Beynac family and a staircase up to the battlements. From here the sentries could keep a constant watch on other nearby castles, which was essential if they were in enemy hands and advisable even if they were owned by friends. Inspite of all this the main talking point where tourists are concerned is frequently a window seat with a hole in it, fitted with a stone bung, which was the last word in lavatories during the Middle Ages.

❋   The village of **Beynac-et-Cazenac** is predictably attractive with its old houses built on narrow terraces overlooking the water and a spring near the Hôtel Bonnet. At one time householders had to make several trips down to collect their water, refresh their animals, do their laundry in a special trough provided for the purpose or just sit round enjoying a satisfactory gossip. Water is now laid on at a much higher level which makes day-to-day living a good deal easier but does not create anything like the same village atmosphere. The locals maintain that the spring can be relied upon in all weathers and has never been known to dry up or show any tendency to falter, even when everyone else is suffering from the effects of drought. In addition to the Hôtel Bonnet there are a handful of other small establishments as well as two more *auberges* on the road to Vézac and a restaurant with a private swimming pool. From a small

jetty, more or less opposite the spring, pleasure boats equipped with coloured awnings leave at 30-minute intervals for trips along the river. They run every day from May to October, charge quite reasonable prices and identify all the attractions they pass in English as well as French so there is no need to carry a dictionary. The river provides some good fishing, there are canoes and kayaks for hire, tennis, golf and riding are within easy reach, as are some attractive walks but without any immediate access to the Grandes Randonnées.

On the far side of Beynac the road and river part company, the Dordogne following an uneventful if somewhat uncertain course to Sioracen-Périgord while motorists deviate to **St Cyprien**. Anyone who is inclined to view castles, churches and other historic landmarks with a slightly jaundiced eye will probably find this stretch of the river much more acceptable. Obviously there are a lot of buildings left over from the past but almost without exception the villages seem more interested in entertaining their guests than instructing them. For example, St Cyprien, standing slightly back from the water, nevertheless provides all the usual sports facilities. These include canoe trips along the river with a mini-bus for the convenience of anyone who only wants to paddle in one direction, usually downstream. There are two hotels in different price brackets and a disproportionately large church that was originally part of an abbey built by the Augustines in the twelfth century. The whole village clings to the side of a hill surrounded by woodlands and is said to look its best at sundown when the colours in the rock behind take on a strange and fiery brilliance.

Beyond the holiday centre of Siorac-en-Périgord and the old town of Limeuil where the Vézère joins the Dordogne — both included in Chapter 2 Périgord (Périgord Noir) — the next town is **Trémolat**. This is another riverside resort that falls into the same category as the others. Admittedly it has a large and rather dismal twelfth-century church and a stylish little chapel in the cemetery but these play second fiddle to its other attractions. Firstly, there is a quiet and comfortable hotel, set in very pleasant gardens, which offers one or two apartments, provides for guests with a handicap that makes life difficult, has an excellent restaurant and garages for cars. Another *auberge* in the vicinity has less to offer and therefore charges accordingly. The large and very up-market campsite has room for 300 people and provides a very wide range of sports as well as a restaurant and all the expected amenities. It is open from May to September but anyone planning to stay is advised to book in advance. There are also marked footpaths with suggested outings for long distance walkers who would like to study local *châteaux* or prehistory. It is possible to rent a wooden caravan or a *gîte*, hire a bicycle or set out on a voyage in a canoe that can last for up to a week. Rowing and

sailing regattas are held frequently in the Cingle de Trémolat, a splendid loop in the river with a backdrop of white cliffs embroidered with greenery.

From this point onwards the Dordogne becomes wide and lazy, ignoring Badefols-sur-Dordogne whose castle ruins made an ideal hideout for robber bands waiting to attack the loaded barges as they sailed past. There is hardly a bend anywhere as it saunters in to Bergerac, past the ancient port and out the other side with a half-hearted wriggle until it joins the border north of **Ste Foy-la-Grande**. Originally this was a typical *bastide*, built in the fourteenth century, which joined the Protestants in the Wars of Religion and emerged from its various encounters considerably the worse for wear. However, it is a pleasant, ordinary, little town with some perfectly acceptable hotels and a small airport.

The river and the border keep each other company, passing an occasional *château* and joining the road from Bergerac to Bordeaux south of **St Michel-de-Montaigne**. This small hamlet grew up round an imposing *château* which a merchant named Ramon Eyguem bought, rather than inherited, at the end of the fourteenth century. His great grandson, Michel Eyquem de Montaigne, was born there in 1533. He was a bright lad who studied law at the University of Toulouse, practised at the bar for a while but eventually gave it up to write the essays that were to make him famous. Throughout his life Montaigne preached as well as prac-

Beynac Castle

ticed tolerance, managing to be a staunch Catholic without losing his Protestant friends including Henry of Navarre. However all his attempts to introduce a modicum of common sense into the Wars of Religion failed miserably and only resulted in making him a convenient target for critics of both persuasions. The original *château* was burned down in 1855 but fortunately the Tour de la Libraire escaped the blaze. He described this tower, where he did most of his writing, as a sanctuary with a chapel at ground level, a bedroom above and his li-

A typical display of pottery for sale near Beynac-et-Cazenac

brary on the top floor. It is now attached to a *château* of more recent vintage which is out of bounds to sightseers although the tower itself is open to visitors.

The Dordogne and the main route to Bordeaux take leave of each other at **Castillon-la-Bataille**, a name which should be known to both the English and the French, although few have ever heard of it. It was here, in 1453, that the English finally lost the Hundred Years' War. The French, commanded by the Count de Penthièvre and Jean Burau, changed their previous tactics and dug themselves in so that when the English infantry under John Talbot were forced to attack they were wiped out by field artillery and both Talbot and his son were killed. The story goes that Talbot's body was so badly disfigured that his herald could only recognise him by his teeth. However the French claim to have identified him to their complete satisfaction and removed a Holy Thorn from his body which is now regarded as a sacred relic and kept in its own chapel at the Château de Mont-Réal. The battle was fought on a plain outside the town where the event is recalled by two monuments, one to the French captains and the other to John Talbot which stands a trifle forlornly on the river bank.

About 10km (6 miles) further up the road there is a turning off to **St Emilion**, the famous wine centre built on a hilltop and surrounded by vines and ancient fortified walls. Originally a Roman settlement, it got its name from a monk who establised a hermitage here. The village that grew up round it received its charter from King John of Magna Carta fame. He appointed a twenty-four-man *Jurade* to keep an eye on the village and maintain the standards of its wines, which their successors have been doing ever since. St Emilion is an atmospheric little town where travellers can find accommodation, a good restaurant and sample the light red wines which the British still insist on calling claret. Its other attractions include the medieval Château du Roi, a strange monolithic church carved out of solid rock by the monks and a small local museum filled with items like a giant wine press and other old fashioned implements.

Road and river meet again at **Libourne**, an inland port founded by an Englishman called Roger of Leyburn to handle wine shipments to England and Holland. There are still traces of the old fortifications like the Tour du Grand Port which stands on the left bank of the River Isle at the spot where it flows into the Dordogne. The streets of the ancient quarter are more or less parallel and cross each other at right angles in the manner of a *bastide*, with a typical arcaded square and a Renaissance *hôtel de ville*. The town boasts a modest *auberge* or two and a couple of small museums. One is concerned mainly with archaeology and local history while the other houses works by Princeteau whose most famous pupil was Toulouse-Lautrec. Although the port is still open for business on a somewhat reduced scale there is little point in arranging a river trip because there is practically nothing of interest along the final stretch of the Dordogne to the Bec d'Ambès where it joins the Garonne. It is here that they both lose their identities to form the Gironde which flows out into the Bay of Biscay 100km (62 miles) north of Bordeaux.

PLACES TO VISIT

Beynac-et-Cazenac

Château de Beynac
☎ 53 29 50 40
Open: 10am-12noon and 2.30-
6.30pm March to mid-November.
Closes 5.30pm March & November.
River trips from Beynac every 30
minutes 10am-7pm May to October.

Bort-les-Orgues

Barrage de Bort Powerhouse
Open: daily 9am-6pm.

Château de Val
Open: 9am-12noon and 2-6.30pm
mid-June to mid-September.

Castelnau-Bretenoux

Fortress
☎ 53 29 57 08
Open: 9am-12noon and 2-6pm, April
to September. Closed Tuesday.
Otherwise 10am-12noon and 2-5pm.

Libourne

Musée Princeteau
Hôtel de ville
Open: 10am-12noon, 2.30-5.30pm.
Closed Saturday and Sunday.

Musée Robin
32 Rue Thiers
Open: 10am-12noon and 2-5pm.
Closed Sunday.

Puy de Sancy

Cable car to the summit operates
9am-12noon and 1.30-5.30pm.

Roque-Gageac, La

Château de la Malartrie
☎ 53 29 54 40
Open: 11am-3pm and 6-9pm early
July to mid-September.

Souillac

Château de Belcastel
Open: mornings and afternoons July
to September. Enquire at *château*.

Château de la Treyne
☎ 65 32 66 66
Open: chapel and gardens 9am-
12noon and 2-6pm June to September. Closed Monday.

Lacave, Grottes de
☎ 65 37 87 03
Open: 9am-12noon and 2-6pm April
to mid-October. August 9am-7pm.

St Emilion

Musée Archéologique
☎ 56 24 72 03
Open: by appointment.

Ste Foy-la-Grande

Museum of Prehistory
31 Rue de la Langalerie.
Open: Wednesdays 3-6pm.

St Julien-de-Lampon

Château de Fénelon
☎ 53 29 81 45
Open: March-October 10am-12noon,
2-6pm. Open to 7pm July and August.

St Michel-de-Montaigne

Tour de la Libraire
In château grounds
☎ 53 58 63 93 or 53 58 60 56
Open: 9am-12noon and 2-7pm.
Closed Monday, Tuesday and mid-
January to mid-February.

Trémolat

Boat trips of 1½ hours. 5pm July and
August.
☎ 53 22 81 18

Périgord 2

Périgord claims, with complete assurance and considerable justification, to be the Cradle of Mankind. However this rather depends on what you expect to find in the cradle. There were man-like creatures living in East Africa about 2,000,000 years ago, followed by Homo Erectus who was hunting large animals and using fire for cooking in Europe, Asia and Africa about 1,000,000 years afterwards. The Neanderthal man had a good innings but seems to have given up the struggle around 40,000 years ago, leaving the field clear for Homo Sapiens. These ancestors of ours may well have originated in several different parts of the world but it is true to say that the earliest remains so far discovered were found in France — in Périgord. In spite of having had to fight hard for survival the ancient inhabitants found time to decorate the walls of their caves and the paintings at Lascaux, which only came to light in 1940, are generally agreed to be the world's finest collection of prehistoric art. The area all round is a treasure trove of primitive cliff dwellings where experts have uncovered everything from Stone Age tools to skeletons and burial sites to vivid pictures of encounters between hunters and their prey which took place some 30,000 years ago.

By no means were all the troglodytes prehistoric. Their caves were dry, relatively warm in winter and cool in summer and comparatively easy to defend, so subsequent generations saw no particular reason to change their way of life. They added various refinements such as doors and windows, the English turned some of these once-desirable cliff residences into fortified outposts during the Hundred Years' War and in this day and age the residents sport television aerials, window boxes and, where possible, plant roses or apples in the front garden. Here and there a large cave, opening conveniently off the road, makes an ideal garage for a well-kept modern car. At the same time other local inhabitants opted for a change in their surroundings. They congregated in small towns and villages, clustered round ancient castles, perched on hilltops, hid themselves away in fertile valleys or built their picturesque hamlets like stone waterfalls spilling down the side of a deep gorge or ravine. Elegant *châteaux* popped up all over the countryside to such an extent that there are said to be more of them concentrated throughout the region than anywhere else in France. Each community still takes enormous pride in its own church, be it an ornate cathedral, the last vestige of an ancient abbey or a minute construction that has survived since Roman times. Agriculture is a way of life for a large proportion of the population whose crops include cereals and tobacco, walnuts, strawberries and grapes for the table or, more usually, for wine. The pastures are full of sheep and cattle, extensive woodlands provide timber, dogs and pigs forage round under the oak trees for truffles and a surprisingly large number of smallholders have a gaggle of geese and a sign offering *foie gras* for sale.

The *département* is divided into four sections. In the north is Périgord Vert, crossed by the River Dronne with towns like Nontron, Brantôme and Ribérac. Périgord Blanc occupies a strip right across the middle, more or less bisected by the River Isle which runs through Périgueux, the ancient capital that was home to both the Gauls and the Romans. Périgord Pourpre, also known as Bergeracois, lies along the lower reaches of the Dordogne, shares its southern boundary with Lot-et-Garonne and revolves to a large extent round the town of Bergerac. Last but by no means least is Périgord Noir, climbing up towards the Massif Central in the east, sliced through by the Dordogne with its profusion of castles and *châteaux* and by the Vézère, remarkable for its prehistoric caves and atmospheric villages.

The *département* is not particularly large, in fact Périgueux, almost exactly in the middle, is only 49km (30 miles) from Nontron, 47km (29 miles) from Bergerac and 66km (41 miles) from Sarlat-la-Canéda, the principal town in Périgord Noir. There are some people who rush straight through, taking advantage of the main roads which are pleasant and extremely well maintained, seeing little except, as one visitor remarked, 'so many different shades of green'. Others take their time, often following an itinerary suggested by the tourist office which can last for anything from four to seven days with recommended stops at convenient intervals. A few explore each area thoroughly, discovering their own small *auberges* and making a point of visiting every historic building, attractive site and little local museum, frequently so full of articles that it takes quite a while to inspect all the items on display.

There are several different ways of travelling round Périgord. The quickest and easiest is obviously by car, especially as the roads, including the minor ones, are usually in an excellent state of repair and the byways are seldom crowded, except perhaps at the height of the holiday season. Local buses are another option and during July and August special coaches are available for excursions to the region's most important tourist attractions with a guide to explain their significance and draw attention to the finer points of each historic church and *château*. More energetic visitors will find that there are bicycles for people who want to pedal about on their own as well as organised outings complete with a guide and someone to transport the luggage from one hotel or campsite to the next overnight stopping place. This service is included in the overall price, along with bed, breakfast and dinner, plus tents where necessary, but cyclists should take along enough money with them to pay for lunch and to cover the entrance fees to the various places of interest along the route.

Horsedrawn caravans appeal to anyone with a gipsy streak in their nature and are readily available in Périgord Vert and Le Bergeracois. They can be hired for a weekend or by the week from the end of March to mid-October and the horse, like those on offer for those who prefer riding to driving, usually has a pretty good idea of where to go. Riders will find that they can make their own arrangements for a week or more on horseback at any time of the year or take advantage of organised seasonal trips starting on Sunday and lasting seven days. The price, including such things as saddlebags, depends on whether the party is camping out, putting up at a small *auberge* or *chambre d'hôte* or staying in style at a country manor. Canoe trips fall into much the same categories. They are available mainly on the Dordogne and the Vézère, can be do-it-yourself excursions or guided tours and come complete with tuition where it is required, advice on conditions and strategically placed campsites, or as package deals covering tents, a picnic lunch, dinner and even a bus where necessary.

The many people who prefer walking have various options. The first is a choice of routes known as Les Sentiers de Grande Randonnée which wander about all over the *département*, as they do throughout the rest of France, just missing the major towns but calling at a host of attractive smaller places such as St Jean-de-Côle, Le Bugue and Belvès, before crossing the border at a dozen different carefully selected points. If back-packing sounds too much like hard work it is possible to hire a donkey to carry the bags. Once again the visitor can wander at will or join a party having paid in advance for

bed, breakfast and dinner, a picnic lunch and the services of a guide.

Having decided where and how to go, the next question is what to do. In addition to visiting all the local attractions, both natural and man-made, there are plenty of other suggestions worth considering. For example, how about inspecting the area from a hot-air balloon? One such offer will set you back a bit as the price also includes a bedroom in an historic *château*, a candlelit dinner in the ancient guardroom, lunch on the terrace if the weather is fine and an opportunity to walk, cycle or even work up an appetite on the tennis court. Alternatively it is possible to keep both feet on the ground and spend the time learning how to paint, make pottery or jewellery, work with silk, leather, metal or wood, sculpture, weave or even turn out a couple of baskets which are bound to come in useful if one is staying in a *gîte*. There are also recommended *chambres d'hôtes* that are quite reasonable and, somewhat unusually, may include both wine and coffee in the price.

Open-air enthusiasts can try their hands at parachuting, but only after a doctor has given his consent, while others can play golf, indulge in windsurfing, go climbing or rafting, learn archery or explore underground caves and potholes. Special courses are open to people who want to try out local recipes, with plenty of opportunities for fishermen to contribute something to the pot. Things are not quite so simple for anyone out after pheasants because shooting

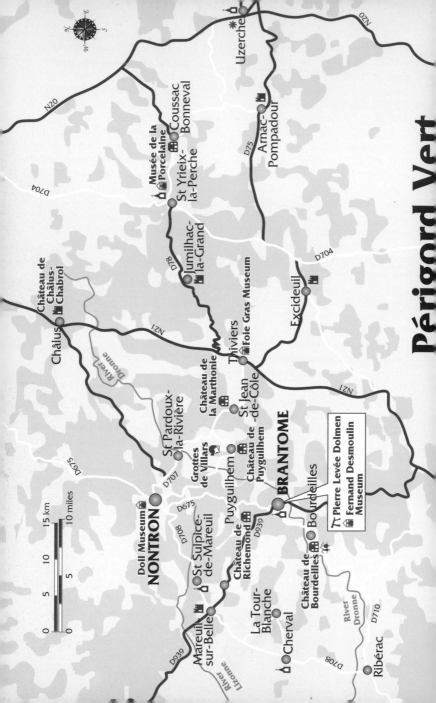

Périgord Vert

Uzerche

N20

Coussac-Bonneval

Musée de la Porcelaine

St Yrieix-la-Perche

D704

Arnac-Pompadour

D75

Jumilhac-la-Grand

D78

Château de Châlus-Chabrol

Châlus

River Dronne

Excideuil

D704

Thiviers

Foie Gras Museum

D704

L'IZ

St Pardoux-la-Rivière

Château de la Marthonie

St Jean-de-Côle

D707

Grottes de Villars

Puyguilhem

Château de Puyguilhem

BRANTÔME

L'IZN

Doll Museum

NONTRON

D675

D708

St Sulpice-de-Mareuil

Château de Richemond

Puyguilhem

D939

Bourdeilles

π Pierre Levée Dolmen
🏛 Fernand Desmoulin Museum

Château de Bourdeilles

La Tour-Blanche

River Dronne

D710

Mareuil-sur-Belle

Cherval

D708

Ribérac

River Lizonne

D939

15 km

10 miles

0   5   10

0   5   10

N20

Brantôme market

Pierre Levée, the remains of a prehistoric burial chamber, near Brantôme

is only allowed during December and January. The sophisticated visitor will not find a great number of luxury hotels or up-market entertainments although there are some old manor houses and antiquated mills which have been turned into charming, comfortable and well-run hotels. Anybody who is prepared to be one of a crowd, often a large and vociferous one, has a choice of festivals during July and August, ranging from the traditional Félibrée, which takes place in a different town every year, to events such as pantomime in Périgueux, classical music in Brantôme and drama in Salat.

PÉRIGORD VERT

Périgord Vert is aptly named, especially in the spring with fresh green leaves on the trees, meadows filled with flowers and the River Dronne making its way calmly and sweetly towards the River Isle, joining forces with it beyond the border in the general direction of Bordeaux. The main town is **Nontron**, not the most memorable of tourist centres although it stands on a ridge between two gorges, thereby commanding a worthwhile view. There is one adequate hotel and a charming little museum full of antique dolls, some of them in historical tableaux like the Salon Récamier and Napoléon and Marie Louise, as well as the Maison de Poupées, theatres, toys and old fashioned games, housed in the *châteaux* nearby. In addition to all this the town occasionally lays on an exhibition or some other event for those who happen to be in the vicinity. The countryside thereabouts is pleasant and undemanding, making it a good place for those who enjoy walking, particularly as three Grandes Randonnées — the GR4, GR36 and the GR436 — are not far away. A happy choice for families who prefer the freedom of a *gîte* to staying in a hotel would be the nearby holiday village of **Les Fontaines** where some forty chalets are scattered about under the trees surrounding a reasonably-sized lake. Further north, at **St Estephe**, a campsite on the edge of the Grand-Etang can accommodate up to 200 people. It provides them with all the usual facilities including an accessible restaurant, adds things like sail boards and pedalos for good measure and is open from mid-June to mid-September. Alternatively it is possible to book a studio in a secluded house overlooking the water and thereafter spend the time walking, bathing, fishing or inspecting places of interest in the immediate area. Not that there are a great many of them apart from **Varaignes** which boasts a Museum of Arts, Popular Traditions and Weaving that is open throughout the year and **Teyjat** which has a small prehistoric grotto all to itself. An added bonus is that a guide is on hand in the village right through the year. Be this as it may, people with concentrated sightseeing in mind would probably be better advised to continue on southwards to Brantôme and explore all the nearby attractions from a base which is closer to hand.

Brantôme itself is an enchanting place, decidedly overcrowded during the season but very inviting at other times of the year. To start with the old section is completely surrounded by two arms of the River Dronne, overlooked by a large abbey which has had quite a chequered career. It was founded in 769 by Charlemagne who wanted a home for the relics of St Sicaire, one of the Holy Innocents murdered by Herod in a vain attempt to rid himself of the infant Christ. As a result it attracted large crowds of pilgrims until it was sacked by the Vikings, only to be recreated in the eleventh century by the Abbé Guillaume. His buildings were altered for the first time 300 years later and again quite extensively in the eighteenth century, after which the whole complex looked very much as it does today.

The church, elegant rather than ornate, has a fifteenth-century dome, a slightly older stone relief of the Baptism of Christ, an even older one of the Massacre of the Innocents and the remains of a chapterhouse which can just be seen from one of the galleries. But the most impressive sight is the four-storey bell tower, built on a rock behind the church in the eleventh century and undoubtedly the best example of its kind in Périgord. The main building, a long white structure facing the river, was an abbey 300 years ago but now gives house room to the town hall and the Fernand Desmoulin Museum. This takes its name from a painter who was born near Nontron in the mid-1800s and, apparently, only practised his art under the influence of a medium. The results can be seen in one of the rooms but are not really to everybody's liking. There are other works by local artists as well as an archaeological section devoted to various items found in the area. Also worthy of note is the beautiful old staircase leading to the original dormitory. The rocks behind the abbey are full of caves once used by the monks for activities such as baking bread and making wine as well as storing their provisions. The biggest of them is memorable for two large groups sculptured out of the rock face and depicting the Crucifixion and the Last Judgement. They are more than a trifle world weary after nearly 600 years and, sadly, the atmosphere has been somewhat ruined by the addition of a stage and some rather hard chairs plonked down, theatre-wise, in front of them.

In an open courtyard on the far side of the complex a bust of Pierre de Bourdeille, a purely administrative Abbé de Brantôme, gazes out over the rather mundane St Sicaire fountain. He is a good looking man with a goatee beard and a moustache, a buttoned shirt and a small ruff, every inch a courtier. But he was many other things besides. Born in 1540, the third son of a count, he spent his formative years under the watchful eye of Marguerite de Valois, the queen of Navarre, before completing his education at the University of Poitiers at the age of 15. Like so many other young men of his day with a taste for both intrigue and adventure he became a soldier of

Brantôme Abbey

fortune and in 1561 was chosen to escort Mary Queen of Scots across the Channel to Holyrood House after the death of her husband, the Dauphin of France. Three years later he turned up in Morocco after which he gave the Knights of Malta a hand in their battles with Suleiman the Magnificent, popped up in Italy, fought for the Spaniards in Africa and faced the Turkish invaders in Hungary before siding with the Catholics against the Huguenots back in his own country.

In addition to his other qualities Bourdeille must have been a wily and accomplished diplomat. On two different occasions he managed to persuade the Protestant leader Admiral de Coligny, a one-time comrade in arms, to change his mind about sacking Brantôme Abbey. This is even more remarkable in view of the fact that Coligny was bloodthirsty enough to lock 300 peasants inside the nearby castle at La Chapelle-Faucher and then set fire to it. However there is absolutely nothing diplomatic about Bourdeille's famous chronicles, produced under the name *Brantôme*. He started writing these memoirs after the battle of Jarnac in 1569, filling them with adventures liberally spiced with the gallantries and scandals of the French nobility. He wrote easily and graphically, mixing satire with humour and ruining any number of reputations in the process. There followed another spell at court, possibly to catch up on the latest gossip but officially to become chamberlain to Charles IX. He even found time to visit Queen Elizabeth in England in 1579. But then his luck ran out. He was crippled after a fall from his horse and retired to the abbey where he continued to write until his death there in 1614.

Facing the fountain from the other side of the road is a small Renaissance pavilion guarding the end of an elbow bridge that dates from the sixteenth century and leads across the Dronne to the abbot's rose garden. Originally it was a kind of summerhouse reserved for important members of the clergy but these days it serves a more general purpose as the office of the Syndicat d'Initiative. Still further on along the road are several houses, some of them very eye-catching indeed, occupying caves in the side of the cliff. Quite a few could do with a bit of attention, new doors and a coat of paint, whereas others are totally fascinating, covered in creepers with small wooden staircases and bushes growing out of the hillside above their heads.

The old quarter of the town is filled with elderly buildings, none of them especially memorable, little narrow streets and small shops crammed with merchandise of every description. On the far side of the town, a couple of kilometres down the road to Thiviers, is a dolmen called Pierre Levée. It consists of the usual large flat stone balanced on smaller ones with, rather incongruously, a modern supporting pillar added for safety and all but hidden by a strategically planted creeper.

Brantôme is well aware of its importance as a tourist centre and has a clutch of very comfortable hotels to prove it. Some visitors maintain that the Moulin de l'Abbaye, with its old waterwheel turning slowly in the river close to the ancient bridge, is the most picturesque, while others give their vote to the Moulin du Roc, a bare 6km (4 miles) from the town. It is a seventeenth-century walnut mill, furnished with items that would not look too out of place in a museum and now provides traditional dishes second to none in Périgord. Unfortunately both of them are very small and extremely popular, but there are several other places to choose from which are most acceptable, each in its own way. In addition to the hotels, and even a restaurant with rooms to let, there are *chambres d'hôtes*, a selection of *gîtes*, other furnished accommodation and a municipal campsite.

Sporting enthusiasts will find that they can play tennis, table tennis or *boules*, hire a horse or a canoe, practice judo or karate, take a gentle stroll or walk for miles, either through open country or along the GR36 or the GR436, both of which are close at hand. Special entertainments during the summer season include equestrian events, concerts, lectures and dances and even a Franco-British *fête*. The weekly market, held every Friday morning on the banks of the Dronne, is an extremely colourful affair, spilling over the bridge into the old quarter in a flurry of awnings and trestle tables groaning under the weight of fresh fish, duck, fruit, vegetables and flowers, hats, shoes and almost anything else you care to mention.

South-west of Brantôme and only a short distance away is **Bourdeilles** with its historic *château*, the family home of the famous chronicler. It is, in fact, two buildings standing high above the River Dronne with an atmospheric little hamlet clustered round the walls. The original castle was ceded to the English in 1259 by St Louis, the ninth French king of that name. This caused enormous friction throughout the barony. Some members of the family and their followers supported the Plantagenets while the others remained faithful to the Capetians, then the royal house of France. There were plots and counter plots, lawsuits and the like until Géraud de Maumont took matters into his own hands and recovered the castle by force. With the approval of the king, then Philip the Fair, he proceeded to turn it into a fortress after which it was constantly in the wars and had to be patched up or repaired after each ferocious encounter.

The castle is a very workmanlike building with walls up to 2m (7ft) thick, a massive octagonal keep and a large gallery that comes in useful for exhibitions in these less turbulent days. The family were still in residence when, in the mid-sixteenth century, Catherine de Medici decided to take her son Charles on a tour of their possessions. Jacquette de Montbron, who was married to Brantôme's brother André, decided to build a special *château* for her ex-

pected visitors, but they failed to turn up and the project was abandoned before it was completed. The *château* is a somewhat austere three storey building standing at right angles to the castle but inside it has been liberally decorated and furnished with items provided by two of its patrons. A series of wooden chests on the ground floor includes several from the fifteenth and sixteenth centuries and even sea chests used by the corsairs which may at one time have been brimming over with pirate jewels and gold. Among other items of interest are a replica of the Holy Sepulchre from Montgé Priory, a carved panel entitled *The Teaching of the Infant Jesus* and a collection of arms and armour. The first floor is particularly memorable for the Salon Doré, a large splendidly decorated room hung with enormous tapestries one of which shows François I indulging in a spot of falconry. There are also paintings by Ambroise le Noble who was a court artist at Fontainebleau, as well as contemporary furniture, carpets and one or two *objets d'art*. The floor above has a decidedly Spanish flavour with paintings, furniture and, as its prize possession, an extremely ornate bed that was slept in by the Emperor Charles V. The two buildings are protected firstly by a fortified curtain wall, then by a second wall surrounding the outer courtyard and finally by a third edging the esplanade which also has a no-nonsense air about it. But the view is especially attractive, the more so if you peer over the wall at the river below. The most eye-catching things at that level are a medieval bridge and an old water mill, built to look like a boat, moored to the bank by a fairly wide path and festooned with flowers. Bourdeilles is definitely a place not to be missed and has the added advantage for canoeists of overlooking their route down river to a useful campsite just outside the town.

To the north of Brantôme, off the road to Nontron on the western side, is the **Château de Richemond**. This not very prepossessing pile was built by Pierre de Bourdeille who lived there for a time and is buried in the chapel at the foot of the tower. It is reached by way of an atrocious road and through two archways beyond which is a courtyard, open on two sides and containing a decorative old well. At the moment the whole property is rather run down but there are signs that it is being refurbished and restored. It should then emerge as a pleasing manor house set in attractively wooded grounds. The area all round is mildly hilly with little roads that make their way through farmlands to hamlets like St Crépin-de-Richemond, tucked neatly into a valley beside the river with a graveyard containing some rather ostentatious mausoleums.

Further to the north-west the perfectly acceptable, fairly busy but not very exciting D939 saunters across the plains to **Mareuil-sur-Belle**, past old cottages and a peppering of wildly spaced twentieth-century buildings including several modern homes. Like Bourdeilles, Mareuil

was an important barony in the Middle Ages when its fortified castle must have been very difficult to defend. It stands in flat open country, slightly aloof from its attendant village, with the remains of a moat, an entrance fort and a ramp leading to the *château* itself. The main section has been restored and a guided tour, lasting about three quarters of an hour, takes in the dungeons, a Gothic chapel that was damaged during the Revolution and living quarters overlooking a garden enclosed by the ramparts. Apart from some attractive furniture and pictures there is a room devoted to Maréchal Lannes who was one of Napoleon's outstanding generals. On display are some of his letters and portraits, his sword and, hardly surprisingly, a bust of Napoleon whom he helped in his successful bid for power in 1799. Another good reason for visiting Mareuil-sur-Belle is that there are some attractive little places scattered about this pleasantly wooded area. A case in point is **St Sulpice-de-Mareuil**, well-known for its twelfth-century church and especially for the carved doorway all set about with the most unlikely animals, some unidentified figures and an occasional scroll. The churchyard is a picture with flowers on nearly every grave and although the majority turn out to be artificial this does not seem to deter the bees at all.

Vieux-Mareuil, quite an ordinary little hamlet with a faintly warlike church dating from the thirteenth century, makes a good stopping place if you book into the Auberge

The boat-shaped mill in the River Dronne below the castle walls at Bourdeilles

l'Etang Bleu some 2km (1 mile) away. As the name implies it stands, smothered in creepers, beside its own lake, has large grounds and a little train to take visitors on a tour of the property. Meanwhile **Argentine**, in the opposite direction and close to the border with Charente, sits on a limestone plateau so riddled with caves and quarries that it has been likened to a Swiss cheese. **La-Roche-beaucourt-et-Argentine** is somewhat bigger, has no hotels to speak of and only the slightest possible link with history. A member of the local community, one Pauline de Tourzel, was thrown into the Templar Prison with Louis XVI and his family, thereby gaining honourable mention in the chapel as well as in the grounds of the castle which was burned down in 1941. Collectors of small churches would do well to call at **Cherval** where there is a perfect example, expertly restored, whereas searchers after ancient ruins will find what they are looking for at **La-Tour-Blanche**, complete with a medieval keep and a village full of elderly houses but little else besides.

Château de Puyguilhem

Still to the west of Brantôme, although a trifle further south, is **Ribérac**, a pleasantly functional small town with some nice little shops, several *gîtes* and a good many British residents. The area is concerned mainly with raising cattle and growing cereals but it also provides tennis, riding and fishing and is a great place for markets and country fairs. There are a couple of modest hotels while Siorac-de-Ribérac weighs in with the odd room or two, but all this is hardly enough to earn it a place in the official list of popular tourist resorts. Most of the hamlets round about have a privately owned *château* not open to the public or a moderately interesting small church.

The most viewable of these are at Vanxains and St-Privat, also known as **St-Privat-des-Prés**. The latter was not only closely connected with a twelfth-century Benedictine priory but is also the proud possessor of a Centre of Popular Arts and Traditions of the Dronne and Double Regions. It is an enterprising little museum which has recreated scenes from the past such as fully equipped workshops, a hairdressing establishment and a grocer's shop. In addition it displays a host of other articles like farm tools, household items and everything that was necessary to run a nineteenth-century school.

Having more or less exhausted the possibilities to the north, south and west of Brantôme the time has come to travel east. Here the first stopping place would probably be the ruined **Abbaye de Boschaud**, provided of course one was approaching the sign from the right direction. Like so many of these roadside identification boards it does not appear to be unduly concerned about traffic coming up on its blind side so it is necessary to drive slowly and keep a weather eye open. The only alternative is to keep backing the car or finding somewhere to turn round and thereby locate it from the opposite direction. The abbey started life in 1163 in a valley called Basco Cavo (Hollow Wood), and it is thought that this could possibly have been the origin of its name. It was a Cistercian house with all the usual buildings including a domed church. However, as in the case of so many other religious centres, the monks were turned out at the time of the Revolution and there was no-one left to prevent it falling down. Fortunately just enough remained standing for restoration work to begin in 1950 and although this has made good progress it still has a long way to go. On the other hand, **Puyguilhem**, practically next door, is a splendid early sixteenth-century castle built by Mondot de la Marthonie, the first president of the Paris Parliament. It looks as though he inspected every *château* on the Loire before deciding exactly what he wanted. This turned out to be an elegant country seat which pretended, not very successfully, to be a fortress. There are towers whose

duty it is to provide room for staircases, the mock battlements, decorated with oak leaves, and the windows designed to light the interior instead of giving the defenders a limited view of their enemy. The whole place was in a sorry state when the Fine Arts Department bought it in 1939. Since World War II it has been done up completely, furnished in character and staffed by guides whose job it is to show visitors over the premises.

Another attraction practically on the doorstep is the series of caves known as the **Grottes de Villars**. There are prehistoric wall paintings many thousands of years old showing bison, hunters and horses, as well as stalactites, some of which are surprisingly white, and a couple of small pools, all reached by way of a passage through the rock. A detailed inspection takes roughly half an hour and is a good prelude to the larger and more impressive caves further to the south.

The last place of note in this group is the enchanting village of **St-Jean-de-Côle**, standing on a tributary of the River Dronne. It is old and very atmospheric with a humpbacked bridge closed to traffic, an unusual church and the imposing Château de la Marthonie. The church was once a chapel attached to an eleventh-century priory and is remarkable for both its oddly-shaped bell tower and the old covered market built on at one end. Tourists are inclined to treat this open space with respect but the locals park their cars inside, out of the sun. One of the most noticeable things about the church is the wooden ceiling covering a large hole in the nave, left open to the elements when the dome fell in. There is some 300-year-old wood carving in the chancel, a faceless figure lying on a tomb in one of the chapels and a painted eleventh-century statue of the Virgin and Child in a niche on the opposite wall. Anyone who walks over the bridge, or even paddles across the shallow ford alongside it, is rewarded with a glimpse of the original cloisters beyond a grassy field protected by a solid stone wall. The **Château de la Marthonie** has a long history but not a great deal to show from its earliest days. The tower and the foundations go back to the twelfth century but the windows were added some 300 to 400 years later when the whole place was rebuilt, whereas the stone staircase climbing up through the archways inside is a seventeenth-century addition. Guided tours are laid on during the summer and include a gallery set aside for old publicity posters and a collection of handmade paper. St-Jean-de-Côle is right beside the GR436 which means that long distance walkers have absolutely no difficulty in calling there and even spending the night at the modest *auberge.*

Thiviers, a bustling market town on the N21 to Limoges, is renowned for its markets, *foie gras*, truffles and the Château de Vaucocour. The castle has been altered and restored so many times that only a few people are disappointed to discover that it is not prepared to accept visitors.

However there are other attractions including the Foie Gras Museum, bicycles for hire in the Rue Lamy, an occasional exhibition, concert, *fête* or event based on folklore as well as a brace of small hotels.

From here a brief and easy excursion would be to **Excideuil**, on the border with Périgord Blanc. It is a busy little town with the remains of a feudal castle that held out against Richard Coeur de Lion on three separate occasions in 1182. Eventually it fell to the English during the Hundred Years' War, only to be recaptured by the redoubtable Bertrand du Guesclin. The fortress was sold by Henry III in 1582, upon which the new owner built himself a more comfortable *château* next door. This has been refurbished on occasions and even had some extra turrets and windows added for good measure, with the result that it is apparently in two minds about whether to open its doors to the public or not. At the moment it is closed, although sightseers can walk right round the property or simply admire the ruins and the *château* with far less effort from a convenient spot on the river bank. The local church was attached to a Benedictine priory at the time that Richard Coeur de Lion had his eye on the site. It was altered quite considerably 300 years later and is now the home of Our Lady of Excideuil. She is apparently only too pleased to listen to prayers and requests for assistance and many supplicants have expressed their gratitude by surrounding her with ex-votos in the accepted man-

St-Jean-de-Côle; Château de la Marthonie on the foundations of a twelfth-century stronghold

St-Jean-de-Côle; the ancient bridge and ford over the River Côle

ner. St Médard-d'Excideuil is just a stone's throw from the Château d'Essendièras once the home of André Herzog, better known as André Maurois. As a result of his experiences during World War I he wrote his best seller *The Silences of Colonel Bramble* followed by a series of biographies whose subjects included Queen Victoria, Byron, Cecil Rhodes and Sir Alexander Fleming who discovered penicillin.

Just north of Thiviers the attractive D78 leaves the main road and keeps company with the River Isle to **Jumilhac-le-Grand**, perched on a rock overlooking the gorges. One of the most fantastic things about it is the castle, built originally by the Knights Templar in the thirteenth century. It was bought in 1579 by a family who had amassed a fortune making arms and armaments and were determined to turn their home into something out of a fairytale. They festooned it with towers and turrets and decorated them with the sun and moon, angels and iron birds. Not content with all this a subsequent owner added two more wings in the seventeenth century which resulted in an extraordinary conglomeration of ideas that loses nothing by being floodlit during the season. Guided tours at various times from mid-March to mid-November invariably include the so-called Spinner's Room. It is said that Louise de Hautefort was shut up in this little space after her husband discovered that she had been unfaithful to him. Nothing daunted she arranged for her lover to be smuggled in at inter-

vals and spent the rest of the time spinning and painting pictures all over the walls. There is a small *auberge* in the village and at least one *gîte* that sleeps half a dozen people and offers opportunities for riding, tennis, fishing, and swimming in the vicinity. It is also a good place for walking, especially in spring when the meadows are full of flowers and the woods are fresh and inviting, but there are no marked footpaths and the Grandes Randonnées are a considerable distance away.

Across the Border in Limousin

As there is seldom anything to mark the border between the different provinces and *départements*, with many places of interest on the far side of these invisible lines, it would be a pity to ignore some of the nearby attractions simply because they happen to be in Limousin. A case in point is **Châlus**, on the main road from Limoges to Périgueux. It is not a particularly outstanding village and might well escape notice altogether were it not for the fact that Richard Coeur de Lion was fatally wounded during an attack on the castle in 1199. The Château de Châlus-Chabrol, as it is called, is a hilltop fort, hidden by trees, which was built in the eleventh century to guard against all too frequent attacks from the south-west. There are guided tours from July to mid-September which are concentrated mainly on the original fortress but also include part of the mansion that was added 600 years later. A small museum divides its attention between the history of the castle and the life of King Richard. The Château de Montbrun, north of the road linking Châlus with Nontron, was another fortress that resisted the attentions of Richard Coeur de Lion. It is a functional looking place, partly surrounded by water, which has been largely restored since a fire caused considerable damage in 1917.

In the opposite direction a most acceptable and not particularly busy road runs south-east past Le Chalard with its old fortified church to **St-Yrieix-la-Perche**. This energetic little town occupies the site of a Gallo-Roman settlement called *Attanum*. An abbey was founded there by Aredius in the sixth century but it gradually crumbled away to be replaced by the impressive Collégiale du Moûtier roughly 600 years later. This splendid church is beautifully decorated both inside and out and possesses as its most important treasure a reliquary bust of St Yrieix. It was fashioned from wood and precious metals in the fifteenth century, given a jewelled collar that was already 200 years old, and placed in a niche in the heart of the church. There are a number of other items that are well worth inspecting although it is necessary to call at the *hôtel de ville* in order to see a superb eleventh-century Bible which is housed there permanently. In 1771 kaolin was discovered in St-Yrieix-la-Perche. Within a remarkably short time busy little workshops were turning out exquisite porcelain that soon became famous all over the world. There is an interesting collection in the local Musée de la Porcelaine with pieces collected from many parts of France but especially from Limoges where the industry started. Shops throughout the area are filled with this most attractive china that can be either delicate and painted in pastel shades or jewel-coloured with elaborate little scenes enlivened here and there with 22 carat gold. Anyone who feels inclined to stop for a while will find an up-market hotel with an excellent restaurant about 12km (7 miles) outside the town. There is also a restaurant in the Boulevard de l'Hôtel de Ville with a dozen or so rooms at less than half the price. Bicycles are available for hire and visitors are encouraged to ride, swim or play tennis as well as sample the Madeleine cakes, a delicacy of which the local bakers are inordinately proud.

To the east of St-Yrieix-la-Perche, and only 12km (7 miles) distant, is **Coussac-Bonneval**, a fourteenth-century *château* belonging to an illustrious family whose most unusual member was undoubtedly Claude-Alexander de Bonneval, sometimes known as Achmet-Pacha. He was born in 1675, fought at the head of an infantry regiment during the Italian campaigns but then transferred his loyalties to Prince Eugène of Austria who made him a general. He returned to France in 1717 where he married but refused to settle down. Back in the service of Austria he had a difference of opinion with the prince and left in disgrace for Constantinople. Here he was converted to Islam, put his talents at the disposal of the sultan, helped to reorganise the Turkish army and then scored more than one victory over the disconcerted Austrians. Attempts were made to persuade him to change sides again but he refused to return to France and eventually died in Constantinople. The contents of the *château* where he was born, and which was refurbished in the eighteenth and nineteenth centuries, include several reminders of Bonneval-Pacha as well as some eye-catching tapestries and Louis XVI furniture. The village also boasts a *lanterne des morts* dating from the twelfth century which once illuminated the entrance to the cemetery and served as a landmark for anyone unfortunate enough to be travelling at night. The local church is of the same vintage but was much restored and redecorated about 200 years ago.

On the way south it would be a definite oversight to miss **Arnac-Pompadour**, which is also within quite easy reach of Thiviers and therefore Brantôme. It has two main claims to fame, a very obtrusive castle and an important Haras, which accounts for the fact that the town is known as both 'The Horse Lovers' City' and 'Cradle of the Anglo-Arab Breed'. The castle was a present from Louis XV to his mistress of the moment, Antionette Poisson, in 1745 along with the title of Madame de Pompadour. Some people maintain that she never even found the time to look at it, let alone live there, whereas others insist that she was seen in the vicinity, if only briefly and on very rare occasions. Either way it is certainly true that she would be a complete stranger to the present *château* because the main building was destroyed during the Revolution when only the outer walls and towers survived.

A short time before Madame de Pompadour died in 1764 the king set up two special farms, one for stallions and the other for mares, more or less in the shadow of the castle. Today they form part of the national stud and can be visited on weekday afternoons, as well as on Sunday mornings and public holidays, but only from the beginning of July to the end of February. The *château* provides offices and living accommodation for members of the staff who arrange for visitors to be shown round the gardens almost any morning or afternoon but seldom if ever invite any of them inside. The terraces are also open to the public on race days when crowds line the walls to get an uninterrupted view of the events taking place on the course situated on the far side of the road. The only other local attraction is the Eglise d'Arnac, a rather forbidding little church which traces its history back to the twelfth century. Inside it can just rustle up a limited amount of art work and a few statues and is therefore hardly worth visiting unless one has plenty of time. Guests staying at one of the small hotels can ride, play tennis or swim but from the point of view of sightseeing there

Porte Bécharie at Uzerche, the only original gateway still surviving

is really nothing to rival the charms of Uzerche, a short drive away.

Even when viewed from a distance it is easy to see why **Uzerche** is often referred to as the Pearl of Limousin. This extremely picturesque little town climbs somewhat precariously along the side of a ridge, caught in a sharp bend of the River Vézère. It is a solid mass of small streets and ancient houses, slate roofs, towers and turrets which could double as hat rests for a witches' convention, and an occasional balcony. Right at the top is the large twelfth-century church of St Pierre dominated by its original bell tower. This, with a little bit of help, has survived intact in spite of all the troubles it has had to put up with from both friends and enemies. Among the things to see inside are some interesting carved stone capitals and an ancient tomb which has been in the crypt so long that no-one has discovered who is buried there or why. Most of the early ramparts have disappeared apart from the Porte Bécharie, reached by way of a narrow road between solid stone houses, at least one of which is decorated with a coat of arms. On the other side a steep flight of steps leads down to the river far below. The gateway, with its surprisingly modern statue of the Virgin Mary, is close to another, less demanding little stairway called the Escalier-Notre-Dame. This provides access to the Place des Vignerons, the market square of the former days, with the ancient Notre-Dame chapel in one corner and the Black Prince's Tower

a stone's throw away. It is impossible to appreciate all that Uzerche has to offer without taking a stroll down the Rue Gaby-Furnestin where Napoleon's surgeon, Alexis Boyer, used to live and on past the decorative doorways lining streets named after Pierre Chalaud and Jean Gentet, to end up admiring the view from the Esplanade de la Lunade which looks out over the valley. There are one or two small hotels providing bedrooms with private baths in addition to restaurants where the menus are mainly traditional. The local campsite has a few chalets as well as places for tents and caravans which makes it a convenient stopping place before heading south along the main route to Brive-la-Gaillarde or selecting any of the minor roads that amble about through hilly country on their journey back to Périgord.

PÉRIGORD BLANC

Périgord Blanc, vaguely resembling a short, decorative boot striding across the centre of the *département*, gets its name from the grey and white limestone that is immediately apparent all over the area. The river valleys, of which the most important is the Isle, are taken up mainly with agriculture and animal husbandry although there are one or two light industries such as cement works and factories producing textiles and shoes. Double, north of the Isle, was once exceedingly marshy and there are still plenty of little pools dotted about, interspersed with forests of oak, chestnuts and pine which provide a certain amount of timber. Deposits washed down from the Massif Central on to the countryside round Vergt, south of Périgueux, have proved ideal for growing strawberries. The fruit from here is particularly delicious so it comes as no surprise to find that the district is considered to be the most outstanding strawberry producing area in France.

Périgueux, the capital of the *département*, is more or less in the centre with main roads that radiate out in all directions, linking it with Limoges, Angoulême, Bordeaux, Agen, Cahors and Brive-la-Gaillarde, often described as the gateway to the south. There are domestic flights to Paris, trains take about 5 hours to Lyon, 4 hours to Paris, 3 hours to Toulouse and about 75 minutes to Bordeaux, but no motorail facilities are available at the moment. The buses are local rather than long distance with the addition of special services running comprehensive tours during July and August. Tickets are obtainable from either the railway station or the Syndicat d'Initiative near the post office but it is as well to remember that lunch is not included in the price. There are cars for hire and bicycles can be found in the Avenue Maréchal Juin and the Cours St George. The city boasts a fairly comprehensive selection of hotels with three in the very comfortable bracket and a dozen or so other perfectly acceptable establishments, including restaurants with rooms attached. The majority make a point of listing the various pastimes open to their guests, ranging from tennis, golf and riding to billiards and table tennis, as well as drawing attention to a children's playground close at hand. There are some excellent restaurants and plenty of little shops, especially in the Rue Limogeanne.

Although Périgueux is a reasonably sized town with a tendency to sprawl along both sides of the River Isle, it is easier to think of the old section as two ancient quarters that joined forces at some time during the Middle Ages. The older was, and is, known as La Cité whereas the other shares its name with the white-domed cathedral of St Front. La Cité was originally a Gaulish settlement where the *Petrocorii*, meaning 'Four Tribes', established a fortified settlement near the sacred spring they called the *Vésone*. When Julius Caesar arrived on the scene the people sided with the Arverne chieftain, Vercingétorix in a vain attempt to halt the Roman advance. After one spectacular success he was defeated and the area found itself well and truly in foreign hands. However this soon proved to be no bad thing. The Romans renamed the settlement *Vesunna* and proceeded to build furiously until the new town with its temples and villas, arena, forum and baths, not to mention an aqueduct more than 7km (4 miles) long, was considered to be one of the best places to live in Aquitaine. It was also one of the first to be sacked by the Alemans in AD3. In spite of the fact that the inhabitants immediately fortified themselves against further attacks, turning the arena into a bastion and pulling down most of the other buildings to put up ramparts, *Vesunna* continued to suffer at the hands of the Visigoths, the Franks and the Vikings. At last there was hardly anything left to justify its name and the remnants were referred to, if anyone did happen to mention them, as 'the town of the Petrocorii' or, more briefly as La Cité.

Fortunately one or two relics have survived from the days before La Cité fell on these increasingly hard times. The **Tour de Vésone**, a solidly built round structure, roughly a quarter of which has fallen down, is all that remains of a temple dedicated to a Roman goddess and sited in the heart of the old forum. Once it was sheathed in marble and had a splendid stairway flanked by colonnades, but now it stands all on its own surrounded by lawns and trees. Legend has it that the damage was caused by St Front when he cursed the temple and all its pagan associations, but historians are more inclined to believe that the missing stones found their way into the ramparts. As long as no-one is expecting a curse to take effect miraculously and immediately this, of course, could amount to exactly the same thing. Close by is all that is left of the **Villa de Pompeïus**, unearthed in 1959 and surrounded by a high chainlink fence. It was built in the first century AD but had to be raised up 100 years later because the area

was prone to flooding, although this did not seem to damage the foundations to any serious extent. It is still possible to make out the various sections of the baths, trace the brick channels that were used for central heating and spot an odd fresco or two.

Unfortunately the arena did not escape so lightly. It is now an attractive garden with a fountain and a few bits and pieces of antiquated stonework round the edges, approached along any of a number of short roads rejoicing in such names as Rue de l'Amphithéâtre and Rue des Gladiateurs. From being one of the largest Roman arenas in Gaul it was demoted to a place in the ramparts and then turned into a fortress with English sympathies during the Hundred Years' War. This building was eventually dismantled on the orders of the French king Charles VI in 1391 and until comparatively recently was used as a quarry to provide building materials for houses going up in the town. The **Porte Normande** dates from AD3, was fashioned out of pieces of stone from temples, tombs and monuments that were conveniently close, giving it a somewhat jigsaw puzzle appearance, and is said to have got its name after an attack by the Vikings on their way up river in the ninth century.

Some 200 hundred years later **St Etienne-de-la-Cité** was built on the site of a temple to Mars and remained a cathedral until 1669. However it suffered at the hands of the Huguenots during the Wars of Reli-

The Roman Tour de Vésone in Périgueux

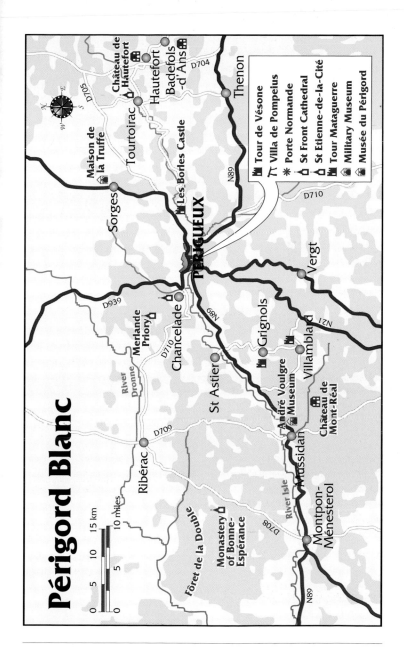

Périgord Blanc

Legend

- Tour de Vésone
- Villa de Pompelus
- Porte Normande
- St Front Cathedral
- St Etienne-de-la-Cité
- Tour Mataguerre
- Military Museum
- Musée du Périgord

Map locations:

Château de Hautefort, Hautefort, Badefols-d'Ans, Thenon, Tourtoirac, Maison de la Truffe, Les Borles Castle, Sorges, PÉRIGUEUX, Vergt, Merlande Priory, Chancelade, Grignols, Villamblard, St Astier, André Voulgre Museum, Château de Mont-Réal, Mussidan, Ribérac, Fôret de la Double, Monastery of Bonne-Espérance, Montpon-Ménesterol

River Dronne, River Isle

Roads: D704, D705, D710, D704, N89, D710, D939, D709, D708, N21, 69N, N89

Scale: 0 5 10 15 km / 0 5 10 miles

gion, losing two of its domes and its bell tower at the same time as the episcopal palace next door was destroyed. Restoration work started in the seventeenth century and today the church is fairly sombre with a carved altar piece, an arch from the tomb of the bishop Jean d'Asside, an ancient font and a 200-year-old organ that was repaired quite recently.

The present **St Front Cathedral** is a much more extrovert affair, largely because it was reconstructed at the end of the eighteenth century by Paul Abadie, a determined architect who was convinced that he knew best. Some might forgive him on the grounds that he went on to design Sacré-Coeur in Paris, but it was a pity that he had to try out his ideas in Périgueux. The cathedral is a massive building, one of the largest churches in south-west France, but it started life as a chapel in the sixth century, marking the burial place of the saint who gave his name to the old quarter. The chapel was replaced by a larger construction, consecrated in 1047 but this was destroyed by fire about 73 years later. The next basilica turned out to be even grander, calling to mind St Mark's in Venice and the Church of the Apostles in Constantinople, but it was torn apart by the Huguenots in 1575, its treasure stolen and the tomb of St Front obliterated. There is no doubt that the whole place was badly in need of attention when Abadie was given the job of restoring it. As far as he was concerned this meant creating the kind of building he wanted to see on the site rather than patching up

the one already there. Amongst other things he pulled down the old refectory, added a number of turrets and up-dated the decorative work, even going so far as to design the new chandeliers. However the altar piece did come from the Jesuit College while the stalls were once part of the abbey at Ligueux. The cloisters started life in the twelfth century and have hardly changed during the last 400 years whereas the chapterhouse is full of all sorts of bits and pieces that did not quite fit in with Abadie's grandiose ideas.

There are many other places of interest to see in Puy-St-Front, starting perhaps with the thirteenth-century **Tour Mataguerre**, believed to have received its name from an Englishman who was imprisoned there during the Hundred Years' War. It is the only remaining tower of twenty-eight which once guarded the medieval city but it has been rebuilt so often that it would be equally true to say that it dates from 1477 or thereabouts. The Rue des Farges leads past the elderly Maison des Dames de la Foi to the **Military Museum** which traces Périgord's warlike past from the Middle Ages to the present day. It is full of everything from weapons to uniforms and would be particularly absorbing for anyone with yesterday's battles in mind. A bevy of fascinating old houses line the narrow streets beyond the cathedral, each with a special feature such as a courtyard, a staircase or a balcony to catch the eye. The Maison Tenant, for example, also known as the Pastrycook's House, has a thought-provoking Latin inscription over the arch. Roughly translated and condensed it declares — 'Let he who takes pleasure in speaking ill of those who are no longer with us know that this house is forbidden to him'. This might have caused trouble in an area that had had so much to put up with in the past, and so many people to blame for its misfortunes, but causes no soul-searching among today's sightseers because the house is not open to the public anyway.

The **Musée du Périgord** on Allées de Tourny occupies the site of an old Augustine convent and is considered to be one of the most important museums of prehistory in France. The items on display cover a remarkably wide range of subjects. There are Stone Age tools, a 70,000-year-old skeleton found near Montignac and a much younger one from Chancelade who perished amongst all his worldly possessions a bare 15,000 years ago. There are axes, earthenware and jewellery which were in existance before and during the Iron Age and exhibits from as far afield as Africa and the Pacific Islands known collectively as Oceania. Coming a bit more up to date, an altar dedicated to the earth goddess Cybele, used for sacrifices and found near the Porte Normande, has pride of place in the Gallo-Roman section. Under the heading of 'Popular Arts and Traditions' are enamels from Limousin and decorative terracotta figures from Thiviers while illustrated manuscripts, paintings and other such exhibits have a department all to themselves.

Finally it is worth taking a stroll along the river bank, past a series of old houses beyond which there is not only an antiquated mill left over from the original granary but also somewhere to leave the car. Périgueux has underground car parks, pleasant shops, statues and fountains and guided tours of the city, details of which can be obtained from the Syndicat d'Initiative in the Avenue d'Aquitaine. Sporting enthusiasts who shudder at the very thought of art or architecture are invited to take part in activities such as tennis, golf and swimming, fishing, shooting, flying and gliding while gourmets can sample some of the most delicious food in Périgord. Colourful markets are held twice a week, in the morning, in the shadow of the cathedral, mainly for the the townspeople although they are crowded with visitors during the season. Some of these will have left their tents and caravans on a campsite not too far away. There are one or two to choose from, mostly well equipped, that tend to become overcrowded at the height of the season.

In addition to the pantomime festival in August there is usually something going on in the town such as an exhibition, a concert which can be anything from classical music to jazz, a theatre production, a tennis or *boules* tournament or an equestrian event. In order to find out what has been arranged, where and when, it is a good idea to get hold of a brochure called *La Fête en Périgord* produced by the Département de Tourisme. It is full of up-to-the-minute informa-

tion covering the whole *département* and is particularly useful with regard to opening and closing times. Châteaux, museums, caves and so on may well change their minds from year to year and having the latest facts and figures avoids unnecessary aggravation, particularly if long trips are involved. There are also details of all sorts of different tours as well as a section listing the times and locations of every event scheduled for the current months.

Taking Périgueux as a convenient base it is very simple to plan excursions to the places of interest in Périgord Blanc, the rest of the area, or much further afield. For a short trip head north along the road linking the capital with Brantôme in order to visit **Chancelade**. This is the site of an Augustine abbey founded in the twelfth century. The monks were thrown out when the English captured it during the Hundred Years' War, only to lose it again briefly to Bertrand du Guesclin, one of the most successful French soldiers of his day. Then, having recovered it without too much trouble, they hung on grimly until the mid-fifteenth century. Even after all this the abbey's troubles were not over because it was partly destroyed by the Protestants during the Wars of Religion and eventually taken over lock, stock and barrel by the Revolutionaries. However it did have a short breathing space in the early seventeenth century when Alain de Solminhac was appointed abbot and set about reforming and restoring Chancelade. As a reward for a job well done he was appointed Bishop of Cahors by Louis XIII but kept an eye on his previous charge, returning after death to be buried a short distance from the church. Although a good deal of the structure is original the same cannot be said of the interior. Some doubt even appears to surround two weary looking frescoes in the chancel, believed to be of St Christopher and Thomas Becket, the ill-fated Archbishop of Canterbury, who had an altar consecrated in his name by the monks after he was canonized in 1173. In contrast to the normal relics one expects to find in a church a pair of shoes, well worn by Alain de Solminhac, are displayed in a glass case in the nave. Some of the abbey buildings are still standing, including a laundry room which is used as an exhibition hall, while part of the presbytery is given over to a Museum of Sacred Art. It is full of items collected from other churches in the vicinity including vestments of various kinds, statuettes, reliquaries and pieces of church plate.

Some 8km (5 miles) away, down a small right-hand turning off the D1, is all that remains of **Merlande Priory**, standing a trifle forlornly in a clearing in the Forêt de Feytaud, surrounded by oaks and chestnut trees. The priory, founded by the monks of Chancelade at the same time as the

---

Opposite: St-Front cathedral, Périgueux

abbey, has completely disappeared apart from a little fortified chapel and the prior's house, both of which have been restored. From here on, towards the north-west, there is not very much to see until the road crosses the River Dronne into Périgord Vert. Once there it takes in Montagrier, a succession of attractive views and Grand-Brassac with its interesting fortified church, before putting on a final spurt to reach Bourdeilles.

An alternative choice for a day out in the country would be to follow the River Isle westwards to the border, with occasional deviations to places such as **St Astier**. This is a well established little town with some old houses and the obligatory church but it is unfortunately over-shadowed by the local cement works. **Mussidan**, on the other hand, is worth visiting in order to see the André Voulgre Museum of Popular Arts and Traditions. It is housed in an attractive long, low, white mansion which was once Dr Voulgre's home and is imaginatively filled with hundreds of different items, many of them collected during his lifetime. A series of rooms are furnished to give an authentic picture of what life was like for a reasonably well-off family in the nineteenth century. The main bedroom is almost ready for someone to move in with a carpet, chairs, a washstand and chest of drawers as well as what appears to be a very comfortable four-poster bed draped with curtains. Life-size figures sit on either side of the kitchen fire, dressed country-style

down to their wooded shoes, the man of the house wearing his hat and holding a skein of wool for his wife who is busy winding it. An older woman can be seen spinning and all around are articles of furniture, and household utensils. In addition a number of different trades are represented with scenes that would have been familiar to people like the local blacksmith and the shoemaker. There is an extensive array of tools and agricultural implements including a 1927 engine driven by steam and a tractor which was provided with tracks from tanks that were surplus to requirements at the end of World War I. An exhibition hall has been added as a home for brass, pewter and pottery as well as a number of stuffed birds and animals while a ceramic workshop, staffed by local artists, produces a selection of useful and decorative articles. Mussidan has a clutch of pleasant, modest *auberges*, the GR646 passes a short distance away en route from St Astier to Montpon and swimming, fishing and canoeing are all available in the surrounding area.

The **Forêt de la Double** starts on the opposite side of the River Isle and stretches almost as far north as St Privat in Périgord Vert. At one time the area was avoided whenever possible, partly on account of its fever-ridden swamps and partly because it was inhabited largely by wolves and criminals. However things have changed quite dramatically. Any pools that were not drained in the nineteenth century are used for breeding fish; pheasant shooting is positively encouraged during the season, the forests produce timber, there are several dairy farms and a centre for water sports has been established on the Grand Etang de la Jemaye, roughly in the middle. It is a pleasant enough lake but still has a long way to go before it could be described as a thriving tourist centre. However it does offer a some fishing, windsurfing and walking as well as opportunities for picnics under the trees.

The only building of interest hereabouts is the Trappist Monastery of **Bonne-Espérance**, near the village of Echourgnac on the D38. It is really quite new, having been founded in 1868 by monks from Port-du-Salut who were hoping to bring a little much needed prosperity to the area. They set up a farm and began collecting local milk to make a cheese they called Trappe. The monks were obliged to leave in 1910 but in 1923 their place was taken by nuns who continued the good work. As one might expect, Trappe is very similar to Port-Salut and is yet another of the seemingly interminable variations that call to mind a remark once made by President De Gaulle. He is said to have pondered aloud on the problems involved in governing a country that produces 400 different kinds of cheese! **Echourgnac** has nothing to get excited about in the way of hotels but it is possible to rent a comfortable *gîte* and spend a holiday swimming, fishing, riding and playing tennis in the vicinity. It would also be an idea to organise a day out at **Parcoul**, on the border

with Angoumois. The hamlet itself has very little to offer apart from a small church but the **Parc de Loisirs du Paradou**, 2km (1 mile) to the south, is specially designed to keep its visitors fully occupied. Amongst the attractions are things like tennis, mini-golf, a lake augmented by some ingenious water slides and a small train inspired by its forerunners in America's Wild West.

East of Mussidan an attractive minor road follows the River Crempse as far as Issac and beyond. On the opposite bank is the **Château de Mont-Réal**, a typically up-dated feudal castle which is supposed to have given its name to Montreal, in Canada. The story goes that the man responsible was Claude de Pontbriand, lord of Mont-Réal, who was with the explorer Jacques Cartier on his second voyage across the Atlantic. Cartier led three expeditions to the New World but his chief claim to fame lies in the fact that he discovered the St Lawrence River in 1536. The *château* is rather an impressive building with a chapel added in the sixteenth century to house one of the Holy Thorns. This is said to have been taken from the body of John Talbot, the Earl of Shrewsbury, at the Battle of Castillon, the English defeat near Bordeaux which ended the Hundred Years' War.

From Issac there is a choice of minor roads, at least four of which converge on **Villamblard** whose fifteenth-century fortress is in ruins. Others of comparable size cut across country to the fortified castle of **Grignols** whose function it was to guard the road from Périgueux to Bordeaux. Built in the thirteenth century on a crest overlooking the valley of the Vern, it was partly demolished some 300 years later but had a number of new buildings added in the seventeenth century. There are some rooms which are definitely past their prime as well as a keep, a couple of moats, some furnishings and a guide to show visitors round from June until late September. Neither Villamblard nor Grignols are all that far from **Vergt**, the centre of the strawberry growing area. However there is not a great deal to see here. The beds are frequently hidden under ubiquitous plastic sheets and the market turns out to be a series of large warehouses where the crop, packed safely into wooden boxes, is loaded on to lorries for distribution all over the country. It would probably be more entertaining to head back towards Périgueux with, perhaps, a slight deviation to Atur for no other reason than to inspect its old *lanterne des morts*.

There are a number of places to visit in the elongated strip of Périgord Blanc east of Périgueux. Among them are the **Château de Caussade**, a rather splendid little fifteenth-century fortress surrounded by a moat, and **Les Bories Castle** overlooking the River Isle. This is well worth seeing both inside and out. The silhouette is not really what one would call exceptional, consisting as it does of a main building with a vast square tower accompanied by two smaller but equally functional round ones. The interior, on the other hand, is truly memorable. There are small rooms, one above the other, in the centre of the square tower with a monumental staircase leading up to them. Many of the ceilings are vaulted and it is possible to get an uninterrupted view of the wooden framework that supports the roof. The kitchen boasts two enormous fireplaces while the great hall is furnished with pieces from the time of Louis XIII. Guided tours lasting nearly an hour are available during the season but visitors who would like to be shown round at other times of the year have only to telephone for an appointment to view.

Sorges, a short drive to the north along the N21 from Périgueux to Limoges was famous as a truffle market in the last century. Anyone who is interested in this particular delicacy would be fascinated by the Maison de la Truffe, a small museum attached to the Syndicat d'Initiative. It is full of maps and photographs, books and films explaining all about this rather ugly but highly aromatic fungus. To start with, there are about thirty different varieties, of which the most sought after comes from Périgord. It is really an underground mushroom that looks rather like an ebony-coloured brain and is found amongst the roots of one or two different types of trees, although it obviously prefers the oaks to anything else. In fact truffle oaks are being planted all over the region in the hope of stepping up the supply, but even that happy prospect is unlikely to bring down the price. The truffles are ready for harvesting from December through to February when sows and dogs are put to work finding them and digging them up. A well developed truffle weighs round about 100g which is about 3½oz and is used to flavour anything from *foie gras* and *pâté* to poultry, omelettes and *ballotines*. It can also be cooked and eaten on its own provided there is a sufficient quantity to hand and if one's bank balance will allow for such extravagance. It is said that nothing will grow immediately above a truffle, an observation worth remembering by anyone who plans to take advantage of an offer to follow the marked path leading to the truffle beds 2km (1 mile) away. However people who want to try a spot of hunting on their own will have to plant an oak, train a dog and then hope to high heaven that the whole venture was not a complete waste of time. As additional strings to its bow Sorges has a Romanesque church, a small *auberge* with private baths and showers, a swimming pool and fish that hang about waiting to be caught.

Tourtoirac, east-south-east on the banks of the Auvézère, is a market town with royal connections, partly legitimate but mainly spurious. A Benedictine abbey was founded there in the eleventh century, suffered considerably in the years that followed and was practically reduced to rubble at the time of the Revolution. All that remains of the royal abbey church is the transept with its square bell tower, the original nave and chapterhouse having been extensively altered and re-

stored. The old cloister is in ruins but there is a small priory church with the monks' bread oven next door and a cemetery where Antoine Orélie de Tounens, the self-styled king of Araucania and Patagonia, is buried.

The story began with his birth in 1825 but really took off some 33 years later when, as a small time lawyer in Périgueux, our hero developed totally unexpected delusions of grandeur. He borrowed a substantial sum of money and set off for Chile where he had already decided to establish his own kingdom on the Argentinian border. Here he was warmly welcomed by the Indians and in 1860 he proclaimed himself Orélie-Antoine I, King of Araucania. He might have got away with it if he had not drawn up a constitution and raised an army which, not unnaturally, landed him in trouble with the existing authorities. He was arrested, put in prison and then repatriated. In no way discouraged by all this he rustled up sufficient backing for a second expedition and landed secretly in Patagonia in 1869, when history more or less repeated itself. Back in France he made two more abortive attempts to establish a kingdom in South America before he died in Tourtoirac in 1878.

The splendid **Château de Hautefort** quite close by has an equally colourful but by no means such an unusual history. In the first place it is not the original castle although it occupies the site of a stronghold built by the ruling family of Limoges in the ninth century. Three hundred years later the castle, having passed into the hands of the aristocratic Borns, was the birthplace of Bertrand, the most famous of all the troubadours. He divided his time between writing poems, that were either amorous, warlike or political, and meddling in other people's affairs. He joined forces with Henri Court-Mantel, the eldest son of England's Henry II and Eleanor of Aquitane, and was with him on his various escapades culminating in an attack on Rocamadour. Court-Mantel died almost immediately afterwards, whereupon Bertrand de Born shut himself up in Hautefort, was besieged by the irate king, surrendered and was condemned to death. He used his literary talents to save his neck but although Henry forgave him Dante did not and consigned him to the depths of hell in his *Divine Comedy*. Throughout much of his life Bertrand kept up a running battle with his brother Constantine, a close friend of Richard Coeur de Lion who had little time for his own brothers either. Eventually, taking advantage of Bertrand's absence from home in 1186, Constantine attacked Hautefort and destroyed it. This proved too much for the troubadour who decided that he had had enough and promptly became a monk. But his place in history was assured and a likeness of him, along with another troubadour, Giraud de Bornheilh, stands in a Périgueux garden, in addition to a boulevard that was named after him.

One castle after another was built to replace the original fortress, the last and most ambitious of them in the mid-1600s, but this was badly damaged by fire in 1968. The present *château* is the result of careful restoration during which very few changes were made. The great staircase was repaired, sixteenth-century Flemish tapestries hang, as others had done, in a gallery of their own while an altar used at the coronation of Charles X can be seen in a chapel in the south-east tower. Part of the south-west tower houses the Eugène Le Roy Museum, recalling the writer whose father was bailiff there in 1836 when he was born. Another room acts as a kind of glory hole, filled with items that were saved from the fire. The design of the *château* is really quite conventional and consists of a vast square of honour with a tower at each corner, two of which are domed. Elegant buildings, reminiscent of the châteaux of the Loire, enclose two sides of the square, the third is pierced by a fortified entrance while the fourth is nothing more than a plain wall separated from the small village by what must have been an exceedingly wide moat. The water has long since disappeared, to be replaced by formal gardens, and these in turn are surrounded by high walls. The original drawbridge, having outlived its usefulness, has been replaced by a stone one that blends in just as well. On the opposite side to the village an undulating panorama of fields and woods with a few small houses in the distance stretches nearly as far as the eye can see.

Either of the little roads that wander down through pretty rather than exceptional scenery to **Badefols-d'Ans** would be a happy choice. This is a small market town with a twelfth-century church and a typical country inn where passers-by can stop for lunch. The local *château*, once owned by the Born family, was burned by the Germans in 1944 but, like Hautefort, it has been carefully restored. However, as a respite from ancient castles visitors can take a swim in Lake Coucou or paddle a canoe through the gorges of the Auvézère. Others might prefer to follow the D71, attractively shaded by poplars and walnut trees, which skirts round an occasional homestead without stumbling over a single village that boasts selfconsciously about the bad old days. The whole area is ideal for driving round, especially as it receives comparatively few visitors, even when the acknowledged tourist resorts are full.

Alternatively drivers can easily join the road running down from St-Yrieix-la-Perche as far as its junction with the frankly uninteresting main route from Brive-la-Gaillarde to Périgueux. This virtually marks the border with Périgord Noir and takes in the market town of **Thenon**. There is a small lake equipped with rowing boats for anyone who wants to work off some surplus energy. Thenon has an *auberge* which stays open right through the year and has access to riding stables, a tennis court and a swimming pool. This is more than can be said for Ajat, on the opposite side of the road which, nevertheless, is an attractive little place. Apart from a *chambre d'hôte* at Eyliac, there does not seem to be anywhere else to stay or much more to do before the short run back to Périgueux.

PÉRIGORD POURPRE

Périgord Pourpre, like Périgord Blanc, is long and fairly narrow with a river running across the centre. In this case it is the Dordogne which has become placid and, in places, rather staid. This is partly due to all the reservoirs and dams which have been constructed on the upper reaches, but even in its unfettered days the river widened out quite considerably when it reached the plains of Aquitaine. Here the valley is extremely fertile and so provides crops such as cereals, maize, tobacco and sunflowers, with vineyards covering the gentle slopes on either side. The weather on the whole is moderate although it can fluctuate on occasions, becoming exceptionally warm at the height of the summer or blanketing some parts with snow in a hard winter. The region is officially described as being half way between the north pole and the equator and equi-distant from the Atlantic coast and the Massif Central, implying that it has the best of all worlds.

The main town is **Bergerac**, associated by most people with Cyrano and his nose despite the fact that he had little, or perhaps nothing, to do with Périgord. The real, live Savinien de Cyrano was born in 1619, according to some sources near Paris although others insist that it was

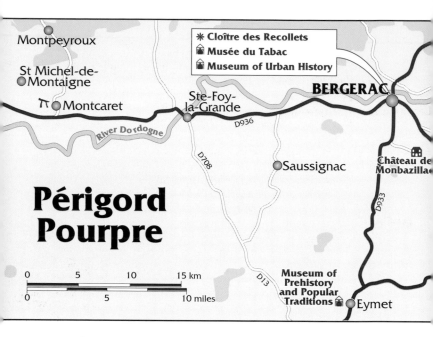

Montpeyroux

St Michel-de-Montaigne

Montcaret

Ste-Foy-la-Grande

BERGERAC

River Dordogne

D936

D708

Saussignac

Château de Monbazillac

Périgord Pourpre

| 0 | 5 | 10 | 15 km |

| 0 | 5 | | 10 miles |

D13

Museum of Prehistory and Popular Traditions

Eymet

somewhere in Périgord. An adventurer at heart, he became a famous swordsman who, between duels and wars, wrote impassioned love letters and a highly successful *Comic History of the States and Empires of the Moon* in 1656, with a sequel, which gave the sun the same treatment, in 1661. Nearly 250 years after his death in 1655 the playwright Edmond Rostand used this colourful soldier-cum-writer and dramatist as the model for his hero in the widely-acclaimed play *Cyrano de Bergerac*, written entirely in verse. Soon the place and the man became firmly intertwined; the town adopted him enthusiastically and another popular misconception came into being.

Bergerac today has a small airport in daily contact with Paris, is linked by train to Bordeaux and Brive-la-Gaillarde among other places and is crossed by busy main roads running north and south as well as east and west. The Dordogne river wends its way through the middle, past the ancient port where vessels used to tie up in the olden days to load cargoes of wine destined for both England and Holland. Wine is still a very important local product, along with tobacco and, less attractively, nitro-cellulose for use in such things as paint and plastics. At first glance the town is not exactly prepossessing but anyone who takes the trouble to investigate will find a good deal to admire.

For the most part the old quarter

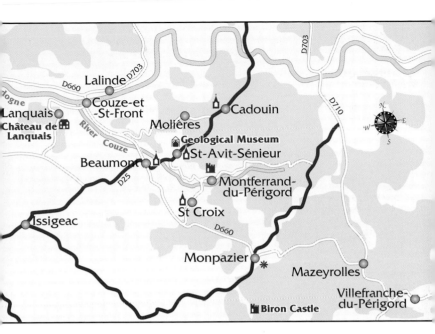

is confined to an oblong area near the port where several of the small streets and comparatively large squares are overlooked by medieval houses left over from the days when Bergerac was the capital of Périgord. The **Maison Peyrarède** is a case in point. This fifteenth-century mansion was up-dated in 1603 in plenty of time to entertain Louis XIII when he stopped off there some 20 years later, thereby bestowing on it the title of the French King's House. It is now the home of the Musée du Tabac which traces the history of tobacco from the time when it was introduced from the New World by explorers like Sir Walter Raleigh in the sixteenth century. Among the earliest exhibits are pipes used by the American Indians who believed that smoking was not only good for them but also helped to establish friendly relations with strangers who invaded their territory. However it was some time before the general population in Europe became familiar with the invitation to 'put that in your pipe and smoke it', either literally or figuratively.

Tobacco was introduced into France in the form of snuff in 1560 when Jean Nicot, the Ambassador to Portugal, sent some to Catherine de Medici in the hope that it would help to cure her headaches. Once the idea caught on there was no holding it and people even started puffing away in church. The fact that Pope Urban VIII excommunicated smokers and Louis XIII slapped a tax on it did absolutely nothing to prevent the habit spreading. The snuff arrived in a solid lump which then had to be grated but by the end of the eighteenth century it was being sold in powder form, stored in large and often very decorative jars. Every young man of fashion immediately started collecting snuffboxes which he was determined should be more extensive, more beautiful and more costly than those belonging to anyone else. Pipes, which were already being used in Holland, were considered vulgar until they were adopted by people like George Sand, after which they too became as ornate and imaginative as possible. At last, in the mid-nineteenth century, wonderfully carved and decorated cigarette holders started to make their appearance, often consisting of ivory, amber and gold. Outstanding examples of all these items are on display along with appropriate paintings, contrasting sharply with a less artistic section which concerns itself with the life of the plant from its seedling stage to the point at which it is ready for sale. Next door is the Museum of Urban History, full of old maps and documents, pottery, furniture and a good many other things that are useful in tracing the history of Bergerac.

A short walk away are two interlocking squares, the Place du Docteur Cayla and the Place de la Myrpe. The latter is surrounded by picturesque old houses with a garden in the middle and an extremely unattractive statue of Cyrano. It is white, gives the impression of being rather less than half finished and suggests a clown rather than a romantic hero. The **Cloître des Recollets**, a delightful half-timbered house overlooking the Place du Docteur Cayla, was once a convent and still has a chapel attached in spite of the fact that it is now the headquarters of the winemaking industry. The Guild holds its receptions in the vaulted cellar but climbs up a stone staircase with a delicate wrought-iron bannister to attend official meetings in the Great Hall on the first floor. Apart from this most of the rooms are given over to the Musée du Vin, de la Batellerie et de la Tonnellerie. The wine section concentrates its attention on the history of the vineyards and the lives of the men and women who worked with the grapes. A certain emphasis is placed on barrel making, an art which is obviously more rigidly controlled than the average outsider would expect. For many people the floor above could prove even more fascinating because it shows models of the various types of river boats that would arrive at Bergerac with assorted merchandise to be replaced by cargoes of wine. A series of photographs show the old port hard at work in the middle of the nineteenth century as well as paying due attention to the activities of fishermen who earned their living from the Dordogne.

Off the Place Pélissière, created when several semi-derelict houses were pulled down, is the church of St Jacques which was once a stopping place for pilgrims on their way to

Compostella, on the far side of the Pyrénées. Also in attendance are a small Museum of Sacred Art and a well-preserved inn dating from the fourteenth century. Other places of interest include the church of Notre-Dame, built in the last century, where the weekly open-air market spills over into the Place Gambetta, making life a trifle complicated for people in search of somewhere to park the car. There are several attractive little shops in the streets all round and a clutch of perfectly acceptable hotels within easy walking distance, the slightly drab-looking Cyrano having one of the best restaurants in town. There are other hotels and restaurants including some on the outskirts, the most comfortable of which is to be found on the road to Villamblard complete with a tennis court and a private swimming pool. Bergerac is undoubtedly well placed for touring Périgord Pourpre. It can point walkers in the direction of the Grandes Randonnées, suggest a good place to hire a horse, a kayak or a canoe and even arrange for parachutists to get a bird's eye view any weekend between February and the end of September. There is a small theatre, concerts and recitals are held at frequent intervals and events concerned with folklore are by no means uncommon, especially during the holiday season.

Comparatively little of interest can be found to the west of Bergerac where the road and the river only partly succeed in keeping each other company as far as **Ste-Foy-la-Grande**.

This was one of the *bastides* built by Alphonse de Poitiers to keep the English at bay and still has the remains of its ramparts and a handful of old houses clustered round the neo-Gothic church. **Montcaret**, a short drive further to the west, has a much longer history. It was originally a Celtic settlement, taken over by the Romans in the first century AD. At least one impressive villa was built there at the time of Constantine the Great but there is not much left of it these days apart from some intricate and colourful mosaics reminiscent of those found at Piazza Armerina, in Sicily. A small eleventh-century church managed to survive the attentions of its enemies but the Hundred Years' War and the Wars of Religion left the rest of the little hamlet rather high and dry.

St-Michel-de-Montaigne nearby would be easy to ignore if it were not for the somewhat grim Tour de la Libraire in the grounds of the *château*. The same applies to **Montpeyroux**, sitting a trifle smugly on the top of a small hillock dominated by an attractive little church and a seventeenth-century *château* (not open to the public). Also in the vicinity is the Château de Gurson, presented to Jean de Grailly by England's Henry III in his capacity as Duke of Aquitaine in the thirteenth century. It was rebuilt about 100 years later and still has some of its fortifications and a small attendant lake. **St-Martin-de-Gurçon**, on the other hand, has nothing in the way of a castl, but its much decorated twelfth-century church is of interest.

A day trip to the south of Bergerac is rather more rewarding. The first place of interest beyond the airport off the N21, or via the much prettier D13, is the **Château de Monbazillac**, surrounded by vineyards in every direction and famous for its sweet white wines. The ancient, semi-fortified castle, once protected by a moat, was built in 1550, opted for the Protestants during the Wars of Religion and was eventually bought by the local wine co-operative who have turned part of it into a museum. The *château* is worth seeing for itself and for the Great Hall with its painted ceiling, the splendid large fireplaces, the Flemish tapestries and the seventeenth-century furnishings. There is an opulent bedroom that once belonged to the *chatelaine*, a more down to earth collection of rustic furniture and a selection of books and documents tracing the history of Protestantism in France. The original cellars have been turned into a wine museum, full of elderly bottles and pieces of equipment that were commonplace in an earlier day and age. A barn opening off the courtyard is now home to a pleasing restaurant, open to visitors from June to September but available for special functions throughout the year. There is also a shop where customers can sample the various wines before deciding which ones to take home with them. The choice is quite extensive and includes ordinary grape juice, reds and rosés from the Bergerac region as well as the Monbazillac white wines that are not unlike Sauternes

and, according to local experts, should be served very cold indeed. It is also claimed that they make extremely good cocktails when mixed with ingredients such as Grand Marnier, Curaçao or Campari.

The south-western part of Périgord Pourpre is devoted almost exclusively to vines, marching in orderly rows across the countryside, dotted here and there with clumps of trees usually accompanied by a *château* or a farmhouse. As one would expect the majority are kept very busy producing wine. Only a small proportion are open to visitors in the tourist sense but few can resist the opportunity to give passers-by a chance to taste the end product. At Colombier, for instance, there is a small tasting room outside the gates of the Château la Jaubertie, once owned by the king of Navarre but now the property of the Ryman family who know as much about grapes these days as they do about stationery. The Château de Panisseau, dating from the thirteenth century, threw in its lot with the Black Prince and apparently never regretted it, although it is better known these days for the quality of its red wine.

Saussignac has a nice little *auberge*, with a good restaurant and facilities for tennis in the vicinity, which would make a good base for those intent on extending their knowledge of wine. For long distance walkers an added advantage is that the GR6 passes the door on its way from Lot to Gironde with plenty of opportunities to deviate along the way. Other sights to see in the area include the

The covered market, Monpazier, the most impressive of the *bastide* towns

✳ **Moulin de Malfourat**, an old mill standing on a hillock without its sails but still commanding a pleasant view, and the sixteenth-century 🏰 **Château de Bridoire**. The original fortress suffered considerably for its Protestant leanings during the Wars of Religion but it was well restored a little over 100 years ago.

There is no particular reason to visit Thénac unless it is to join the picturesque, though admittedly small, D18 which runs south to **Eymet**. This village is another of the *bastides* founded by Alphonse de Poitiers in the mid-thirteenth century. It was owned by one nobleman after another and never quite knew which side it was meant to be supporting during the Hundred Years' War. The result of this was that it was

battered by each of them in turn, lost the whole of its castle apart from the keep, while any other fortifications that managed to survive were destroyed on the orders of Louis XIII. However things started to improve after the Wars of Religion and it is now well known for the *foie gras* and other delicacies produced by the local food factories. The Place Centrale with its elderly houses and 300-year-old fountain is surrounded by arcades with two rather basic inns nearby and a folklore museum 🏛 tucked away in the fourteenth-century keep. **Issigeac**, to the east on the far side of the N21, falls into much the same category. It only has one *auberge* but has retained both its castle and its church. The latter was built by the Bishop of Sarlat in the early 1500s but it was left to one of his successors to add the Château des Evêques towards the end of the seventeenth century. This large building with a tower at either end is now occupied by the *hôtel de ville*.

Beaumont is yet another *bastide*, built this time to protect the interests of England's Edward I. It suffered along with all the rest, losing most of its fortifications but somehow managing to preserve the large thirteenth-century church of St Front. This is a decidedly militant building, more of a fortress than a house of God, with four entirely functional towers and a parapet from which the archers could shower arrows down on anyone who broke through the outer defences of the town. For some reason it was given a softer look when restoration work was carried out around 100 years ago but even this cannot hide the fact that its primary aim was to protect both itself and the townspeople who depended on it. The market square is typical of its type and times, set fractionally off-centre with antiquated houses and arcades all round. Beaumont was also luckier than some of its contemporaries because one of the original gateways, the Porte de Luzier, and a section of the curtain walls are still standing.

Monpazier is considered by many to be the most impressive and the most atmospheric of all the *bastides*, regardless of who built them in the first place. Nor does it miss a trick when it comes to living up to its reputation. Everything about the little honey-coloured town is carefully preserved including one or two incidents from the past which help to make its background even more interesting. It has a brace of small *auberges*, one of which occupies a thirteenth-century house, a restaurant or two and a campsite in addition to providing tennis, riding and fishing for holidaymakers who decide to stay for a while. The GR36 from Cahors edges its way past in the direction of the Dordogne, making it an ideal stopping place for anybody on a walking tour.

Monpazier was founded on 7 January 1284 by Edward I of England who was also Duke of Aquitaine. The *bastide* was a combined effort by Edward and Pierre de Gontaut, the lord of Biron, and although the project started off quite well it soon ran into trouble. Gontaut and the local people could not get along any better than the royal houses of England and France so Monpazier naturally became an even greater bone of contention than it might otherwise have been. The uneasy peace that followed the English defeat at Castillon lasted for just over 100 years. Then, in June 1574, Monpazier was betrayed to the Protestants and occupied by Geoffroi de Vivans, the wily Huguenot captain who went on to capture both Sarlat and Domme. When the Calvinist Jeanne d'Albret called in on her way to the wedding of her son Henri of Navarre and Marguerite de Valois she was greeted with enormous enthusiasm. Records kept at the time say that the streets and squares were thoroughly cleaned and every bit of refuse was removed. However the town had grown accustomed to hedging its bets and therefore put on just as warm a welcome soon afterwards for the Catholic Duke of Anjou. This was probably a very wise move because he went on to become Henry III of France. The peasants, who were no doubt heartily sick of being mixed up in other people's wars, made their feelings felt in 1594 and staged a full scale revolt 43 years later. Their leader, a man called Buffarot, was captured, brought back in chains to the *bastide* and broken on the wheel in the main square.

The atmosphere these days is infinitely more peaceful but the village looks just the same. The main square, with its solid stone houses, functional archways and arcades, has an elderly covered market at one end complete with measures that were used for grain. Behind the arches are shops of every description which close promptly at midday so that the owners can trot upstairs for lunch as the shopkeepers before them had obviously been doing for hundreds of years. The streets are designed on the grid system, the longer ones running parallel to each other and crossed at right angles by alleys with narrow spaces between the houses to minimise any damage which might be caused by fire. The church of St Dominique is original, though much restored, and the whole place is surrounded by the remains of the protecting walls, pierced by three of the six fortified gateways that completed the outer defences of the town. Markets are still held at regular intervals, there is a fair on the third Thursday of every month along with an occasional flea market, a fashion parade or some such event as well as concerts of classical music which take place in the church.

Less than 10km (6 miles) to the south-west of Monpazier is **Biron Castle**, a forbidding conglomeration of towers and turrets, medieval fortifications and Renaissance afterthoughts which fourteen generations of the Gontaut-Biron family altered, extended and improved upon as and when the spirit moved them. The site was originally chosen for an eleventh-century fortress that became an Albigensian stronghold until the sect was wiped out by Simon de Montfort on the orders of Pope Innocent III. It is hardly surprising that the pope took exception to the Albigenses who, although ferociously Christian, had no time whatever for the Church of Rome. They did not believe that Christ ever existed as a man and were convinced that the world and everything in it was the work of the devil. In their view mankind's only hope of salvation lay in abstinence and self denial. This did not suit the hierarchy at all and when the sect refused to toe the official line they were hounded and persecuted without mercy until, eventually, their headquarters at Mont Ségur was captured in 1245.

A new Biron Castle was built to replace the original one, but this had a very bad time during the Hundred Years' War and was severely burnt in the Wars of Religion. After casting more than a casual eye over his battered property Pons de Gontaut-Biron decided that what he really wanted was an elegant *château* that would tone in with the medieval remains and make living a good deal more comfortable. He therefore set about restoring, enlarging, renovating and up-dating his ancestral pile. In 1598 Biron was raised to the status of a barony and when Charles de Gontaut-Biron succeeded to the title he was made a Marshal of France and Governor of Burgundy. But he was an insatiably ambitious man and almost immediately started plotting with Spain against the king. His treason was discovered but Henry IV pardoned him. However, when he got up to his tricks for the second time, and refused to confess in order to save his skin, he was arrested and taken to the Bastille. Charles lost his head, along with the barony, in 1602 and it was roughly 120 years before the family were given back their title. Gradually it began to dawn on the owner-occupants that the castle's upkeep was playing havoc with their finances and they decided reluctantly to sell. The castle was bought by the local authorities in 1790 since when they, in their turn, have been restoring and refurbishing, adding such attractions as an art centre and planning an appropriate museum.

The outer courtyard of Biron Castle encompasses the old receiving house and the salt room, a place of great importance in the Middle Ages, a fortified tower which makes a lodge for the caretaker, and a two-storey chapel dating largely from the sixteenth century. The lower part can be reached directly from the village and was the original parish church, whereas the upper floor was deliberately built on top of it, opens off the courtyard and was reserved for the family. Two of its most outstanding treasures, a *Mise au Tombeau* with seven beautifully carved figures and five angels surrounding the body of Christ and a most expressive Pietà, were sold to Pierpont Morgan and are now in the New York Metropolitan Museum. However the recumbent figures of Armand de Gontaut-Biron, the Bishop of Sarlat, and his brother Pons who rebuilt the castle are still in evidence, although both were damaged during the Wars of Religion.

A stairway and a vaulted corridor lead up to the court of honour, overlooked by the *château* itself. Surprisingly it only takes about 45 minutes to look round when the main things on view are the Great Hall of State and the enormous kitchen, paved with stone slabs under a barrel roof, which served as the garrison's refectory. The family's living quarters have been restored and used for art exhibitions while plans are afoot to add a museum about the Hundred Years' War. There are some attractive views from the castle over the small village below which, incidentally, has no hotels and no mention of Lord Byron, an extremely distant relation whose ancestors are said to have crossed the Channel with William the Conqueror.

The most distant place of interest,

The massive church and cloisters at Cadouin were restored after the Wars of Religion and the Revolution

in the furthest south-eastern corner of Périgord Pourpre, is **Villefranche-du-Périgord**, a Catholic *bastide* that was constantly at loggerheads with Protestant Monpazier. Their history was one of raids and counter raids during which neither succeeded in capturing or even incapacitating the other. However, in the midst of all this death and destruction, they did manage to provide at least one moment of light relief. This was recalled by the Duc de Sully, the chief adviser to Henry IV, who left behind some very illuminating memoirs. Apparently the citizens of Villefranche decided to launch a surprise attack on the people of Monpazier who, unknown to them, had had the same idea and chosen the same night for it. As luck would have it they planned to take entirely different routes. As a result both sets of soldiers arrived at their objectives, found them defenceless, collected as much loot as they could carry and settled down to enjoy an easy victory. It was not long before everybody realised exactly what had happened. Peace was declared, at least temporarily, the spoils of war were returned to their rightful owners and the troops marched back to their respective homes with nothing except red faces to show for their midnight sortie. Villefranche-du-Périgord is still very obviously a *bastide* with a large covered market in the square and the usual arcades all round it. The village still vies with Monpazier by having two pleasant little *auberges* which both offer baths en suite and reasonably priced meals served, whenever possible, in the open air.

A spiders web of small, winding and well surfaced roads offers several alternative routes back towards Bergerac with plenty of excuses to stop along the way. The first might well be **Montferrand-du-Périgord**, a delightful little hamlet built on terraces above the River Couze. Its old castle is in ruins but there is a twelfth-century keep, a group of very viewable old houses and a covered market. In addition some medieval frescoes can be seen in the chapel that stands slightly apart in the cemetery. **St Croix**, on the other hand, makes a point of publicising its own attractions in the shape of a twelfth-century church and the remains of an ancient priory. **St-Avit-Sénieur**, a trifle to the north, has a slight edge on both of them. Its large fortified church was part of a Benedictine abbey, built at about the same time as William of Normandy was constructing his White Tower in London. The abbey was dedicated to the memory of St Avitus, the soldier who turned his back on war in order to become a monk and was put to death in consequence. The church is deliberately severe with the towers and watchpath that were so essential if the inhabitants were to have any hope of survival during the Middle Ages. The abbey has all but disappeared apart from the monks' dormitory above the chapterhouse, now the home of a small geological museum. The hamlet of **Molières** was originally intended to be an English *bastide* but for some reason no-one ever got around to finishing it. This in itself is a point of interest and, while there, it is worth casting an eye over the fairly typical old church.

Even visitors who are short of time or who have had enough of ancient buildings, should make a point of driving to **Cadouin**, where the skillfully restored church and cloister are sights not to be missed. The Abbey of Cadouin was founded in 1115, became a Cistercian house and was a force to reckon with in the Middle Ages. This was largely on account of the so-called Holy Shroud, a piece of cloth discovered in a church in Antioch at the time of the Crusades and brought back in triumph to France. Everyone apparently believed that it had been used to wrap the head of Christ after the Crucifixion and as such it was a relic of incalculable importance to Christians everywhere. Once it had been lodged in the abbey pilgrims started to converge on Cadouin in ever-increasing numbers, amongst them Richard Coeur de Lion, St Louis, the French king who died in Tunis on his way to liberate Jerusalem and, a good deal later, Charles V. When the English seemed likely to overrun the abbey during the Hundred Years' War the Holy Shroud was sent first to Toulouse and then to Aubazine for safekeeping. Once the danger was passed nobody wanted to hand it back and it took the combined efforts of the pope, Louis XI and the law to force its protectors to return the priceless relic. Cadouin immediately started celebrating by adding a number of new buildings but these were damaged later by the Huguenots. An element of doubt about the authenticity of the Holy Shroud began to creep in during the nineteenth century when one of the monks insisted that the inscription along the edge was part of a Moslem text. This was confirmed in 1934 who added that the fabric was only 800 or 900 years old. In the face of such evidence Cadouin ceased officially to be a place of pilgrimage.

The impressive abbey church and the cloister, built with the help of Louis XI and restored after the Revolution, are so full of detail that it takes quite a while to inspect them properly. The church itself is relatively uncluttered whereas the cloister combines serious religion with moments of almost ribald humour. A case in point is where a small dog belonging to a well dressed and obviously affluent couple appears to have been told to bite a dispirited looking itinerant monk while a face winks knowingly through an opening in the pillar behind. Aristotle is shown in company with a courtesan in complete contrast to the large, sadly damaged fresco depicting the Annunciation. The Royal Door, one of four leading into the cloister, is decorated with the arms of both Brittany and France, a permanent reminder that Anne of Brittany, who had Cadouin's welfare very much at heart, was married to both Charles VIII and Louis XII who succeeded

him as king of France. The abbot's throne is in its accustomed place but the chapterhouse and a couple of other small rooms, all restored quite recently, have been turned into a Pilgrim Museum. It is filled with such things as banners and flasks, reliquaries and other similar items including, of course, the Holy Shroud. There are some people who choose to ignore both carbon dating and the Arab text, not to mention the fact that nothing seems to have been known about the cloth before the thirteenth century. As one visitor put it quite simply 'If God wants to cloud the issue for some reason that is quite all right with me'. The gardens in the centre of the cloister are everything that a walled garden should be with shrubs, lawns and a few trees in addition to the stone paths which converge on a circular raised flowerbed in the middle.

Couze-et-St-Front has quite a different claim to fame. It has been making paper for the past 400 years and had thirteen mills in full production during the eleventh century when it was the most important centre of its kind in Aquitaine. All but two have now closed down. One of the survivors, the Moulin Larroque, still uses the old methods and is quite willing to show visitors over the premises any weekday as long as it is in working hours. The art of making paper originated in China where more than one hundred rules were laid down governing its production. The Arabs became interested in the eighth century AD and started up their own mills near Damascus where the crusaders picked up the idea and decided to try it for themselves. The process hardly changed over the next 500 years until a Frenchman called Louis Nicolas Robert came up with a machine that would make paper in rolls instead of in flat sheets as before. A British manufacturer bought the prototype and produced the first working model in 1812.

A short drive away, towards Bergerac, is the remarkably self-possessed **Château de Lanquais**. The site is believed to have been occupied since prehistoric times but there is nothing to see which pre-dates the medieval section of the building. This started life as a fortress but was adapted later when the Renaissance half was being built. The two are linked by a tower that is taken up by a spiral staircase in the best tradition of isolated castles which no longer expected to be called upon to fight for their existence. The 'new' wing is by far the most ornate. Amongst other things there are two beautifully carved stone fireplaces with matching doors on either side, some of the ceilings are painted and the dining hall is hung, somewhat unusually, with cotton print.

On the opposite side of the Dordogne is **Lalinde**, a rather nondescript little market town which has nothing much of historic interest but does not seem to mind this in the least. It was, in fact, one of the early English *bastides* which served its purpose before being badly knocked about when the Catholics and the Protestants flew at each others' throats. After the battles were over it went about its business quietly and efficiently until the Germans burnt it down in 1944 to get their own back on the Marquis who had been making life as difficult for them as possible. There are half a dozen small hotels, the most atmospheric of which is housed in a thirteenth-century *château*. It is a trifle short on amenities but makes up for this by serving meals out on the terrace overhanging the river. Those who prefer self-catering can rent a *gîte* or pitch a tent or park a caravan on the official campsite quite close by. The town is reasonably well equipped as a holiday resort, inviting its guests to play tennis, golf or mini-golf, ride, fish, play *boules* or hire a kayak or a canoe on the river. As far as hikers are concerned it is conveniently placed for the GR6 while motorists have a choice between driving 22km (14 miles) along a flat, fairly built-up road to Bergerac or heading northeast into Périgord Noir.

PÉRIGORD NOIR

Périgord Noir, the last of the quartet, is really no bigger than the others but manages to cram a great deal into a confined space. The area gets its

---

Opposite: Maison de la Boétie and the Passage Henri-de-Ségogne at Sarlat-la-Canéda

name not, as one might expect, from caves and grottoes or rich black soil but from the woodlands which have persisted almost everywhere. The holm-oak, with its profusion of dark leaves, is largely responsible although there are many other types of trees with lighter foliage such as poplars, chestnuts, willows, beech and walnuts. The main rivers are the Dordogne and the Vézère, fed by lesser known tributaries, some of which are rather too small to be included in any ordinary map. The valleys, although not as wide as the Dordogne in Périgord Pourpre, are equally fertile, producing many of the same crops such as wheat, maize and tobacco. Walnuts are cultivated for their oil as well as for the nuts themselves, both of which are important ingredients in traditional cooking along with mushrooms and the even more highly prized truffles. However, as far as the visitor is concerned, Périgord Noir is best known for its prehistoric caves and grottoes and especially for the amazingly life-like animal paintings that have survived for many thousands of years.

Sarlat-la-Canéda, the main town in the area, is a fascinating place to visit, in addition to which it makes an ideal base. Like any other provincial centre it has outgrown its ancient boundaries in order to provide space for little suburban houses, an odd factory or two, shops and supermarkets, filling stations and the like. However, because of the lie of the land and the way the medieval town was constructed in a hollow, very little of this has impinged on the old

quarter, parts of which are magical. It is possible to drive right up to the cathedral, and even park the car if a space is available, but in order to get the full flavour of Sarlat it is essential to walk. Several of the streets and alleys are closed to traffic, partly because not more than one vehicle at a time could get through some of them anyway, but more probably because a conscious effort has been made to preserve the original atmosphere. A great many of the old buildings, some of them half timbered, others of stone with elaborately carved windows, turrets and gables, have been skilfully and painstakingly restored. So have the little passageways, occasionally with their own arches, that pass within nodding distance of small courtyards, old staircases and tiny shops where craftsmen display their wares in the hope of making a sale. There is certainly a commercial side to the town, personified by some very run-of-the-mill souvenirs, but this is outweighed by all the unexpected little touches such as an old horse-drawn carriage, that draws attention to a small museum.

St Sacerdos Cathedral is a good a place to start exploring. It began life as an ordinary small church in the twelfth century to provide a resting place for the body of the saintly Bishop of Limoges. He was very highly respected, especially as he apparently had the power to cure leprosy which, with the plague, was one of the most dreaded diseases of the period. Nevertheless Bishop Armand de Gontaut-Biron decided to pull it down in 1504 to make way for a cathedral but he was transferred 15 years later and work stopped for the better part of a century. The present building started to take shape after that but unfortunately St Sacerdos was not around to see the project completed because the Protestants under Geoffroi de Vivans removed his body, burned it and tossed the ashes away.

On the far side of an adjoining courtyard, part of which was an ancient cemetery, the Chapel of the Blue Penitents is virtually all that remains of the Benedictine abbey founded by Charlemagne in the ninth century. Standing slightly back from the cathedral is a circular tower with a conical roof called the **Lanterne des Morts**. It dates from the twelfth century but nobody seems to know quite why it was built or how it got its name. One popular belief is that it was intended to mark the visit by St Bernard in 1147 at the time when he was given the job of bringing sects like the Albigensians back into the Catholic fold. To add weight to his mission he said that anyone who ate the bread he had blessed would recover from whatever ailments were bothering them, ignoring the Bishop of Chartres's rider that this had to be done in perfect faith. Apparently St Bernard achieved his object in Sarlat but, if this is so, it does seem odd that miracle cures should be immortalised by building a 'Lantern of the Dead'. Another theory — that a lantern was kept burning at the top — appears to be even more unlikely because it was

practically impossible for anyone to get into the upper room to keep it working properly. A third explanation, and one which could be closer to the mark, is that the tower was a kind of funeral parlour on an unusually grand scale, but after such a long time it is really anybody's guess.

Opposite the cathedral is the **Maison de la Boétie**, without any doubt one of the most eye-catching houses in Sarlat. It was built and much decorated in the sixteenth century and gained additional fame as the birthplace of Etienne de la Boétie, a young parliamentarian and writer of considerable ability who had a profound influence on his friend Michel de Montaigne. After Boétie's early death in 1563 Montaigne wrote his famous *Essay on Friendship* which helped to keep the young man's memory alive. The town also did its share by putting up a statue of him in the Place de la Grande Rigaudie near the law courts and a stone's throw from the Cour des Fontaines. Running down the side of the house is the Passage Henri-de-Ségogne with a recently installed plaque to André Malraux. He was also a writer but his place in history is much more widely based. During World War II he became an outstanding member of the Resistance Movement but following his capture by the Germans he was imprisoned for some reason instead of being shot. After the war he became Minister of Cultural Affairs and in this capacity introduced a new law designed to protect historic buildings and even whole sections of ancient towns like Sarlat, Rouen and

Sarlat's cobbled main street

Colmar. Restoration work began in 1964, 11 years before his death, and Sarlat is a perfect example of the wisdom of his ideas.

Practically next door to the Maison de la Boétie, at the other end of the Passage Henri-de-Ségogne, is the Hôtel de Maleville. It also dates from the sixteenth century, when three existing houses were knocked into one, and now provides a home for the Office de Tourisme. This looks out on the Place de la Liberté, encrusted with shops and cafés in addition to the *hôtel de ville* and all that remains of the ancient church of Ste Marie. The chancel no longer exists so the open space where it used to be makes an ideal stage for the annual Theatre Festival held there every summer. The conventional theatre is housed in the former bishops' palace, built in about 1533 next door to the cathedral. Beyond the Place de la Liberté is another collection of atmospheric houses grouped round the Place des Oies. This 'Goose Square' is aptly named because a market is held there each Saturday morning where, among a host of other offerings, crowds gather to buy the odd goose along with by-products such as *foie gras*. As well as the various medieval town houses dominated by the Plamon Tower there is a little fountain dedicated to Ste Marie which plays away happily in a vaulted grotto and, according to one elderly resident, has never been known to run dry. Other places worthy of mention are the creeper-covered Présidial which was the Court

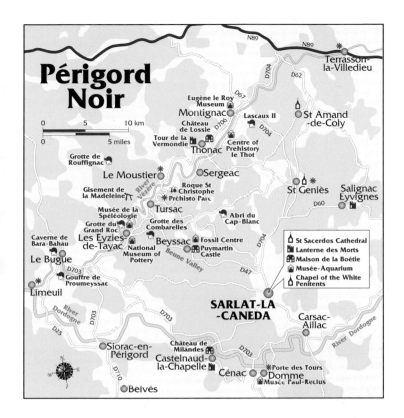

Périgord Noir

Terrasson-la-Villedieu

Eugène le Roy Museum

Montignac · Lascaux II · St Amand-de-Coly

Château de Lossie

Tour de la Vermondie · Thonac · Centre of Prehistory le Thot

Grotte de Rouffignac

Le Moustier · Sergeac

Gisement de la Madeleine · Roque St Christophe · Préhisto Parc

St Geniès · Salignac Eyvignes

Musée de la Spéléologie · Tursac · Abri du Cap-Blanc

Grotte du Grand Roc · Grotte des Combarelles

Caverne de Bara-Bahau · Les Eyzies-de-Tayac · National Museum of Pottery · Beyssac · Fossil Centre · Puymartin Castle

Le Bugue

Gouffre de Proumeyssac

Limeuil

SARLAT-LA-CANEDA

Carsac-Aillac

St Sacerdos Cathedral
Lanterne des Morts
Maison de la Boétie
Musée-Aquarium
Chapel of the White Penitents

Siorac-en-Périgord

Château de Milandes

Castelnaud-la-Chapelle · Cénac · Domme · Porte des Tours

Musée Paul-Reclus

Belvès

River Vézère · River Dordogne · Beune Valley

0 5 10 km
0 5 miles

N89 · D704 · D62 · D67 · D706 · D704 · D60 · D704 · D47 · D703 · D25 · D710 · D703

---

of Justice in the reign of Henry III and only moved out during the Revolution, the Rue des Consuls and the Rue Jean-Jacques Rousseau.

The **Chapel of the White Penitents**, a comparative newcomer because it was only built about 300 years ago, is now a Museum of Sacred Arts housing a wide variety of exhibits from the sixteenth century onwards. The only other listed museum in town is combined with the aquarium and is to be found on the Rue du Commandant Maratuel, well away from the old quarter. It is divided, roughly speaking, into three sections. There are hundreds of fish living in large glass tanks which visitors are instructed not to touch, for their own sake as much as anything else. The function of water in the environment is examined very thoroughly and this leads on naturally to things like navigation on inland waterways and, of course, fishing. Anyone who gets tired of walking round can study the subject in comfort by watching films and audio-visual programmes.

Quite naturally Sarlat is well blessed with hotels, the best of which are located on the outskirts of the town but shut quite firmly for long winter holidays. There is hardly anywhere to stay in the old quarter but the compensation for living in more modern surroundings is that one can swim, play tennis or golf, ride, fish or take a do-it-yourself trip along the river in a kayak or a canoe. The GR6 lies to the north of the town with a short-cut that joins the GR64 near Domme on the opposite bank of the Dordogne. Special tours are arranged during the season and details of these as well as the dates, times and locations of current exhibitions or visits to the local pottery are available from the Office de Tourisme. There are cars for hire and bicycles are obtainable during the season at a handful of different places including the railway station with plenty of places to visit afterwards.

Because Sarlat is fairly close to the departmental border there is not a great deal to see travelling eastwards before crossing into Quercy, more widely publicised these days as Lot. However there is a short, quite attractive circular route that begins at **Temniac**, due north of the town. It has a small, twelfth-century pilgrim's chapel with a good view to the south and the remains of a ruined castle that belonged to the Knights Templar before it was taken over as a country residence by the bishops of Sarlat. From here the road heads more or less north-east with a side turning off to the ruined eleventh

century Château du Claud. Next is **Salignac-Eyvignes**, a small hamlet with a moderately grim castle perched on the rock above its head. Parts of the castle date from the twelfth century but it was improved and modernised behind its encircling ramparts at irregular intervals over the next 500 years. Although it is still owned by the same family Salignac Castle is delighted to welcome visitors, providing guided tours at the height of the season but allowing people to wander around on their own at some other times of the year. A number of the rooms on view have been furnished in keeping with their surroundings.

An attractive minor road takes leave of the D60 and continues merrily on its way, well surfaced and winding through wooded country, edged on either side by ferns. It passes Carlucet with its old cemetery and St Crépin whose manor house replaced a fortified *château* 400 years ago, before heading north to **St-Geniès**. Many people consider this to be one of the most attractive villages in Périgord Noir. Its manor house is surrounded by little contemporary houses with the Chapelle du Cheylard perfectly sited on the top of a rise. The frescoes inside are a bit unusual because, instead of saints and angels, they are more interested in people who lived thereabouts and the way they spent their time. **St-Amand-de-Coly**, on the other hand, has the severe remains of a fortified church that do their best to dwarf the houses all round. It was once part of the defences built by the

Augustine Order to protect an abbey and its complement of 400 monks established there in the twelfth century. Apart from a carved doorway there is very little decoration, either inside or out, but it is interesting to see how it fitted in to the overall design. There is an audio-visual presentation organised by Les Amis de St-Amand-de-Coly in the old presbytery opposite.

On the way back to Sarlat, which is quite straightforward and therefore very undemanding, it is an idea to branch off westwards along the D47 in order to visit **Puymartin Castle**. This is quite a gem as castles go, built of honey coloured stone with the conventional round towers, turrets and curtain walls. Somehow it does not look fierce enough to have been a Catholic stronghold which defied the Protestants who captured Sarlat during the Wars of Religion but perhaps that is because it was fully restored a century or so ago. An added attraction is that Puymartin is open to visitors with guided tours that last for about half an hour. There are some very worthwhile things to see inside: half a dozen Flemish tapestries trace the history of the Trojan War while the eighteenth-century murals are more interested in mythology. The furniture is a pleasing mixture of the styles that were in vogue from the reign of Louis XIII until the Revolution. In addition the guardroom has its full quota of pictures while the small chapel apparently is older than everything else.

Sarlat is only about 10km (6 miles) from the Dordogne, far enough in the eighth century for it to escape the notice of anyone travelling up the river with looting in view. The main road down to Gourdon, in Lot, is the easiest and quickest way of crossing the river, even allowing for time to pause at **Carsac-Aillac**. This is a pleasant if rather nondescript little village with a couple of modest *auberges* and an attractive small church. The most unusual things about it are the modern stained glass windows and a Stations of the Cross along with texts taken from the works of Paul Claudel, the writer and diplomat who died in 1955. The village lists its attractions as tennis, mini-golf, riding, canoeing, fishing, billiards and *boules* but omits to mention the Grande Randonnée practically on the doorstep. Instead of carrying on towards Gourdon a small, scenic road makes its way through rocky outcrops, past the Château de Montfort which was badly mauled on several occasions in the past, and crosses the river above **Cénac**, a village that was practically obliterated by the Protestants in 1589. All that remains of the priory is a small, much restored eleventh century church that is only open during the summer. Whoever carved the old capitals must have been extremely fond of wildlife because nearly every biblical story has a strong animal connection such as the lions which refused to attack Daniel when he was thrown into their den.

Domme, reached by means of a road that snakes its way up the side of a crag, was a *bastide* built on the orders of Philip the Bold towards the

Domme; one of the ancient gateways leading to the old town

end of the thirteenth century. By balancing it on top of a rock there was no way the French could lay it out on conventional lines, although they did manage to straighten out a few streets. The focal point, as with all *bastides*, is the main square with its splendid covered market and rather oddly shaped Governor's House, now the home of the Syndicat d'Initiative. Under the market, whose first floor balcony is decked with flowers and supported by solid stone pillars, are the caves where the villagers took refuge in times of trouble — a frequent occurrence in the Middle Ages. In this respect they were only following the example of prehistoric animals that took shelter in the grottoes and sometimes died

there. Bones that were discovered when the caves were being prepared as a tourist attraction have been left in situ, along with stalactites and stalagmites that decorate the small galleries. Also facing the Place de la Halle is the Musée Paul-Reclus, an old house full of items tracing the history of Domme. This well thought out little museum includes reproductions of typical living quarters as well as clothes, household utensils and farm implements augmented by pictures and documents.

The Grand Rue is the place to look for souvenirs provided one is willing to pay quite high prices and jostle for position with all the other tourists who congregate there during shopping hours. At the far end is the Porte

The *bastide* town of Domme

﹡ de la Combe with a promenade following the line of the ramparts
﹡ round to the Porte del Bos which lost its portcullis a great many years ago. It is pleasant to amble back through streets of expertly restored houses with wrought-iron balconies, vine-covered terraces, stairways and flowers to the thirteenth-century
﹡ Porte des Tours. This gateway, with its huge semi-circular stone towers, has been better preserved than either of the other two original entrances. Philip the Fair intended the towers to be guardrooms but at least one served as a prison for the Knights Templar who carved their names and insignia on the walls. The Belvédère de la Barre and the Promenade des Falaises undoubtedly have the best view, looking out across farmlands to the Dordogne. At one end is a well kept public garden with a viewing table beyond which is an
﹡ elderly mill. The main, and almost the only, hotel shares the same view and provides some bedrooms with baths and small balconies as well as a restaurant where the menus are both good and imaginative. All the usual outdoor activities are on offer but anyone planning to spend some time there during the season should book well in advance.

Although Domme's first duty was to resist any English attack during the Hundred Years' War its moment of truth came in 1588. The Catholic inhabitants were so convinced that their isolated position made the fortress virtually impregnable that they hardly bothered to take anything other than the basic precautions. On the night in question it seems probable that the troops, like the villagers, were soundly asleep in bed, leaving an odd sentry dozing at his post. Unfortunately they reckoned without Geoffroi de Vivans. At the head of a small group of men he climbed up the Barre under cover of darkness and opened the gates to his main forces who were waiting outside. After consolidating their position, burning down the church and destroying Cénac Priory close by, his garrison held the old *bastide* until the beginning of 1592. By that time the Wars of Religion were starting to run out of steam so Vivans sold Domme back to the Catholics for 40,000 livres, but he was sly enough to make sure that there was nothing of any great use to them after his forces moved away.

The ruined castle of **Castelnaud-la-Chapelle** had an equally chequered history beginning, to all intents and purposes, when it was captured by Simon de Montfort in 1214. Less than 50 years later Louis IX handed it over to England's Henry III, thereby providing the enemy with a formidable stronghold which they held on to for most of the Hundred Years' War. When at last that was over the castle was in a pretty bad way and a great deal of time and money was spent on restoring it. However enough of the family fortune was left to make little Anne de Caumont an extremely wealthy heiress after her father died in 1572. At the age of 7 she was kidnapped by her guardian and forced to marry his son who was killed 5 years later in a duel. The idea of so much money and real estate in the hands of a child upset the Duc de Mayenne who kidnapped her in turn with the same object in view. Six years later history repeated itself and Anne found she was tied to an even less desirable husband than before. Eventually she left the Comte de St Pol and when their son was killed at the siege of Montpellier she gave up the unequal struggle and went into a convent. Her mother, who had apparently taken all three abductions in her stride, retaliated by disinheriting the unfortunate girl and handing over the castle to one of her cousins. In the end the Revolution caught up with Castelnaud and it was left abandoned and in ruins until restoration work started in 1969.

The castle, still looking rather the worse for wear, stands on the top of a hill, separated from the road by a number of small houses built on narrow terraces. No attempt has been made to dress it up like a medieval *château*. Instead the main building has been turned into a museum which demonstrates the methods used in siege warfare during the Middle Ages. The cannon which were introduced at about this time were infinitely more effective than the weapons they replaced and this is emphasised by tableaux in the artillery tower, with the addition of ancient samples including some original cannon balls. Two audiovisual presentations trace the history of the castle in particular, and medieval warfare in general, while a

reconstructed twelfth-century catapult in the grounds shows what the earlier defendants had to face. The view from the castle is magnificent with the river far below and the Beynac fortress glaring at it from an equally commanding position on the opposite bank.

Although part of the damage suffered by Castelnaud during the Hundred Years' War was repaired by Brandelis de Caumont, his son and heir, François, decided that he wanted to live in a more elegant home when he married and settled down. The result was that he built the **Château de Milandes** on a less formidable hilltop a few kilometres away. It is an attractive Renaissance mansion, covered in creepers, with towers and gables, casement windows and a great deal of greenery in the formal gardens all round. It got through the Wars of Religion without much difficulty and even escaped intact during the Revolution, thanks to the tactful intervention of the staff. However the family were unable to hold on to it and it was auctioned by the Republicans. The buyer, a man called Claverie, updated the *château*, added a small wing and laid out fresh gardens but the whole place needed doing up again when it was bought by Joséphine Baker, La Perle Noire of the Folies Bergères. During World War II she had joined the Resistance Movement and provided a refuge for Allied servicemen, for which she received the Legion of Honour, but her abiding ambition was to create a world village for orphaned children,

Château de Milandes

Rural museum at Milandres

regardless of their race, colour or creed. Les Milandes was exactly the sort of place she had in mind. She and her husband, Joe Bouillon, worked hard to make this dream come true but the upkeep was exorbitant and she was forced to sell the *château* in 1964. The Château de Milandes gives visitors an opportunity to see pieces of furniture, *objets d'art* and other items that belonged to Joséphine Baker as well as possessions left behind by the original owners after the Revolution.

A great many little roads, linking villages of no particular merit, thread their way south through the woods to the border with Lot. The only one worth mentioning from an architectural point of view is **Besse** which has a private *château* and a small church with an elaborately carved doorway that touches on a variety of subjects from hunting to the Seven Deadly Sins. However **Mazeyrolles**, slightly to the west on the D710, puts in an entirely different plea for attention. It is a medieval hamlet with a thirteenth-century English blockhouse and a small *auberge* that is open right through the year. Apart from such amenities as its own swimming pool, somewhere for golfers to practice their strokes, a ping-pong table and a place to play *boules* there are facilities for tennis, riding, fishing and canoeing nearby. However the main attraction is that horsedrawn carriages are available for anyone who wants to spend the day exploring all the local byways, either on their own or accompanied by a guide. The *caléche*, a lightweight

vehicle rather like a governess cart, will hold up to five people and the idea is to leave at 10.30am, returning at about 6pm. There is no need to worry about finding somewhere to stop for lunch because a picnic can be provided, adding slightly to the cost but including such things as *hors d'oeuvre*, meat, cheese, pastries, mineral water and wine.

Anyone with neither the time nor the inclination to spend a few days rusticating will find that it is only a short drive from Les Milandes across country to **Belvès**. This is a most attractive little town overlooking the Nauze Valley where the old houses are adorned with turrets and the terraces are full of shrubs and flowers. The Place d'Armes is home to both an old belfry and a covered market which has a pillar where wrongdoers were tied up to be flogged. A former Dominican monastery looks out on the Place de la Croix-des-Frères, which undoubtedly borrowed its name from the monks. The two squares are separated by lines of elderly houses, some of which have been restored with the ground floors adapted to make room for a series of rather nice little shops. Markets are held quite regularly in the main square, growing in size and importance towards the end of the year when large quantities of walnuts are brought in from the forests all round.

From Belvès a comparatively major road follows the course of the Nauze past Sagelat with its forgettable little church, to **Siorac-en-Périgord** on the banks of the Dordogne. Although the village has both a large *château* and a small church it is regarded principally as a holiday resort. The houses are strung out along the water's edge, facing what is called a beach, but in reality it is like any other river bank. It is certainly a great place for kayaks and canoes, especially as it is possible to explore 200km (124 miles) of waterways without a barrage in sight. Craft can be hired for an hour or more but it takes about a week to complete the journey to Argentat in Limousin, although rather less to Terrasson in the north-eastern corner of Périgord Noir. The stopping points are about 14km (9 miles) apart and quite a few of them are worth visiting. Other outdoor activities include golf, riding and fishing with a private tennis court for those staying at the right hotel. There are three of them in Siorac, at least one of which is willing to arrange sightseeing trips in a hot air balloon. Those who prefer a tent or trail a caravan will find a good campsite on the river bank.

It is at this point that the motorist is faced with a choice of routes, each one different and each one extremely fascinating in its own way. Anybody who plans to be back in Sarlat for dinner would probably opt for the road along the northern bank of the river through St-Cyprien and past the magnificent castle at Beynac — both of which are included in Chapter 1 The Dordogne. The traveller whose plans are more fluid would be just as likely to put up somewhere for the night and start off bright and early in the morning for the Vézère which joins forces with the Dor-

dogne at Limeuil. The river has come a long way from its source on the Plâteau de Millevaches in Limousin, passing through such memorable places as Uzerche, but the last part of its journey is without doubt the most historic. From Montignac southwards the hills on either side are literally riddled with caves and shelters, inhabited for the better part of 30,000 years. Newcomers to the scene added an odd castle or two, mostly during the Middle Ages, but since the cave drawings and paintings were discovered hotels and museums have flourished alongside all the attractions that go hand in hand with a flourishing tourist industry. The time it takes to cover this comparatively short distance depends entirely on the person concerned — a casual observer would probably manage it in one day quite easily whereas other people might need a week or more.

The third choice falls somewhere between the other two. It entails a short run from Siorac-en-Périgord to **Le Buisson-de-Cadouin**, another little resort with fewer amenities less than 20km (12 miles) downstream. From here a fairly main road heads due north with a turning off to **Limeuil**, built on a promontory between the Dordogne and the Vézère. ✳ This is yet another small town with a long history and a few reminders from the distant past to prove it. There is a picturesque right angle bridge spanning both rivers beyond which the old houses nudge each other along narrow streets that climb, sometimes laboriously, up the side of the cliff. The village was well fortified in its youth, with gates and ramparts, some of which have survived, along with a modest castle and the twelfth-century church of St Martin. This was built with the approval of Richard Coeur de Lion, dedicated to Thomas Becket, damaged during the Wars of Religion and restored afterwards but contains nothing of outstanding interest. The main reason for driving up to the topmost point, called Haut Limeuil, hoping all the time not to encounter another car travelling in the opposite direction, is to see the view. At one time the village was a busy port with boatbuilding, fishing and weaving, whereas today it is more interested in holidaymakers. There are canoes for hire, a couple of small *auberges* and sports facilities.

Ignoring both the Dordogne and the Vézère a minor road sets out for **Paunat**, to the north-west. It is a small hamlet tucked away in a valley which does not get a great many visitors in spite of having a twelfth-century church left over from an ancient monastery. The church is decidedly severe, but none the worse for that, and during restoration work that began in 1977 traces were discovered of a previous building which may have been older by some 300 years.

There are several different ways of getting from Paunat to Rouffignac and as many good reasons for heading in that direction. The most southerly of these is the **Grotte de Rouffignac**, about 5km (3 miles) short of the town. The grotto, also known as the Cro de Granville, is one of the largest with galleries and caves stretching for more than 8km (5 miles). However only about half the area is open to the public who do their sightseeing in comfort from a small electric train. The location of the grotto has been known since the fifteenth century but it was only in 1956 that Professor Nougier discovered the drawings and paintings of mammoths, bison, ibex, rhinos and horses. There is rather an endearing, sleepy looking rhino with double horns standing in a queue with two others but the most unusual picture shows a battle between two herds of mammoths, nearly a dozen in all, which has been christened The Patriarch.

Rouffignac itself has nothing much in its favour, apart from the church, but the area round about justifies a visit. The sixteenth-century church was the only building that escaped when the Germans set fire to the town in 1944. Interesting features are the twisted columns that help to hold up the roof and the female figures, including mermaids, in the stone work. This was considered to be almost blasphemous in the Middle Ages unless, they happened to be either saints or angels.

South of Rouffignac is the **Château de Fleurac** which was completed in the nineteenth century. Apart from the interior of the *château* with its antique furniture there is an automobile museum.

The ruins of **L'Herm Castle** are another local attraction. The fortress was built in 1512 and had a rather more unsavoury history than most

Fayrac, one of the many *châteaux* overlooking the River Dordogne

others of its ilk. The first occupant, Jean III of Calvimont, was killed there and so was his daughter Margaret whose husband murdered her in order to marry Marie de Hautefort in 1605. This bloodthirsty couple are said to have committed nearly a dozen other murders between them so it is small wonder that nobody really wanted the castle after that. Marie de Hautefort's niece bought it for some reason or other and then walked out, leaving it to its own devices. Inspite of being both unloved and abandoned the *château* can hardly be described as brooding, although it does look a trifle lonely, standing by itself in the forest. Two extremely dilapidated carved men-at-arms mount guard at the doorway

but the beautiful spiral staircase has weathered remarkably well along with its tower, parts of the original building and some decorative chimneys. There is little else to inspect in the vicinity but the forest makes a delightful place to walk, especially as there are a number of marked footpaths. Less energetic visitors might just as well head for **La Douze**, a few kilometres to the west of the D710. Like Rouffignac the village has a small church with some unusual features. They include an altar made from one huge stone, carved rather on the lines of a painting with the Baron of Ladouze and his lady accompanied by their patron saints. There is also a font perched on top of a decorative Roman column. A few kilometres to the south a fork in the road gives motorists a choice between driving on to Le Bugue or taking an equally acceptable route to Les Eyzies-de-Tayac, both of them with prehistoric connections and both on the River Vézère.

A thorough exploration along the valley of the Vézère is certainly rewarding but it is also extremely time consuming. For this reason the majority of people are inclined to select a few of the most outstanding caves, museums and castles and leave the rest for a later date. Some return, others do not and therefore miss a great many very interesting sites. Each one has its own peculiarities but the subtle differences are more likely to appeal to the expert than to a family party on a conducted tour.

Travelling from south to north, and determined not to miss a thing, the first encounter after leaving Limeuil and passing the twelfth-century Chapelle St Martin, is with **Le Bugue**. This is a pleasant, unassuming little town that welcomes tourists. There is one very comfortable hotel beside the river with all the expected facilities including a good restaurant, a few studios, easy parking and a private swimming pool. The various *auberges*, about five in all, are smaller and less ambitious. The town is bidding fair to become a popular tourist centre with good campsites and watersports. For anyone on a serious hiking holiday Le Bugue is on the GR6, making it easy to travel west beyond Lalinde, east to Souillac in Lot or along the Vézère Valley on the GR461.

Less than 2km (1 mile) from Le Bugue is the **Caverne de Bara-Bahau**. There is not a lot of it so a conducted tour should only last about half an hour and still allow time to see the outlines of bears, wild oxen and other animals which were discovered in 1951. They were apparently drawn with sharp flints roughly 20,000 years ago and have not worn as well as some drawings elsewhere that date from the same period. The **Gouffre de Proumeyssac**, about 4km (2 miles) in the opposite direction, has been described as the Cathédrale de Cristal because of the stalactites dripping from the roof like some gigantic fringe. A tunnel drilled through the rock leads to a viewing platform with a stream underneath and peculiar formations growing up all round. There is plenty of parking space outside, a picnic area, a small shop, a bar and a minuscule museum. **Campagne**, about the same distance away along the road to the north, has not a single cave to its name. However there is a much restored fifteenth-century *château* which is not open to the public, standing in extensive grounds which are. They are full of ancient sequoias and cedar trees with a stairway known as the Chemin des Dames pointing the way through the forest.

Les Eyzies-de-Tayac is sometimes referred to as the 'Capital of Prehistory', a title which might possibly have rubbed off from its very interesting national museum of the same name. This is housed in a thirteenth-century fortress, updated 300 years later, which peers down at the village from beneath a rock half way up the cliff. The view is shared by a statue of a prehistoric man which does not do justice to our ancestors nor even to the ape-like creatures who preceded them. On the other hand the museum is overflowing with fascinating exhibits going back some 30,000 years. It has sections devoted to such things as the art of shaping flints, not widely practiced these days but fairly commonplace something like a million years ago. There are carved limestone slabs, spears, hunting knives, ornaments of various descriptions, cave paintings and copies of items on display in other national museums. The area all round Les Eyzies-de-Tayac is somewhat overcrowded with caves and shelters, each of which has added something to our knowledge of prehistory. The Abri de Cro-Magnon contributed three skeletons that won the unqualified approval of Paul Broca, the surgeon and anthropologist who founded the School of Anthropology in France. The Grotte de St Cirq provided one of the earliest carved human figures to be discovered so far, which was immediately dubbed the Sorcerer of St Cirq. This cave also contained a selection of paintings and tools whereas the Grotte de Carpe-Diem had to be content with oddly shaped stalactites and stalagmites in a variety of different colours. The Grotte de Font-de-Gaume has been known for nearly 200 years and has some exceptionally beautiful polychrome paintings, especially of deer, bison, horses and reindeer. It comes as no surprise to find that Les Eyzies has nearly as many hotels as it has caves. Some are very comfortable, overrun with tourists, especially in the high season, and offering them all the aids to gracious living in addition to private swimming pools with tennis, golf, mini-golf, riding, fishing and canoes in the vicinty. Less affluent visitors can be just as happy in one of the *auberges* but *gîtes* are rather hard to come by and so, to a certain extent, are sites for tents and caravans.

A side trip into the Beune Valley starts with the **Grotte des Combarelles**, a winding corridor decorated with some 300 different animal portraits including a splendid creature on the prowl that looks more like a prehistoric lioness than anything else. Further on the **Abri du Cap-Blanc** was found to contain, among other treasures, two bison and a number of horses beautifully carved so as to take full advantage of the uneven surface of the rock. The pretty little sixteenth-century Château de Laussel nearby was built almost on top of the site where an unattractively buxom relief known as the Venus with the Horn of Plenty was discovered. Nowadays she and her companion, called the Hunter, are safely installed in the Musee d'Aquitaine in Bordeaux. Other attendant attractions include the ruined **Château de Commarque** which was a constant bone of contention during the Hundred Years' War, and a Fossil Centre in the grounds of the Château de Beyassac on the banks of the Petite Beune.

Returning to the Vézère, and crossing over to the western bank, potholers will gravitate towards the **Musée de la Spéléologie**. It is set up in the rock fortress of Tayac, looking across the river towards a small fortified church of the same name on the opposite side. The museum is full of equipment, models and geological information that might possibly make anyone other than a confirmed addict feel a trifle claustrophobic. Not far away is the **Gorge d'Enfer**, a splendid open grotto with two shelters, one of which is justly famous for the carved relief of a fish, possibly a salmon, that measures more than 2m (7ft). It also boasts a small safari park, open throughout the year and full of animals distantly related to the ones immortalised in the various caves and grottoes.

Next in order of appearance is the **Grotte du Grand Roc** with steps leading up to caves with stalactites and stalagmites as well as other formations closely resembling seaweed and coral. This particular section of the river ends with **Laugerie Basse** and **Laugerie Haute**. The former was discovered to be full of tools and human remains going back to the time when prehistoric families followed the herds of reindeer as they migrated southwards to avoid the worst effects of the Ice Age. A small museum on the site has a display of such useful articles as needles, arrow heads, harpoons, lamps and pottery. Not to be outdone Laugerie Haute gives ample proof of the fact that the area was inhabited constantly for about 30,000 years. It is one of the places where it is possible to see the cuts made in the rock in order to drain off storm water which might otherwise have flooded the living spaces. It is here that the D47 gets rather tired of prehistoric encounters and makes a sudden dash for Périgueux.

Because there is still a great deal to see in the Vézère Valley it is necessary to recross the river and follow the D706 that starts off along the opposite bank. Beyond **Tursac** with its typical Romanesque church and a campsite, the road pauses at the entrance to the **Préhisto-Parc**. This is a large wooded area with paths that snake their way through long grass and trees so that other sightseers can be heard but frequently not seen. Every so often one comes face to face with a perfect model of a sabre toothed lion, a woolly rhinoceros or some other prehistoric beast, or catches a glimpse of early hunters bringing back the body of a deer they have killed. There are lifesize tableaux showing men pitting their strength and skill against mammoths, armed with nothing much more than clubs and stones. Fishermen are out looking for something to vary their somewhat monotonous diet, while outside a natural shelter a whole family are hard at work, leaving a cave artist to decorate his walls with different types of animals. Everything in the park is accurately reproduced and vetted by experts which makes it almost possible to believe that the people who lived and hunted over the same ground have somehow been frozen in their

A statue of Cro-Magnon man looks down on Les Eyzies-de-Tayac

tracks for the benefit of the twentieth century.

A few kilometres further on the road stops again, this time to inspect the **Roque St Christophe**. This is a sheer cliff, some 80m (262ft) high and stretching for 1km (half a mile) or more, which is riddled with caves and shelters stacked up in five layers like a prehistoric apartment block. It was obvious from the tools and other items discovered here that it was occupied some 20,000 years ago but by no means all the walkways and terraces date from that time. In around AD10 it made a useful fortress when the Vikings pushed their way up the river. Later it was pressed into service during the Hundred Years' War and suffered further indignities during the Wars of Religion. Work is still in progress, partly of a scientific nature and partly cosmetic for the sake of tourists. It is not unusual to see workmen suspended on ropes half way down the face of the cliff trimming any bushes that are likely to obscure the view. The narrow paths are edged with handrails to prevent anyone falling over

One of the prehistoric animal paintings discovered in the Lascaux caves

as the crowds climb laboriously up to the higher levels, disappearing every so often into tunnels in the rock. There is plenty of space to park but, so far, no obtrusive restaurants or souvenir shops to spoil the atmosphere.

It is remarkably easy to lose one's way in this part of the valley because so many small roads wander off in search of other places of interest. However they all seem to arrive eventually at some well signposted crossroads or other, although it is not unknown to discover oneself back at the same point beside the river, where the D706 takes advantage of a convenient bridge to visit **Le Moustier** on the other side. If the name sounds familiar that is because part of the Middle Paleolithic Age has been called the Mousterian Pe-

riod. This came about when excavations started under a shelter in the village and turned up a human skeleton and flints of the type that were made and used to good effect by Neanderthal men. **La Madeleine**, a site to the south, is definitely more modern. The period named after it came at the end of the Ice Age something over 10,000 years ago when craftsmen perfected the art of carving wood, bone and ivory in addition to painting on walls. Among the many beautiful examples found in the Gisement de la Madeleine was a splendid bison, with a slightly Cretian look about it, that is now in the National Museum of Antiquities at St Germain-en-Laye near Paris. Like St Christophe, La Madeleine was occupied during the Middle Ages and there are traces of a chapel and living quarters at the foot of a ruined castle about 15 minutes walk from the car park.

St Léon-sur-Vézère, although surrounded by likely looking country, has no caves of its own. Instead there is a very viewable little church left over from a twelfth-century Benedictine priory, a small chapel and two *châteaux*, neither of them open to visitors. Although it has a municipal campsite, anyone in need of a good lunch will have to press on to **Thonac** where there are a couple of *auberges* to choose from and yet more tourist attractions close by. The slightly longer of two possible routes to the north passes the **Tour de la Vermondie** which does its best to ape the Tower of Pisa. Although it is thought to have been badly damaged by the Saracens in 732 romantics have a tendency to attribute its odd angle to quite a different incident. According to legend a young couple were parted when the man was imprisoned in the tower. The girl walked past every day in the hope of seeing him until the tower, possibly getting a little tired of the whole business, bent over so that the couple could kiss each other. The story does not go on to say if he then stepped out, as any full-blooded young prince would do, and made good his escape with her.

The nearest of several other places of interest within easy reach of Thonac is the **Château de Lossie** which is said to have both an echo and an amusing legend to go with it. It seems that when one of the neighbours popped over to see if he could borrow some money the owner demanded, in loud voice, to know if he was a good payer. The word for payer being *pagaire* the echo called back *Gaire...Gaire*. With this warning to be careful ringing in their ears the owner was able to refuse without causing any unpleasantness. Legends apart the *château* has much to recommend it. Built in the sixteenth century it is a no-nonsense type of country mansion with a tower at one end that is decorative rather than warlike and a wide terrace overlooking the river. The rooms are well-equipped with choice pieces from Italy, early seventeenth-century French furniture and some fine tapestries.

Slightly to the north, along the D45, is **Le Thot**, a research establishment founded in 1972 to delve into everything to do with prehistory. It is a modern building with a fascinating museum full of enormous photographs, models and facsimiles. Among other things it shows the methods used to recreate the Lascaux galleries so that people could still see these unique cave paintings without damaging the originals. There is an audio-visual presentation concerned with the discoveries made at Lascaux, Peche-Merle, Niaux and Altamira, a film show and prehistoric settlements copied in the grounds, including a hut made from bones and animal skins that was discovered in the Ukraine. The attendant park is also home to several different animals which are descended from the original wildlife of the region. However, the mini-mammoths are represented by a lifesize robot.

A minor road doubles back from Thonac across the Vézère to **Sergeac**, a small hamlet with a most unusual fifteenth-century cross on the outskirts, some nice old houses including the local manor and the remains of a commandery that was once the property of the Knights of St John of Jerusalem. The little fortified church has nothing particularly outstanding about it although this is certainly not the case with **Castel-Merle** nearby. The complex consists of several shelters, some of them decorated, and a small museum which includes amongst its other exhibits some extraordinarily modern-looking necklaces made from bits of bone, old teeth and shells. One vast shelter, known as the Fort des Anglais, is reached by way of a staircase hewn out of the rock. It was occupied by the English during the Hundred Years' War who made themselves comfortable in the living quarters, kept their horses in the stables and were ready to deal with anything suspicious that was happening on the river.

However impressive all these shelters and caves may be they cannot compare with the **Grotte de Lascaux**, a unique collection of prehistoric art that was discovered by accident in 1940. It was due to a dog that lost its footing and fell down a hole. Four young boys went in search of it with the aid of a lamp and found themselves in a gallery covered in paintings. They told their teacher who passed on the story to the Abbé Breuil. He verified it for himself and in 1948 the four sections which make up the grotto were opened to the public. Sadly, the steady procession of sightseers did more damage in 15 years than nature had caused in as many thousand and in 1963 Lascaux was closed. However a replica was created in a specially-constructed cave some 180m (200yd) away, calling it **Lascaux II**. The Institut Géographique National was asked to help and in 1983 an almost identical copy of the upper section was completed.

The tour starts in two small rooms where visitors can find out something about the history of the galleries, why the paintings had survived in such mint condition and how contact with the outside world and excited human beings was beginning to destroy them. There are also glass cases full of items found in Lascaux such as coloured powders, flints and tallow candles. After that the party, always restricted in number, moves on into the Salle des Taureaux, so called because of its amazingly realistic herd of black bulls including one measuring more than 5m (16ft) from head to tail. There is also one animal that looks vaguely like a unicorn, but was probably inspired by a rhinoceros, as well as some deer and a collection of small horses. The second gallery is one mass of pictures portraying all the various species including horses, some of which are cheerful little ponies with long hair, not all that different from the delightful small creatures made popular by James Thelwell. A bare kilometre away from Lascaux II is Régourdou which was discovered in 1954. Its most important contributions were a human skeleton 70,000 years old, give or take a year or two, and a bears' burial ground which might possibly have had some religious significance.

Only about 3km (2 miles) separate Lascaux from **Montignac**, a small town on the Vézère with a tower that was originally part of a fortress belonging to the counts of Périgord. It was a sleepy little village before the caves were discovered but in the space of a year or two it blossomed into a fully fledged tourist centre, with half a dozen hotels including the up-market Château de Puy Robert and the slightly less self-important but larger Soleil d'Or. During the season it is full to bursting point with tourists in search of prehistoric art, some of whom bring tents and caravans which, provided they have booked in advance, are accommodated on a nearby campsite. Facilities include tennis, swimming, fishing and the Eugène Le Roy Museum. This is conveniently sited alongside the Syndicat d'Initiative and is devoted to traditional arts and crafts as well as local history. It also contains a reconstruction of the study where Le Roy wrote his famous story of the peasant revolt.

Those who wish to leave the river and its caves for a while can drive northwards through Auriac-du-Périgord for a glimpse of the **Château de Rastignac** which is likely to bring

on a touch of *déjà vu*. This is because it looks very similar to the White House in Washington although there is nothing to suggest any connection between the two. It was built at the beginning of the nineteenth century but had to be restored after the Germans set fire to it at the end of World War II. The neighbouring hamlet of **La Bachellerie** is very pleasant and unassuming with a little church that suffered almost as much at the hands of the English during the Hundred Years' War and still has the scars.

The main route north from Montignac follows the course of the river to **Terrasson-la-Villedieu**, another small town that falls into the category of two for the price of one. Terrasson is the old village that clambers up the left bank above its twelfth-century port to the sparse remains of a fortress and a much restored medieval church. La Villedieu is quite modern by comparison and is still growing. The two are joined across the river by a couple of bridges, one old and the other new. It is rather a bustling little place with a modest *auberge* and a market on Thursdays that does a roaring trade in walnuts and truffles when they are in season. From here it is a straight run to Larche on the border with Limousin which has a small, inexpensive inn with baths en suite where motorists can stop for the night only 11km (7 miles) short of Brive-la-Gaillarde.

PLACES TO VISIT

Arnac-Pompadour

Château
Grounds have guided tours morning and afternoon except on 15 August, Sunday afternoons and race days.

Bergerac

Château de Monbazillac
☎ 53 58 30 27
Open: 9.30am-12noon and 1.30-7.30pm June to September. Otherwise 10am-12noon and 2.30-7pm. Wine tasting during these hours. Restaurant open June to September.

Cloître des Recollets
Place du Docteur-Cayla

Musée du Tabac
Maison Peyrarède,
Rue de l'Ancien-Port
☎ 53 63 04 13
Open: 10am-12noon and 2-6pm Tuesday to Saturday. 2.30-6.30pm Sunday. Closed holidays.

Museum of Urban History
Next to the Maison Peyrarède
Open: same times as the Musée du Tabac

Museum of Sacred Art
Rue du Docteur-Cayla
☎ 53 57 33 21
Open: 3.30-6pm daily July and August but closed Monday. Otherwise 3.30-6pm Wednesday and Sunday only.

Wine Museum
☎ 53 57 80 92
Open: daily Tuesday to Friday 10am-12noon and 1.30-5.30pm. Saturday 10am-12noon and Sunday 2.30-6.30pm mid-March to mid-October. Closed holidays.

Beyssac

Fossil Centre
Château de Beyssac
South-east of Les Eyzies-de-Tayac
☎ 53 29 65 16
Open: 10am-12noon and 2-5.30pm April to September. Otherwise afternoons only.

Bourdeilles

Château
☎ 53 03 73 36
Open: daily 10am-7pm July to early September. 10am-12noon and 2-6pm April to June and early September to mid-October. Closed Tuesday. 2-5pm early February to March and mid-October to mid-December. Closed Tuesday and Christmas Day.

Brantôme

Abbey and Caves
☎ 53 05 80 63
Open: 10am-12noon and 2-6pm. Closed Tuesday September to June. Guided tours.

Château de Richemond
☎ 53 05 72 81 or 56 92 64 48
Open: 10am-12noon and 3-6pm mid-July to end of August. Closed Friday. Sunday morning and the morning of 15 August.

Bell Tower
☎ 53 05 81 65
Guided tours afternoons only mid-June to mid-September.

Fernand Desmoulin Museum
☎ 53 05 70 21
Open: 10am-12noon and 2-6pm. Closed Tuesday.

Bugue, Le

Caverne de Bara-Bahau
☎ 53 07 28 82 and 53 07 27 47

Open: 8.30am-7pm July and August.
9am-12noon and 2-7pm April to June,
September and October.

Gouffre de Proumeyssac
☎ 53 07 28 82 and 53 07 27 47
Open: 8.30am-7pm July and August.
9am-12noon and 2-7pm April to June
and September to October. Otherwise by appointment. Closed December to mid-January.

Cadouin

Abbey Church & Pilgrim Museum
☎ 53 63 36 28
Open: daily 10am-7pm July to first
week in September. 10am-12noon
and 2-6pm April to June and second
week in September to mid-October.
Closed Monday. 2-5pm early February to March and mid-October to
December. Closed Monday and
Christmas Day.

Campagne

Château Garden
☎ 53 07 44 74
To see the park apply to the caretaker.

Carsac-Aillac

Church
If closed apply to the *Mairie*.

Castelnaud-la-Chapelle

Castle & Museum
☎ 53 29 57 08
Open: July & August daily 9am-8pm;
May, June & September daily 10am-
7pm; March, April, October to mid-
November and school holidays daily
10am-6pm; rest of year Sunday-
Friday 2-5pm.

Château de Milandes
☎ 53 29 50 73
Open: daily 9am-7pm May to September, also evenings Wednesday
and Saturday July and August. Daily
9am-12noon and 2-6pm mid-March to
April and October to mid-November.

Castel-Merle

Museum & Shelters
☎ 53 50 77 76 and 53 50 79 70
Open: 10am-6.30pm July and
August. 10am-12noon and 2-5.30pm
April to June and September. Closed
Wednesday.

Châlus

Château de Châlus-Chabrol
☎ 55 78 56 61
Guided tours morning and afternoon
July to mid-September. Afternoons
only on Sunday and holidays mid-
April to June.

Château de Montbrun
☎ 55 78 40 10
Open: each morning and afternoon
throughout the year.

Chancelade

Abbey
North-west of Périgueux
☎ 53 04 86 87
Open: daily 2-7pm July and August.

Merlande Priory
Open: daily 9am-12noon and 2-6pm.

Couze-et-St-Front

Moulin Larroque
☎ 53 61 01 75
Paper mill open: Monday to Friday
daily during working hours.

Domme

Caves
Under the covered market
☎ 53 28 37 09
Open: 9.30am-12noon and 2-7pm
mid-June to mid-September. 9.30am-
12noon and 2-6pm April to mid-June
and mid-September to end of October.

Musée Paul-Reclus
☎ 53 28 30 18
Open: 10am-12noon and 3-6pm April
to October.

Porte des Tours
☎ 53 28 37 09
Open: on request. Special tours at 5pm, April to September.

Douze, La
Church
If closed apply to the Epicerie Claude.

L'Herm Castle
☎ 75 31 61 22
Open: daily 10am-7pm July to mid-September.

Eymet
Museum of Prehistory & Popular Traditions
In the *château*
☎ 53 23 92 33 or 53 23 74 95 (Syndicat d'Initiative)
Open: 10am-12noon and 3-7pm mid-June to mid-September. Closed Sunday morning. Otherwise 10am-12noon and 3-6pm. Closed Sunday morning.

Eyzies-de-Tayac, Les
Basse Laugerie Deposit
☎ 53 06 97 12
Open: 9am-6pm mid-March to mid-September.

Gorge d'Enfer
☎ 53 06 94 71
Guide available from Laugerie Haute site. Park open: 9.30am-6pm July and August.

Grotte des Combarelles
☎ 53 08 00 94
Open: 9am-12noon and 2-6pm April to September. 10am-12noon and 2-4pm October to March. Closed 1 January, 1 May, 1 and 11 November, 25 December, also some days in March and April. During high season you must buy tickets at 9am for the morning and 2pm for the afternoon.

Grotte de Font-de-Gaume
☎ 53 08 00 94
Open: 9am-12noon and 2-6pm April to September. 10am-12noon and 2-5pm March and October. 10am-12noon and 2-4pm November to February. Closed Tuesdays and 1 January, 1 May, 1 November, 11 November and 25 December and some days in April and June. In the season it is necessary to buy tickets in the morning.

Grotte du Grand Roc
☎ 53 06 96 76
Open: 9am-7pm July and August. 9am-12noon and 2-6pm mid-March to June and September to mid-November.

Grotte de St Cirq
☎ 53 07 14 37
Open: 10am-6pm May to October. 12noon-4pm October to May.

Haute Laugerie Deposit
☎ 53 08 00 94 and 53 06 92 90
Open: 9am-12noon and 2-6pm April to September. 10am-12noon and 2-3.30pm November to February. Closed Tuesday. 10am-12noon and 2-4.30pm March and October.

Musée de la Spéléologie
☎ 53 29 68 42
Open: 9am-12noon and 2-6pm July and August. Closed Saturday.

National Museum of Prehistory
☎ 53 06 97 03
Open: 9.30am-12noon and 2-6pm April to November. Closed Tuesday 9.30am-12noon and 2-5pm December to March.

Hautefort
Château
☎ 53 50 51 23
Open: daily 9am-12noon and 2-7pm Palm Sunday to to All Saints Day. Otherwise 2-6pm Sunday and holiday afternoons. Closed mid-December to last week in January.

Issac

Château de Mont-Réal

☎ 53 81 11 03 or 53 81 20 94
Open: daily 10am-12noon and 2-6pm
July to September. Otherwise by
appointment only.

Jumilhac-le-Grand

Château

☎ 53 52 58 62
Open: 10am-12noon and 2-6.30pm
July to mid-September, 2-6pm mid-
March to June and mid-September to
mid-November Sundays and holidays
only.

Lanquais

Château

☎ 45 25 02 04 or 53 61 24 24
Open: 9.30am-12noon and 2.30-6pm
April to October. Closed Thursday.

Mareuil-sur-Belle

Château

☎ 53 60 91 35
Open: 2.30-6.30pm July and August.
2.30-6pm March to June and September to October. Closed Saturday.
Possible morning tours for groups on
request.

Manaurie

Caverne de Carpe-Diem

☎ 53 06 93 63
Open: 9am-7.30pm July to September 10am-6.30pm April to June.

Marquay

Abri du Cap-Blanc

☎ 53 59 21 74
Open: 9.30am-7pm July and August.
10am-12noon and 2-5pm April to
June and September to mid-October.

Monpazier

Biron Castle

☎ 53 63 13 39
Open: daily 10am-7pm July to first
week in September. 10am-12noon

and 2-6pm April to June and second
week in September to mid-October.
Closed Monday. 2-5pm early Febru-
ary to March and mid-October to
December. Closed Monday and
Christmas Day.

Montcaret

Roman Villa

☎ 53 08 00 94
Open: 9am-12noon and 2-6pm April
to September. 10am-12noon and 2-
4pm October to March. Closed
Tuesday. Also closed 1 January, 1
May, 1 November, 11 November and
25 December.

Montignac

Eugène Le Roy Museum

☎ 53 51 82 60
Open: 9.30am-12noon and 2.30-
5.30pm. Closed Sunday except
during July and August.

Lascaux II

☎ 53 51 95 03
Open: daily 9.30am-7pm July and
August. 10am-12noon and 2-5.30pm
February to June and September to
December. Closed Monday. Buy
tickets at the Syndicat d'Initiative in
Montignac and arrive at least 45
minutes before closing time.

Moustier, Le

Prehistoric Shelter

☎ 53 06 92 90 (Otherwise enquire at
the Auberge de Vimont near the site).
Open: 10am-12noon and 3-6pm mid-
May to mid-September.

St Christophe, Roque

☎ 53 50 70 45
Open: 9.30am-6.30pm July to first
week of September. 10am-12noon
and 2-6pm mid-March to June and
mid-September to mid-November.

Mussidan

André Voulgre Museum

☎ 53 81 23 55

Open: 9.30am-12noon and 2-6pm
daily except Tuesday June to mid-
September. 2-6pm Saturday, Sunday
and holidays March to May and mid-
September to November. Otherwise
open for groups only.

Grignols Castle
☎ 53 54 28 64 or 53 54 25 40
Open: 2-6.30pm mid-July to mid-
September. Closed Wednesday.

Nontron
Doll Museum
☎ 53 56 20 80
Open: daily 10am-7pm July to first
week in September. 10am-12noon
and 2-6pm April to June and second
week in September to mid-October.
Closed Tuesday. 2-5pm early February to March and mid-October to mid-
December. Closed Tuesday.

Parcoul
Parc de Loisirs du Paradou
☎ 53 91 42 78
Open: until 11pm daily early May to
late September.

Périgueux
Les Bories Castle
☎ 53 06 00 01
Open: daily 10am-12noon and 2-7pm
July to September. Otherwise on
request by telephone.

Military Museum
Rue des Farges
☎ 53 53 47 36
Open: 10am-12noon and 2-6pm
weekdays April to September. Closed
Sundays and holidays. 2-6pm
October to March. Closed Sundays.
2-6pm Wednesday and Saturday
January to March.

Musée du Périgord
Facing the gardens on the Allées de
Tourny
☎ 53 53 16 42
Open: 10am-12noon and 2-6pm July

to September, 10am-12noon and 2-
5pm October to June. Closed Tuesday throughout the year.

St Etienne-de-la-Cité
Near the arena in La Cité
Closed Sunday afternoon.

St Front Cathedral
Near the river in the Puy St Front
quarter
Visits to the cloisters are arranged
with the sacristan.

Tour Mataguerre
In Puy St-Front quarter on the Cours
Fénelon
☎ 53 53 10 63
Guided tours at 2pm Tuesdays to
Fridays during July and August. (This
is part of the Medieval-Renaissance
tour and can be divided into two
sections — La Cité at 2pm and Puy
St-Front at 4pm.) For full details
enquire at the Syndicat d'Initiative.

Villa de Pompeïus
Next door to the Vésone tower in La
Cité
Guided tours Tuesdays to Fridays
during the Gallo-Roman tour. Detailed information is available from
the Syndicat d'Initiative.

Tour de Vésone
La Cité
It also forms part of the Gallo-Roman
tour.

Puyguilhem
Château
☎ 53 54 82 18
Open: daily 10am-7pm July to early
September. 10am-12noon and 2-6pm
April to June and early September to
mid-October. Closed Monday. 2-5pm
early February to March and mid-
October to December. Closed
Monday and Christmas Day.

Grottes de Villars
☎ 53 54 82 36
Open: daily 10-11.30am and 2-

6.30pm mid-June to mid-September, 2-6.30pm on Palm Sunday, then Sundays only to mid-June and during second half of September.

Rochebeaucourt-et-Argentine, La-

Castle Park
Apply at the fish farm.

Rouffignac

Château de Fleurac
Musée de l'automobile
☎ 53 05 95 01, 53 05 95 14
Open: Easter to mid-June Sundays and public holidays 2-7pm. Mid-June to September daily 2-7pm. Mid-July to August also open 10am-12noon daily.

Grotte de Rouffignac
☎ 53 05 41 71
Open: 9-11.30am and 2-6pm July to mid-September. 10-11.30am and 2-5pm Palm Sunday to mid-June and mid-September to end of October.

Salignac-Eyvignes

Castle
☎ 53 28 80 06
Open: daily except Tuesday 10.30am-1pm and 2-6pm July and August. 2-6pm at Easter, the second half of June and the first half of September. Closed Tuesday.

Sarlat-la-Canéda

Chapel of the White Penitents & Museum of Scared Arts
Rue Jean-Jacques Rousseau
Open: 10am-12noon and 3-6pm Easter to end of September. Closed Sunday morning.

Musée-Aquarium
Off the Avenue de Selves
☎ 53 59 44 58
Open: 10am-7pm mid-June to mid-September. Otherwise 10am-12noon and 2.30-6pm.

Musée Automobile
Avenue Thiers
☎ 53 31 62 81
Open: daily 10am-10pm July and August. 10am-12noon and 2-7pm; late March to June and September to October. Otherwise 10am-12noon and 2-6pm weekends and holidays.

Puymartin Castle
☎ 53 59 29 97
Open: daily 10am-12noon and 2-6.30pm April to October, but closes at 6pm April, May and most of September.

St-Amand-de-Coly
☎ 53 51 67 50
Church open: 9am-7pm throughout the year.

Sorges

Maison de la Truffe
☎ 53 05 90 11
Open: daily 10am-12noon and 2-6pm July and August. Daily except Monday 10am-12noon and 2-5pm rest of the year.

St-Avit-Sénieur

Geological Museum
☎ 53 22 32 27
Open: 2-6pm July and August. Closed Monday.

St-Jean-de-Côle

Château de la Marthonie
☎ 53 62 30 25
Open: 10am-12noon and 2-7pm daily July and August.
If the church is closed apply to the town hall or at the bakers shop.

St Geniès

Chapelle du Cheylard
If closed apply to the hardware store, closed Sunday and Monday.

St-Privat-des-Prés

Centre for Popular Arts & Traditions
☎ 53 91 22 87
Open: 3-6pm June to September. To view at other times enquire at the town hall.

St-Yrieix-la-Perche

Château de Coussac-Bonneval
Guided tours afternoons only on Wednesdays, Saturdays and Sundays mid-March to the end of November.

Musée de la Porcelaine
☎ 55 75 10 38
Open: morning and afternoon all through the year but closed on Sunday, Monday and holidays.
To see the old Bible enquire at the *Mairie*.

Teyjat

Prehistoric Cave
☎ 53 06 97 03
Guide available in the village throughout the year.

Thiviers

Foie Gras Museum
☎ 53 55 12 50 (Syndicat d'Initiative)
Open: 10am-12noon and 3-6pm. Closed Sunday and Monday.

Thonac

Château de Lossie
☎ 53 50 70 38
Open: 10am-7pm July to mid-September. Otherwise by appointment.

Centre for Prehistory
Le Thot
☎ 53 50 70 44
Open: daily 9.30am-7pm July and August. 10am-12noon and 2-5.30pm early February to June and September to December. Closed Monday and Christmas Day.

Tour-Blanche, La-

Museum
☎ 53 91 11 98
Open: daily 2.30-5.30pm July and August. Closed Sunday.

Tourtoirac

Abbey
☎ 53 51 12 17
Open: 9am-12noon and 2-6pm June to mid-September.

Tursac

La Madeleine
☎ 53 06 92 49
Open: 10am-7pm July to first week in September. 10am-12noon and 2-6pm April to June and second week in September to mid-October. Closed Tuesday.
2-5pm early February to March and mid-October to mid-November. Closed Tuesday.

Préhisto-Parc
☎ 53 50 73 19 and 53 06 96 76
Open: 9am-7pm May to September 9am-12noon and 2-6pm March, April, October and November.

Varaignes

Museum of Arts, Popular Traditions & Weaving
☎ 53 56 35 76
Open: 10am-12noon and 2-5pm June to September. Closed Tuesday. 2-5pm October to May. Closed Tuesday.

Villefranche-du-Périgord

Ecomusée
☎ 53 29 98 37
Open: daily except Sunday and Monday afternoons 9am-12noon and 3-6pm June to September. Tuesday and Sunday 10am-12noon, Saturday 10am-12noon and 3-6pm April, May and October, otherwise Saturday 10am-12noon.

Lot

3

The present day *département* of Lot, created in 1790, corresponds almost exactly to the ancient province of Quercy and, as before, shares a common border with Périgord. It is part of Midi-Pyrénées, along with Tarn-et-Garonne and Aveyron to the south and east, and has three other immediate neighbours: Auvergne and Limousin in the north with Lot-et-Garonne completing the encirclement to the west in Aquitaine. Lot has characteristics in common with each of them and yet manages to preserve its own identity. In contrast to the mainly pastoral and wooded countryside of Périgord it consists largely of limestone plateaux known as Causses, which are not as stark and lonely as some of those to the east but nevertheless give the same impression of spaciousness.

Sheep do well on the high ground among the scrub and juniper bushes and are bred in large numbers, for both meat and wool, with milk and cheese as a lucrative sideline. At lower altitudes the ground becomes increasingly fertile and is planted with vines, cereals and tobacco as well as orchards, walnut and chestnut trees and pines that provide both resin and a certain amount of timber. The Causse de Gramat, south of the Dordogne, is slashed by deep canyons honeycombed with caves and grottoes. These can stretch for considerable distances and once gave shelter to prehistoric families as well

as mammoths, lions, bears, bison and deer. Cave paintings have been located in the Grotte de Cougnac, north of Gourdon, and at Pech-Merle on the River Lot but not, so far, in anything like the same numbers as along the Vézère in Périgord.

The *département* is well supplied with rivers which have carved out deep and sometimes secretive valleys for themselves. The most important are the Dordogne, which follows a serpentine course in the north on its way through from Auvergne to the coast above Bordeaux, and the Lot with just as many loops and curves between its source in the Cévennes and the point where it joins the Garonne west of Agen. Chief among the many smaller rivers and tributaries is the Célé, considered by many people to be the most beautiful of all, closely followed by the Alzou, the Sagne, the Bave, the Ouysse and the Vers.

There are ample opportunities for fishing, swimming, canoeing and activities such as rafting and windsurfing. Riding holidays are very popular with some 600km (372 miles) of bridle paths. They call at most of the main centres in addition to pausing at more than twenty overnight stopping places, from *gîtes* to specially selected campsites. Ramblers and long distance walkers have a great selection of paths to choose from including several Grandes Randonnées. The GR46 runs from

Opposite: Porte du Figuier, one of Rocamadour's main entrances in the thirteenth century

north to south, joined by the GR64 from Périgord and the GR6 from Figeac in the vicinity of Rocamadour. The GR36 from Lot-et-Garonne makes contact at Cahors, providing a variety of options for those who want to carry on to places further east like Conques or Cordes. Illustrated maps and guides, covering these and less ambitious marked footpaths, are available from the local tourist offices. Cars and bicycles can be hired in the main centres with suggested itineraries for people who have no desire to blaze their own trails. There is also an organisation which will suggest theme holidays, such as caving, lessons in a traditional craft, or tours of places specialising in local recipes, and will arrange the bookings if required.

There are numerous dolmens in the Causse de Limogne, south-east of Cahors, which is reputed to have one of the largest concentrations in France. *Châteaux*, castles, ruins and museums of all descriptions abound and Lot has so many ancient chapels and churches that, half the time, no-one even thinks of mentioning them. Picturesque small villages follow each other in rapid succession along the river courses but are more widely scattered on the higher ground. This is especially true round centres like Labastide-Murat where living off the land is difficult and demanding and many former inhabitants have opted for a less strenuous life elsewhere. Large towns are few with the exception of Cahors and, to a much lesser extent, Figeac, Martel and Gourdon. However there are

many hotels to be found throughout the region, some well equipped and comfortable, others extremely basic but almost invariably cheap and cheerful. There are many *gîtes* and other furnished accommodation, a few holiday villages and numerous campsites, some with bungalows and mobile homes as well as restaurants, swimming pools and a wide range of sporting activities.

Lot is very easy to get to, no matter how you travel. Cahors and Figeac both have their own airports, used mainly for charter flights. There are trains from Paris that cover the distance in about 5 hours whereas Toulouse is only an hour away. Alternative lines run from Limousin eastwards to Auvergne and Aveyron, stopping occasionally along the route, while there are two major roads — the N20 linking Brive-la-Gaillarde with Toulouse by way of Cahors and the N140 that branches off through Martel to Figeac and across the border into Aveyron. A comprehensive network of relatively minor roads and little byways make off in every direction to visit places of interest.

The *département* is divided up into four sections with Quercy in the north, Le Gourdonnaise occupying the western half of the centre, Le Figeacois to the east and La Vallée du Lot and Le Quercy Blanc along the southern border. Each has its own main town and is peppered with atmospheric villages and tiny hamlets that tend to be thickest on the ground in Haut Quercy and along the valley of the Lot. As in Périgord the best and easiest way of seeing the region is to establish a base and explore the surrounding area before moving on to the next convenient stopping place. However, as there are no great distances to cover, one can easily pick a central point and then make one-day sorties in any direction.

HAUT QUERCY

The main town in Haut Quercy is **Martel**, an agricultural centre and a delightful place that lives up to its nickname 'the town of seven towers'. Two wide streets, the Boulevard des Cordeliers and the Avenue du Capitany, have taken the place of ancient ramparts but the Tournemire Tower, which once served as a prison, is still very much in evidence along with two elderly gateways that were initially part of the outer defences. There are not many streets in the old quarter but those that do exist are lined with extremely attractive houses, particularly along the Rue Droite which almost, but not quite, links the well-fortified church of St Maur with the Hôtel de la Raymondie. The church appears to be very much on the defensive with its two watch towers, a line of battlements and a keep-like belfry. There is a sixteenth-century stained glass window in the chancel and a beautifully carved doorway above which a sympathetic Christ sits in judgment while angels sound the trumpets proclaiming the Resurrection. The Hôtel de la Raymondie started life as a fortress in the thirteenth century

but within a short time it was converted into a town house of considerable elegance with a tower at each corner and rose windows overlooking the court of honour. For a while it was home to the law courts but now it houses the *hôtel de ville*, the Syndicat d'Initiative and a small museum. This is full of items discovered on the Puy d'Issolud, which may or may not have been where the Gauls made a last determined attempt to stop Julius Caesar's dreams of conquest in 51BC.

The Place des Consuls with its large covered market has a number of old houses, two of which encapsulate the early history of Martel. The Maison Grise on the Rue Tournemire has a coat of arms which includes three hammers, the emblem of the town. These were the favourite weapons in the armoury of Charles Martel who defeated the Saracens at Poitiers in 732. Some doubt surrounds the story that he caught up with a few stragglers north of the Dordogne, wiped them out and then built a church to celebrate his victories, thereby founding a new town. However it was called after him and the story does account for Martel's importance in the twelfth century. The Maison Fabri takes up the history at this point. The main character is Henri Court-Mantel, the eldest son of Henry Plantagenet and Eleanor of Aquitaine who was rich and beautiful but much too free with her favours. Henry, like her previous husband Louis VII, finally lost his temper but instead of divorcing her he locked her up in a tower. Young

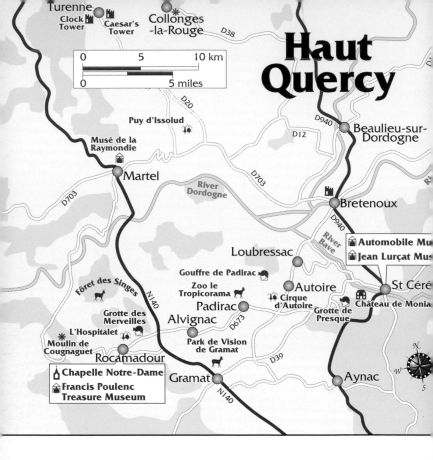

Henri took exception to this and declared war on his father who immediately disinherited him, transferred all his possessions to his brother Richard Coeur de Lion and stopped his considerable allowance. This left young Henri with some monumental problems. In order to get enough money to support himself and pay his soldiers he attacked and plundered a number of abbeys, the last of them being the pilgrim centre of Rocamadour where he stole all the treasures, including the famous sword known as Durandal. Legend has it that as he was leaving the abbey the bell started to toll of its own accord and he took this as a sign from heaven that he had at last gone too far. Overcome with anxiety, fever

Opposite: The doorway of an ancient mansion in the old quarter of Martel

and remorse he made for Martel, installed himself in the Maison Fabri — or an earlier house on the same site — and sent a message to his father asking for forgiveness. The king was engaged at the siege of Limoges at the time but he returned the desired pardon which arrived shortly before Court-Mantel died.

For the next two centuries the town flourished, but it was battered by both sides in the Hundred Years' War, savaged by the Huguenots during the Wars of Religion and lost its official status in 1738 when it was sold to the King of France. Today it makes lavender water and a liqueur known as *eau-de-noi* and is an important market for walnuts, truffles and sheep. Martel has a couple of quite modest hotels and three campsites and is well placed for long distance walkers using the GR46.

The **Puy d'Issolud**, 14km (9 miles) to the east of Martel and close to Vayrac, is a small volcanic cone rising above a plateau with steep cliffs and one or two little streams. Long before the Romans arrived it was a well fortified Gaulish stronghold surrounded by dry stone walls and deep ditches. Some experts think that it was the site of *Uxcellodunum* where the defenders fought valiantly against Caesar's legions and annoyed him so much that he is said to have had every prisoner's right hand cut off to prevent the survivors taking part in any further battles.

There are not many other places of interest north of the Dordogne, apart from all the riverside towns and villages included in Chapter 1.

However, it would be a pity not to spend a little more time visiting **Collonges-la-Rouge**, across the border in Corrèze. It is a tiny, bewitching little medieval hamlet, built of red sandstone, that owes its existence to a priory founded there about 1,200 years ago. By the sixteenth century it was becoming a holiday resort and the local nobility, along with several well-to-do officials from Turenne, chose it as the perfect site for their new country mansions. As a result it has several elegant houses, many of them complete with towers and turrets. The Castel de Vassinhac, which once belonged to the viscounts of Turenne, is strongly fortified below its selection of pepper-pot roofs and so, to a lesser extent, are the Castel de Maussac and the Hôtel des Ramade de Friac. Other buildings of interest include the Maison de la Sirène, so-called because of the mermaid who watches over it with a comb in one hand and a mirror in the other.

The Porte du Prieuré is all that remains of the Benedictine priory that was destroyed during the Revolution but beyond it is the old grain market and a very militant church dating from the end of the eleventh century. It looks like a large fortified manor house with its battlements, a watch-path and even a gun room that proved to be very useful during the Wars of Religion. There is not much to see inside, nor even in the ancient Chapel of the Penitents next door, but the charm of Collonges-la-Rouge lies in the village itself. This is particularly true out of season when it is not so busy with sightseers, although with no chance of seeing it floodlit at night. Cars are not allowed between June and mid-September so it is necessary to park close to the main road and walk down the Rue de la Barrière. The best way back is along the somewhat erratic Rue Noire as it edges its way past a succession of elderly houses, some festooned with creepers. The Relais St Jacques de Compostelle, recalling the days when pilgrims called in on their way to Spain, can provide a room with a private bath but it is usually fully booked during the season and often has queues for lunch.

As Collonges-la-Rouge is only about 20km (12 miles) from Martel, drive back via **Turenne**, which was also part of Quercy in the olden days. It was a place of supreme importance in the Middle Ages but lost its sovereign status when it was sold to Louis XV in 1738. Caesar's Tower (which has nothing to do with the Romans) and the Clock Tower with its thirteenth-century guardroom, are all that remain of the extensive castle which Louis destroyed. The hilltop site is partly surrounded by ancient houses, among them the original Gold Foundry and the large Tournadour Mansion which was once used as a store for keeping salt. There is also a church, rather over embellished in the eighteenth century, and an atmospheric little street called the Rue Droite which clambers up the hillside to the non-existent castle.

South of Martel, just off the N140, is **Rocamadour**, one of the best known and most visited little towns

in Haut Quercy. It is a spectacular collection of churches, ramparts and ancient buildings stapled to the side of a perpendicular cliff which rises 150m (492ft) above the River Alzou. It was, and to a certain extent still is, a place of pilgrimage so deeply enmeshed in myths and legends that it is impossible to separate fact from the fantasy. The story started when a hermit of no fixed abode settled down in a cave, built a small oratory and insisted on being buried underneath it. Centuries passed and his tomb might never have been disturbed if an unidentified resident, who must have been quite an important person, had not chosen the entrance to the Chapel of the Virgin for his last resting place in 1166. The grave diggers got to work and before long uncovered the body of a small man. This was placed beside the altar while it was decided who he was and what to do with him. Within a short time it became apparent that the remains were able to perform miracles so, having decided that they belonged to the hermit, it was essential to put a name to him.

The possibility that he was a holy man from Egypt was considered and then rejected. For a time St Silvanus was thought to be a likely candidate, but in the fifteenth century it was decided that the body belonged to Zaccheus, the little publican who was a friend of Christ and the husband of St Veronica. Meanwhile the news of the body had got round and immediately Rocamadour was inundated with pilgrims, among them Henry Plantagenet, St Bernard and a succession of French kings. Before long the shrine became a serious rival to Santiago de Compostela and extended its influence to southern Spain and Portugal and as far east as Sicily. However fame brought considerable fortune in its wake and with it the inevitable treasure hunters. Rocamadour was attacked and plundered with monotonous regularity, especially during the Hundred Years' War and the Wars of Religion, was laid waste by the Protestants and eventually wiped out in the Revolution. In the nineteenth century many of the buildings were rebuilt and redecorated and pilgrims were encouraged to visit the shrine, then no more than a shadow of its former self. In spite of this Rocamadour should definitely not be missed, regardless of all its tourist overtones and the considerable amount of climbing that is involved.

The heart of Rocamadour is the parvis, or Place St Amadour, a small open space surrounded by no less than seven chapels and churches, the most important being the **Chapelle Notre-Dame**. It stands on the site of the original chapel, destroyed by a rock fall in 1476, and is believed to mark where the hermit was buried. It is the home of the miraculous Black Madonna, a tiny and not particularly attractive figure carved in walnut during the twelfth century with a very elderly-looking Child sitting on her knee. Unlike most statues of the Virgin she is not smothered in silks and laces although both figures have fairly modern crowns. The inside of the chapel is black with soot from thousands of candles and filled with ex-votos including ships and a tiny sailor, emphasising the fact that Our Lady of Rocamadour has been venerated by the seamen of Britanny for the past 900 years. A bell that was said to ring by itself in anticipation of a miracle is suspended from the roof and a sword, reputed to be the Durandal, or a faithful copy of it, is embedded in the rock outside. Behind the chapel is the Basilica St Sauveur with a very unusual crucifix and the crypt of St Amadour where the saint's body was entombed before it was hacked to pieces by the Huguenot captain Bessonies when he found that it would not burn. The Chapelle St Michel, built into the rock face, has some interesting frescoes that are reasonably well preserved, although the paintings in the chancel are definitely showing their age.

Next door to the Chapelle St Michel is the **Francis Poulenc Treasure Museum**, dedicated to the composer who is said to have had a vision while on a trip to Rocamadour in 1963. It contains items of sacred art, documents tracing the history of the town, paintings, stained glass, ex-votos and highly decorated reliquary caskets including one said to have contained the remains of St Amadour. From the ramparts a calvary wends it way up past the caves of the Nativity and the Holy Sepulchre beyond which is the massive Cross of Jerusalem, brought back from the Holy Land by early pilgrims. Quite close by is the Rocher des Aigles, a centre for raising birds

Rocamadour in the evening sunshine

of prey where displays of falconry are held for the benefit of visitors provided the weather is suitable.

No cars are allowed into Rocamadour so everybody must park outside the walls and start the long haul to the top. The only concession made to the twentieth century is a lift near the Porte Salmon, a short walk from the 500-year-old *hôtel de ville* where splendid tapestries depicting the flora and fauna of the area are on view during the summer months. Other places of interest at this level are the old fortified Mill of Roquefrège and the Roland le Preux Museum with waxworks recalling past events and the pilgrims who once worshipped at the shrine. From the nearby Place de la Carreta the Grand

Escalier with its 223 steps leads up to the Place St Amadour. At one time the faithful, often weighed down with chains, covered the whole distance on their knees but nowadays most of them consider it sufficient to bow with every step. No doubt true pilgrims feel that Rocamadour is a holy place, but for the merely curious the atmosphere is considerably diluted by cafés and shops bursting at the seams with souvenirs. The large reconstructed fort at the top of the stairway, now also reached via another lift, was once home to the knights who guarded the shrine and acted as hosts to important pilgrims. However this function has now been taken over by a collection of reasonably well appointed hotels.

Rocamadour is well suited for a variety of different holidays. For hikers it is on the GR46 and the GR6, there are stables in the vicinity with a choice of bridle paths and bicycles can be hired at the station, but fishermen have to look slightly further afield. The modern campsite is fairly well-shaded with a swimming pool, snack bar, small shop and a children's playground, but there are few *gîtes* in the surrounding area. Motorists can set out in almost any direction that appeals. One possibity is the Moulin de Cougnaguet, a fifteenth-century fortified mill a few miles to the west. It is attractively sited at the foot of a sheer cliff, has water rights granted to its predecessor in 1279 and four ancient millstones, one of which is still working.

One of the best views of Rocamadour is from **L'Hospitalet**, an equally ancient hamlet a few kilometres away. It started life in the eleventh century when Hélène de Castelnau founded a small hospital there to care for pilgrims who paused at the town on their way to Santiago de Compostela or, somewhat later, wanted to freshen up before paying their respects to the Black Madonna. Apart from the remains of a fortified gateway and a few traces of the original walls this medieval building has disappeared completely, although there is a small church of no great moment that was rebuilt nearly 600 years ago. Cheek by jowl with the Office de Tourisme on the opposite side of the road is the **Grotte des Merveilles**, discovered in 1920 and reached through a small garden which includes a children's playground. It is a small grotto, hardly larger than the foyer of a modest cinema, but it contains a number of stalactites and stalagmites, an underground pool and a few cave paintings more than 20,000 years old. But the main attraction of L'Hospitalet is the view of Rocamadour further along the canyon which is seen to the best advantage when it is bathed in morning sunlight or after dark, floodlit and twinkling.

A short drive along the D36, in the direction of Gramat, are two quite different attractions that should not be missed. The first is the **Jardin des Papillons** which, at first glance, appears to be just a large plastic-covered greenhouse with a car park. It is, in fact, the home of hundreds of butterflies from all over the world. They are hatched out in the nursery section and then transferred to the main area with its waterfall and ornamental lakes, gravel paths and beds full of exotic plants and flowers. The butterflies come in all colours, shapes and sizes from pitch black, strangely marked with iridescent greens, to pale pastel shades. Giant varieties that only fly at night cling to the walls and roof, looking like paper decorations at carnival time, while the rest fly about in complete freedom, ignoring the visitors. At the end of their short lives several extremely colourful butterflies are mounted for sale. Le Jardin des Papillons is primarily a scientific centre and the money from entrance fees and the sale of souvenirs helps with the research.

Almost next door to the butterfly garden is the **Forêt des Singes**, another much larger scientific centre that is also open to visitors. This covers a wooded area of some 25 acres and is home to about 150 Barbary apes and other macaques, all of whom are natives of southern Asia and north Africa and are in danger of dying out. The tribe lives in total freedom in the park under similar conditions to their native habitat. Although they are wild in every sense of the word the apes are willing to tolerate humans, provided they are neither teased nor frightened when they can turn decidedly nasty.

Another option for those interested in animals is **Gramat** on the main road to Figeac and only a short drive away. It is a pleasant market town with a sprinkling of small *auberges* and a comfortable hotel standing in its own park nearby. Gramat specialises in local fairs where it is possible to buy anything from sheep to nuts and truffles but its main attraction is the police training centre for dogs and their handlers, established there in 1945. Throughout the summer there are conducted tours of the establishment with special displays every Thursday afternoon. An added incentive for many tourists is the Parc de Vision de Gramat which is open throughout the year, although the times vary with the seasons. It covers a large area with a round trip of about 3km (2 miles) calling on all the many residents. These include wild oxen, tarpans and bison whose ancestors were around in prehistoric times, bears, wolves and lynx, deer of various descriptions, farmyard animals and even a New Forest pony or two. Birds have their own quarters not far from the botanical gardens which are being extended to include all the different types of trees and shrubs found on the Causse.

Alvignac is a modest spa where people go to give their livers and digestions a rest or, if necessary, medical treatment. Local hotels offer rooms with private baths at reasonable prices and at least one provides a swimming pool and facilities for the disabled. It makes an ideal base away from the hustle and bustle of Rocamadour and yet is within easy reach of both the town and **Gouffre de Padirac**, another popular showplace in Haut Quercy.

Commercialisation has spread a heavy veneer over this impressive chasm — it has been described as an overrated hole in the ground — but this is far from being the majority verdict. Most visitors find it either beautiful or striking, certainly unusual and even awe-inspiring. Admittedly the tour starts by taking two lifts, which can hardly be described as a romantic introduction, but it saves time and energy which can be put to better use later.

There are several versions of the legend associated with Padirac, all of them arising out of a meeting between St Martin and the Devil. Apparently Satan created the chasm as a pleasure resort for himself where he could relax half way between hell and ground level. The saint, who had been on a trip to the causse with

The ruins of the ancient hospital at L'Hospitalet, near Rocamadour

Opposite: The source of Gouffre de Padirac's underground river

his donkey, stumbled across it by accident when the animal suddenly stopped and refused to go any further. In the confrontation that followed good triumphed over evil, Satan retreated leaving behind a sack full of souls which he had collected and St Martin went on his way accompanied by the repentant sinners. Occasionally the attention of a doubting tourist will be drawn to the hoof prints ostensibly left by the donkey when it was persuaded to continue its journey. Although people in the Middle Ages had a fear of the supernatural they were even more afraid of being killed or wounded in some local battle. As a result they chose the lesser of two evils and used Padirac as a safe hideout during both the Hundred Years' War and the Wars of Religion. Its existence was a well-kept secret until Edouard Martel rediscovered the chasm in 1889. For the next two years he explored the underground river and its galleries as far as the Hall of the Giant Dome, the area which has been open to the public since 1898. In more recent times expeditions have penetrated still further, discovering some 22km (14 miles) of underground caverns including one filled with the bones of animals that are at least 150,000 years old. They also uncovered a number of chipped flints left behind

by prehistoric hunters a mere 50,000 or so years ago. However none of these fresh discoveries are included in the tour, which already lasts approximately 1½ hours.

At the bottom, near the lifts and about 75m (246ft) below the surface is a large mound created when part of the roof fell in, leaving a hole with steep sides through which can be seen a small patch of sky. From here steps lead down to the subterranean river at the far end of the long Gallery of the Spring where there is a little landing stage. Here small, flat-bottomed boats continue the journey over smooth limpid water that never varies in temperature from 10.5°C for a distance of about 700m (2,296ft or ½ mile). On the far side of the Lac de la Pluie with its giant stalactite, known as the Great Pedant, passengers disembark and follow a narrow passage, named the Crocodile Path, to the Hall of the Great Natural Dams. Apart from a succession of pools separated by limestone outcrops and a lofty waterfall there is a large catchment known as Lac Superieur and the Hall of the Great Dome, 91m (298ft) high with a viewing platform built into the rock face about half way up. The return journey, first by boat and then by a succession of lifts, returns visitors to ground level in far less time than it would take to climb the stairway with its 455 steps.

Out in the open air again there are a modest *auberge*, a restaurant, souvenirs and plenty of space to park.

Anyone with the energy to cope with a few more steps can visit the attendant Zoo le Tropicorama, an at-

tractively wooded area where brilliantly coloured parrots are ready to pose for photographs with anyone who lends them an arm for a perch. There are several different kinds of birds, animals such as deer and monkeys, as well as gardens with sections devoted to various kinds of plants. The village of **Padirac**, less than 3km (2 miles) away, boasts a handful of small hotels while a campsite within walking distance of the chasm offers shaded plots, a restaurant, a snack bar, a small food shop and opportunities for swimming and rambling, with caves and dolmens for additional interest.

The old fortified hamlet of **Loubressac**, to the north-east of Padirac, is worth a brief visit, both for itself and for the view. It consists of a series of interwoven alleys running between elderly houses to a fifteenth-century manor perched at the extreme end of the rocky spur. Below is the River Bave and, in the distance, the roofs and towers of St Céré. **Autoire**, a trifle to the south along a pleasing minor road, is equally picturesque in a different way. There are lovely old half-timbered houses, ancient manors with turrets, and fountains in the little squares. The church is in keeping with the rest of the village, without anything particular inside, but the view from the terrace takes in the Limargue Mill and the rocky Cirque d'Autoire. To see this natural amphitheatre properly it is necessary to park just off the road and follow the path past a series of waterfalls, across a bridge and up through the rocks to a vantage point at the top.

✵ Another local attraction is the **Grotte de Presque** where stalagmites, a few of them unusually fragile and almost snow white, have suggested names for the various caves such as the Hall of Wonders, the Drapery Chamber and the Red Marble Hall.

Those who wish to inspect another ancient *château* should visit **Château de Montal** which, for a very unexpected reason, is in an excellent state of repair. It was built on the site of a feudal stronghold in 1523 by Jeanne de Balsac d'Entraygues, the widow of Amaury de Montal who, at one time, was governor of Haut-Auvergne. She wanted it as a present for her eldest son Robert who was away fighting for the French in Italy. Sadly, he was killed before it was completed but the two main wings linked by a square tower are impressive enough on their own, especially as the inner courtyard is acknowledged as a masterpiece. A complicated frieze decorated with shields, figures, birds, initials and stylised flowers separates the ground floor windows from the ones above. These are interspersed with alcoves, each containing the bust of a different member of the family. Amaury is there looking very intellectual, Robert sports a plumed hat, while his brother Dordé is a young page but the most unforgettable is of Jeanne herself — a middle-aged woman, marked but not defeated by tragedy, who had the words *Plus d'Espoir* (Hope no More) carved into the stonework.

Jeanne lived in the castle for the rest of her life but when the last member of the family died it passed from one owner to another and suffered during the Revolution. In 1879 it was bought and its contents sold to collectors and museums throughout Europe and in the USA. However, in 1908 a petro-millionaire named Maurice Fenaille bought what remained of Montal and spent a great deal of money tracking down most of its treasures and buying them back, often at wildly inflated prices, before giving the castle and its contents to the State. A guided tour lasts almost an hour and takes in the magnificent Renaissance staircase, the guardroom with its eye-catching fireplace and a number of salons hung with pictures and tapestries and filled with original furniture.

The Château de Montal is only 3km (2 miles) west of **St Céré**, a picturesque little market town in the Bave Valley which was an important trading centre in the thirteenth century. Good fortune and astute management brought it safely through the Hundred Years' War, the Wars of Religion and the Revolution, leaving its old quarter virtually intact. The original market square, where fishermen used to display their catch on a stone bench outside the Maison de Jean de Séguier 500 years ago, is known as the Place du Mercadial. It is overlooked by several ancient half-timbered houses and has as its centrepiece a delightful drinking ✳ fountain topped by the figure of a young girl. The Rue St Cyr and the Rue du Mazel are both lined with medieval houses but the church of Ste Spérie was so enthusiastically restored 200 years ago that nothing remains of the building which preceded it.

One of St Céré's most famous citizens was the artist Jean Lurçat of tapestry fame. After perfecting his art in Aubusson, and joining the Resistance during World War II, he settled in St Céré in 1945. Having set up a workshop in the ancient Tours de St Laurent, once part of the formidable outer defences, he continued to produce designs for both tapestries and ceramics until his death in 1966. Later his wife presented a representative selection of his works to the museum, which housed it in one of the towers where he had lived for the best part of 20 years. Other examples are on display in the gallery of the casino where visitors tend to linger before crossing the road to try their luck at the gaming tables. In addition the town has a small but excellently maintained Automobile Museum with some interesting old cars and an elderly light aircraft.

St Céré is an increasingly popular tourist centre. Its Music Festival, held each summer, includes sacred music, song recitals, operas and symphony concerts, some of which are held in the impressive setting of the nearby Château de Castelnau-Bretenoux. Between them a handful of small hotels can provide a number of rooms with private baths, a self-contained studio or two, private swimming pools, gardens and garages. They also offer menus which include a delicious local dishes. Holidaymakers who prefer to cater for themselves can rent a furnished apartment or a country *gîte* and do their shopping at the colourful open-air Saturday market. In addition there is a municipal campsite for tents and touring caravans.

Cars and bicycles can be hired locally and cyclists have a choice of three recommended circuits of 46km (29 miles), 58km (36 miles) and 80km (50 miles) respectively, depending on which part of the area is explored. The Causse is also a good place for walking and although some of the paths can be on the rough side the GR652 is not that far away. Among the more isolated and therefore less frequented local attractions within a radius of 16km (10 miles) or so is the Chapelle de Notre-Dame de Verdale on the far side of **Latoville-Lentillac**. After a pleasant ride or drive along the valley of the Bave a narrow road leads up to a minuscule waterside hamlet on the Tolerme. From here a path climbs fairly steeply, with the help of a couple of rather suspect wooden bridges, to a limestone crag crowned with the little pilgrim chapel. There is nothing memorable about the building itself but the view across the Tolerme gorges is worth the effort involved, especially when the chestnut trees blanketing the surrounding hills are in flower, or later when they are drenched in autumn colours.

GOURDONNAIS

Gourdonnais, which borders on Périgord, has somewhat fewer tourist attractions than Haut Quercy but

A drinking fountain in the centre of St Céré

Exhibits in the Automobile Museum, St Céré

still manages to keep its visitors both interested and fully occupied. It is virtually cut in half length-ways by the N20 from Brive-la-Gaillarde to Cahors and largely ignored by passing motorists who have neither the time nor the inclination to inspect the country on either side. As a result there are not a great many sightseers around and it is usually quite easy to find somewhere to spend the night or park a caravan at one of the well-equipped campsites, except perhaps at the height of the season.

Gourdon, the capital which gives its name to the whole district, is a very pleasant market town that has lost a large percentage of its ancient landmarks but takes great care of the ones it has managed to preserve. In the olden days it was little more than a terraced village clustered round a hilltop castle and surrounded by ramparts, most of which have disappeared. They have been replaced by a circlet of boulevards, pierced by the fortified Porte du Majou, once the main entrance but now firmly closed to traffic of all descriptions apart from pedestrians. On one side is the sixteenth-century chapel of Notre-Dame du Majou with its back firmly up against the non-existent walls, beyond which a street of the same name, lined with antiquated houses, leads up to the domineering church of St Pierre. This is a large, rather sombre looking building with two heavy matching towers, a big rose window and some decorative seventeenth-century carved woodwork inside. Above and beyond it is the esplanade where the castle once stood, its place taken by a viewing table and a terrace looking out across the wooded countryside.

The old quarter of Gourdon is a good place to wander about, discovering attractive little backwaters like the Rue Zig-Zag or finding the way barred by a heavy wooden door set in a carved stone surround. The Rue Cardinal-Farinié with its old turreted houses finds its way up to the Place de la Mairie where the covered arcades make an ideal setting for the local market. At the opposite end of the street, on the far side of the encircling boulevards, is the Eglise des Cordeliers which started life as part of a Franciscan monastery. It is a most impressive old church, partly because there is nothing inside to detract from the pure, soaring lines of the nave with its nineteenth-century stained glass windows at the far end and a beautifully carved font close to the entrance. There are a number of small hotels, two of them with swimming pools, quite a few furnished apartments and a municipal campsite with plenty of trees and facilities for boating and fishing, as well as swimming, about 1km (½ mile) from the centre of the town. Bicycles can be hired at the station and a cycle path in addition to two Grandes Randonnées, the GR64 and the GR652, passes by the door. A summer festival of concerts and theatre performances is one of Gourdon's regular attractions along with a harvest festival that is held during the first weekend in August.

Gourdon has its own prehistoric caves, the **Grottes de Cougnac**, a bare 2km (1 mile) away on the road to Sarlat. They consist of two separate entities, the first of which is a group of three grottoes filled to capacity with tightly packed stalactites. The second is a bit larger and contains the Salle des Colonnes, so-called because of the crystalline columns extending from the floor to the roof, and the adjacent Salle des Peintures Préhistoriques. The cave paintings, mostly in brown and black, include elephants, ibex and deer, something that looks more like a pregnant mountain goat, an odd human figure or two and the imprints of hands and fingers similar to those at Pech-Merle further south.

The **Chapelle Notre-Dame des Neiges** is a simple, sturdy little building, dating originally from the fourteenth century, with a carved doorway and a spring which is believed to have miraculous properties. **Le Vigan**, 4km (2 miles) to the east, has an even older church that was once part of an important abbey founded in the eleventh century. The bell tower, added at the end of the Hundred Years' War, managed to survive the Wars of Religion but only came through the Revolution by the skin of its teeth, along with one or two sculptures inside.

Cazals, to the south-west of Gourdon, was an English *bastide* that has retained a few of its old houses grouped round the main square, to which it has added a modern church with some eighteenth-century carvings. The town provides a selection of furnished accommodation and two campsites, one of them at Frayssinet-le-Gelat on the shores of a lake. Visitors who rest their caravans under the trees can swim, play tennis, fish and ride, hire a pedalo or go shopping in the village a few minutes' walk away. It takes a bit longer to reach **Les Arques** where there are two more small churches, both considerably restored. St Laurent, in the heart of the hamlet, was cut down to size in the nineteenth century but kept its Moorish-type arches whereas St André-des-Arques, standing alone in the woods, has some fifteenth-century frescoes that were only discovered in 1954. They show several of the apostles with their badges of office, St James and his staff, St Thomas holding a set square and St Peter with his keys. Also present are St Christopher and, on the pillar opposite, the infant Jesus waiting to be carried across the river.

The countryside hereabouts is gentle and inviting, an undulating pattern of woods and pastures, sprinkled with little hamlets like Lherm and Goujounac, each with its own particular charm. But the picture changes as you travel eastwards into the Causse south of Gramat. It is the largest limestone plateau in Quercy, a fairly unsympathetic mixture of scrubland, dry stone walls, flocks of sheep and smallish clumps of trees. Some people drive through it quickly whereas others find it fascinating. The villages and homesteads become more widely spaced, linked by byways, some of which have a small stream for company. The landscape alters subtly rather than dramatically, especially in the autumn when the leaves begin to change colour and there is a nip in the air as a prelude to the snows of winter. *Châteaux*, castles and ruined fortresses are few and far between but, by way of compensation, the uplands are dotted with strange little stone buildings whose tiled roofs sweep down to ground level on either side of heavy wooden doors. Windows are conspicuous by their absence, which is only to be expected because they are traditional sheep folds, providing the animals with adequate shelter when the weather is particularly foul.

Labastide-Murat occupies one of the highest points on the Causse de Gramat. It is an unprepossessing little town which might never have found its way into any tourist guide if the son of a local innkeeper had not gone on to become one of the great military heroes of France. Incidentally, he also married Napoleon's sister Caroline, became a Marshal of the Empire and King of Naples before the Emperor abdicated and was exiled on the island of Elba for a while. Murat's father had wanted him to be a priest but at 21 he joined the army, distinguished himself at the Battle of the Pyramids and was given command of the cavalry during the Syrian campaign. In 1808 he was posted to Spain to see what he could do about Wellington but was recalled 2 months later and sent to rule Naples on behalf of his brother-in-law. When Napoleon escaped from Elba Murat rejoined him and marched against Austria but was defeated and took refuge in Cannes.

By this time Naples was back in the hands of the Bourbons and when he landed at Pizzo with 200 men in an attempt to recover his kingdom he was captured, court martialed and shot on 13 October 1815. Labastide-Fortunière changed its name to Labastide-Murat in his honour and, more recently, installed a museum in the house where he was born. This old inn stands in an alley close to the church and contains an interesting collection of memorabilia including a large and rather ostentatious family tree.

There is a small hotel in the town for those who want to explore the surrounding area, not that there is a tremendous amount to see. On the outskirts is a *château* which Murat built for his brother André, although this can only be inspected from the outside at the moment, and a privately owned castle at **Vaillac**, 5km (3 miles) away. It is a large and impressive medieval fortress consisting of the main section, a handful of towers, a keep and enough space in the outbuildings for 200 horses and their equipment. On the other hand, **Montfaucon** is a one-time *bastide*, built on a hilltop, with many of its original houses and a fifteenth-century church containing an unexpectedly ornate retable. It has intricately carved niches for the statues, barley-sugar columns, angels trumpeting, little biblical scenes and rather more than its full quota of gold. **Soulomès**, about the same distance to the southeast, has a small church that was once part of a commandery belonging to the Knights Templar. A

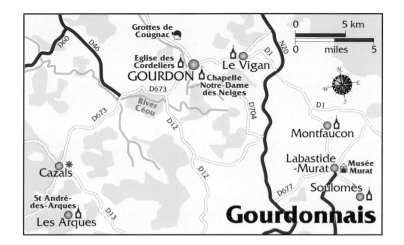

number of fourteenth-century frescoes have been discovered in the chancel depicting various scenes, the Entombment, the Resurrection, a knight accepting the risen Christ as a matter of course and St Thomas looking suitably taken aback. At the risk of overdoing the subject of small churches there is another quite interesting example at Caniac-du-Casse quite close by. It is decidedly short on frescoes but makes up for this with a twelfth-century crypt housing the tomb of St Namphaise, a shrine much frequented by pilgrims in search of a cure for epilepsy.

FIGEACOIS

Figeacois, which shares the central strip of Lot with Gourdonnais, has a great deal more to boast about than its neighbour. There are some extensive uplands with, at a rough guess, more sheep than people, unpretentious little villages, chestnut groves, bridle paths, Grandes Randonnées and an occasional warlike *château*. In addition it has two rivers of considerable repute — the infinitely beautiful Célé and the middle reaches of the Lot marking the border with Aveyron.

The main town is **Figeac** which manages to combine some light industry, and very unprepossessing modern suburbs, with a delightful old quarter on the banks of the Célé. This came into being in the ninth century consisting, in the usual way, of a jumble of tiny houses dancing attendance on a monastery. As the abbey grew in size and importance so did Figeac and the fact that it was a staging post on the pilgrim route to Santiago de Compostela ensured that it was kept both busy and prosperous. In 1302 the church handed over control to Philip the Fair, which did not make much difference to the ordinary citizens but gave the town added status when a Royal Mint was established there. Figeac became a Protestant stronghold in the Wars of Religion and during their 24-year occupation the Huguenots made a predictably nasty mess of its ancient churches. However, once things returned to normal they were restored wherever possible and St Sauveur, in particular, was updated a little over 200 years ago.

The most important of all the ancient buildings is the Mint, a solid, reliable-looking stone construction where money was exchanged in the Middle Ages and where information is dispensed today by the resident Office de Tourisme. It was carefully restored at the beginning of this century, when part of an adjoining house was incorporated, and still has its original archways and one of the few remaining octagonal stone chimneys that, in years gone past, were a feature of the town. The museum inside has a whole variety of exhibits from sculptures and sarcophagi to seals of office and antiquated coins stamped out in nearby workshops. From the Hôtel de la Monnaie, and what better name could there possibly be for a mint, it is only a short walk to the abbey church of St Sauveur. There is very little left from the eleventh century and not a great deal to see inside, whereas the former chapterhouse, now the Chapelle Notre-Dame-de la-Pitié, has a number of decorative wooden panels added about 300 years ago. The Place de la Raison,

where the cloister and the monastery gardens used to be, is separated from the river by the Avenue Maréchal-Foch. It is a busy thoroughfare where, with infinite courtesy, cars will stop short of the traffic lights to allow photographers to record the obelisk dedicated to Jean-Francois Champollion from the opposite side of the road.

Champollion has been described as the father of Egyptology, a brilliant linguist who had a working knowledge of Greek, Latin, Arabic, Chaldean and Syrian before his fifteenth birthday. It is hardly surprising that, within 5 years, he became a lecturer in history at the University of Grenoble. It was round about this time that the English physicist, Thomas Young, was fully occupied in trying to decipher the Rosetta Stone, a tablet of polished black basalt inscribed with Egyptian hieroglyphics, cursive script and Greek. This was discovered by one of Napoleon's officers in 1799 near the banks of the Nile and acquired by Britain after the fall of Alexandria 2 years later. It was Champollion who finally realised that the three inscriptions were identical, confirmed his theories in Egypt and compiled an alphabet from hieroglyphics before his early death in 1832. The Rosetta Stone is safely housed in the British Museum in London but one of the few castings made from it can be seen in the museum dedicated to his work in the house where he was born. It can be found in a square named after him, a stone's throw from the old main square.

Figeac is another of those historic places which are best seen on foot. The Place Carnot, right in the heart of the ancient town, is surrounded by roads lined with photogenic houses, among them the Rue Delzhens which climbs laboriously uphill to the church of Notre-Dame-du-Puy and the Rue Séguire, virtually unchanged since the Middle Ages. In the Rue de Balène two buildings are of special note, namely the Hôtel d'Auglanat with its arched doorway and the fortress-like Château de Balène which contains the Lotois Centre of Contemporary Art and holds exhibitions from time to time.

All around this area are mullioned windows, arches and turrets, stone carvings, half-timbering and *soleihos*, a kind of open-sided terrace under the roof which came in useful as a combined storehouse, veranda and conservatory. The whole quarter is encased in modern boulevards shaded by plane trees beside which is a leisure park with an upmarket campsite with well over a hundred individual pitches, a restaurant and facilities for a wide variety of different types of sport. Neither is there any shortage of furnished accommodation nor of hotels, the latter ranging from a comfortable establishment with all the expected amenities to small hostels without a great deal to offer and therefore charge accordingly. Boats are available on the river, there are riding stables nearby as well as cycle paths, blazed footpaths and relatively good fishing in the surrounding area. Where motorists are concerned the town is ideally situated on the main route from Brive-la-Gaillarde to Rodez, Millau and Montpellier and within easy reach of both Cahors and Aurillac, across the border in Auvergne. On the outskirts are two eight-sided obelisks known as the Needles of Figeac which are thought to have marked the boundaries of the old Benedictine monastery lands but apparently no-one has decided if the Meander Needle, to the south, was intended to serve the same purpose.

The least frequented part of Figeacois lies to the north-east of the town beyond **Cardaillac**, originally the home of one of the most powerful families in Quercy but now little more than a ruin. Two square towers dominate the tiny hamlet as they have done for the past 800 years. The Clock Tower is closed to visitors but anyone with enough energy and enthusiasm can climb the spiral staircase in the Tour de Sagnes for a view of the River Drauzou, the valley and the country thereabouts.

Further north, past **Le Bourg**, where the church is all that remains of an ancient priory, is **Lacapelle-Marival**. Its most obvious attraction is the castle, a well-preserved thirteenth-century fortress built on traditional lines with watch towers at each corner of the large square keep and a *château* added 200 years afterwards. There are also a few elderly houses, a small church of no particular merit, an original gateway and a fifteenth-century covered market but nothing to get excited about in the way of hotels. The church at **Rudelle**, of the same vintage as the castle and built by the same family, might be a good place to work off some surplus energy. It is a solid stone construction that looks far more like a resolute fortress than a place of worship — even a militant one left over from the Middle Ages. The hall at ground level is still used as a parish church with its bells housed in a refuge on the floor above. This is reached up a wooden staircase followed by a ladder, through a trap door, and then up another staircase, this time of stone. The only light filters in through narrow arrow-slit windows that were no doubt much appreciated by its defenders in days gone past but are worse than useless when it comes to admiring the view. For this it is necessary to negotiate another ladder and a further staircase up to the watch path on the roof.

Thémines, north of Rudelle on the N140, has nothing of interest apart from an elderly covered market and a turning off to Aynac, quite close by. The Château d'Aynac has an air of wellbeing and serenity about it, enhanced by white-shuttered windows, small squat towers each with its matching dome, neat lawns and plenty of trees. It is one of two riding schools belonging to the Tourisme Attelé. Not only are guests taught to ride but they learn how to take care of the animals and all the equipment kept on the premises. Fully trained staff hold indoor classes as well as practical lessons and arrange excursions, which can be anything from an hour or more in the saddle to a longer trip which

takes in an historic town, a famous grotto, or an outstanding beauty spot. There are ordinary rooms in addition to dormitories for children, nourishing meals, an infirmary with a qualified doctor and outings in horse-drawn vehicles as well as other entertainments, most of them with an equestrian flavour.

To the west of the N140, and slightly south of Lacapelle-Marival, is **Assier** which owes its fame and fortune to Galiot de Genouillac who wrote numerous books. His career started when he became a page at the court of Charles VIII, advanced considerably in the reign of Louis XII with his promotion to first gentleman of the bedchamber and reached its peak when he became Grand Master of the Artillery under François I. Amongst other things he was Master of the Horse, Seneschal of Armagnac and later of Quercy, Superintendent of Finances and a knight of the Order of St Michel. Nobody could accuse Galiot de Genouillac of being either retiring or modest although there is no doubt about his ability. His extravagant ideas produced some spectacular results such as the Field of the Cloth of Gold which he organised near Calais for the meeting between Francois I and England's Henry VIII in 1520.

The castle he built for himself at Assier was another case in point, a vast and lavishly decorated pile with domed towers, ornamental friezes, carved pillars, statues and state rooms awash with precious metals, silks and tapestries. The historian Brantôme described it as 'the best

The former abbey church of St Sauveur, Figeac, with a game of boules in the adjoining park on the site of the old cloisters and abbey gardens

The old mint at Figeac

furnished house in France' and equal in splendour to the *châteaux* of the Loire. After Galiot's death the castle was abandoned bit by bit by his descendants, who may well have found the upkeep too demanding and expensive, until it was finally sold in 1766 when three wings were demolished. Only the guards' wing was left standing but drawings of the original *château* give a pretty fair idea of what his 'little place in the country' must have looked like when he was in residence.

Although the remaining section is much less overpowering than any of the other three it is still worth seeing with a monumental entrance framed by Doric columns above which is the niche where the medieval arms magnate insisted on a statue of himself on horseback. The frieze on the opposite side that once overlooked the inner courtyard includes scenes from the Labours of Hercules, with whom Galiot obviously felt he had an affinity, along with carved cannons belching fire and a considerable amount of smoke. Inside is a handsome staircase with a carved pillar, divided more or less equally between the owner, Fortune and Hercules, a reclining statue of Anne de Genouillac and a few mementoes of this larger-than-life character.

The church was also quite obviously built by Galiot and decorated according to his instructions. There is a frieze right round the building filled to capacity with cannons of all descriptions, some of them firing from disproportionately small castles while others hurl great cannon balls back at them. There are knights and infantrymen, not to mention gunners, as well as highlights from battles he fought and almost certainly won, due in no small measure to his ability as a tactician. It is not perhaps the ideal decoration for a church but it undoubtedly provides a useful record of the arms, armour and equipment in use during the sixteenth century. Above the doorway two cherubim are shown offering the Virgin his military insignia, the sword he wore as Master of the Horse and the chain of the Order of St Michel. Nor is the atmosphere any less militant inside where Galiot, dressed in all his court finery, lies on a marble sarcophagus below a carved relief showing him in characteristic pose with emblems, a cannon and two gunners apparently waiting for orders to fire. Inscribed in both the church and the castle is his motto 'J'aime Fort Une' which could be variously translated as 'I Love Fortune' or 'I Love One Greatly', whichever seems the most appropriate. After all this there is nothing much else to see in the area unless you count the various dolmens and the world weary Menhir de Belinac at Livernon.

Travelling southwards from the rough, hilly country round Assier it is extremely pleasant to find oneself in the valley of the River Célé close to its meeting place with the Lot at Conduché, in Quercy Blanc. Strictly speaking all the nearby places of interest should be included in Chapter 1, but it would be rather arbitary to cut off the river simply because it takes no notice of an invisible boundary, drawn largely for the benefit of tourists. That having been settled there is nothing much to say about Conduché itself except that, from here, the road edges its way upstream between the overhanging cliffs and the water towards the Valley of Paradise with a first stop at **Cabrerets**. This is a delightful little waterside village surrounded by greenery, situated just beyond the point where the River Sagne joins the Célé. It is a popular stopping place for people exploring the surrounding area on foot and also for motorists visiting some of the local attractions including prehistoric caves, ancient buildings and an open-air museum. Incidentally it is as well to book in advance because the scattering of *logis* and *auberges* dotted about amongst the trees and along the river banks are often filled to capacity, particularly during the summer months.

The **Grotte du Pech-Merle** is the showpiece of the area — an extensive collection of underground caves and passages that were discovered in 1922. The Abbé Breuil described the complex as 'a sistine chapel of the Causse plateau, one of the most beautiful monuments of the pictorial art of the paleolithic age'. It all began when the Abbé Lemozi, a priest who lived in Cabrerets and was a confirmed speleologist and prehistorian, fired the imagination of two teenage boys who decided to do a little exploring on their own. Their adventure started in a small fault which was known to have been used

as a place of refuge by local people during the Revolution. They discovered a narrow, slimy trench leading out of it and followed this for some time, in spite of a host of obstacles, until they reached a cave full of prehistoric drawings. The *abbé* set about investigating the caves scientifically and before long it was decided to open them to the public. However it was not until 1949 that another section was uncovered and found to contain the original entrance used by the early inhabitants some 20,000 years ago.

A tour of the Grotte du Pech-Merle lasts for nearly 2 hours and involves walking for something like 2km (1 mile), through winding subterranean passages, the first of which is known as the Chapel of Mammoths. It is a vast gallery with a frieze approximately 7m (23 ft) long and 3m (10ft) high full of pictures of bison and mammoths. This is followed by the Salle des Disques, an equally extensive cavern adorned with strange disc like nodules and traces of prehistoric footprints petrified for all time in the clay floor. Beyond are some colourful and impressive rock formations and a narrow passage that takes its name from the head of a bear etched into the wall. At a slightly lower level is the picture gallery with its famous spotted horses, facing in opposite directions and surrounded by peculiar symbols and ghostly disembodied hands that resemble modern rubber gloves! They were apparently made when the artist got fed up with painting wild life, lent against the wall with one hand and amused himself by stencilling round it with the other. It is interesting to note that he must either have been ambidextrous or had a friend around to help. Another unusual feature is that female figures are included in the drawings on the roof. Finally, in the Salle de Combel, the roots of an oak tree forced their way down into what seems to have been a type of bears' burial ground.

Back at ground level the **Amédée Lemozi Museum** is a combined research and information centre with workrooms, a lecture hall, a library and a photographic laboratory. The museum itself is open to the public and contains a fascinating array of articles from more than 150 different prehistoric sites. There are collections of bones, flints and tools going back many thousands of years, Iron Age utensils, weapons and even examples of very early jewellery, all of which goes to show that human nature has not changed a great deal after all. Another room is lined with colour photographs taken in various caves throughout the region while a film dealing with local prehistoric art is shown in a small cinema accommodating about fifty visitors.

There are two castles within easy reach of Cabrerets — the ruined Château de Diable, also known as the Castle of the English because they occupied this eagle's nest fortress during the Hundred Years' War, and the fourteenth century Château de Gontaut-Biron. It is an extremely well preserved building with an inner courtyard, a business-like tower and a terrace complete with balustrades overhanging the road some 25m (82ft) above the stream of passing cars. Unfortunately it is not open to the public, but there are no such problems with the Fontaine de la Pescalerie slightly further to the north. This eye-catching waterfall, created by an underground river, appears without warning from the face of the rock close to an ivy-covered mill, half hidden in the trees, and not far from the eighteenth-century manor house which has been turned into a comfortable hotel.

Beyond a tunnel through the cliff the valley widens out and there is a turning off to **Cuzals**, a large and extremely interesting open-air museum. It claims to be the only one of its kind to combine both agriculture and machinery in order to provide a picture of life in the rural areas of southern France. The estate covers 120 acres, was opened in 1985 and concerns itself mainly with the eighteenth and nineteenth centuries. The centrepiece is the ruined Château de Cuzals which only pretends to be antiquated but certainly looks the part. It houses a pottery museum, an exhibition of toys, a restaurant, a bar, souvenirs and an old printing shop. Nearby is a children's playground where even the merry-go-round dates from about 1930. There are two self contained little farms, the first using time honoured methods that were the norm before the Revolution while the second deals with changes that took place up to 1910. Each has its appropriate outbuildings, tools,

Figeacois

crops and even animals.

The Water Museum is a resounding success with young visitors because it contains, among many other things, a selection of working models which they can operate themselves. Also open for inspection are reconstituted workshops dealing with local crafts and craftsmen such as blacksmiths, shoemakers, weavers, carpenters, stonemasons and others of that ilk. A splendid old steam engine and a whole range of farm implements have a corner of their own beyond which are examples of various types of rural architecture including pigeon lofts. These were constructed not so much for the benefit of the pigeons as to collect their droppings that were invaluable when it came to fertilising the land and improving the quality of the crops. Other subjects examined in depth include beekeeping and making honey, growing grapes, tobacco and strawberries along with other types of fruit and vegetables, not forgetting truffles, and repairing such things as early bicycles, wagons and carts. Because there is so much to look at visitors are advised to take their time. Having paid the initial entrance fee they are welcome back at any time during the next 7 days completely free of charge and, as a good many people take advantage of the offer, it is a good thing that there is sufficient parking space for vehicles just outside the main gate.

✳ **Sauliac-sur-Célé** is the next thoroughly worthwhile little village with its old houses glued to the cliff face rather in the manner of swallows' nests. Above them are several fortified caves where the local people took refuge in times of trouble. They could only be reached with the help of ropes and ladders so anyone who was hale and hearty clambered up first and then used baskets to haul the rest aloft, followed by all the necessary provisions .

✳ **Marcilhac-sur-Célé**, larger and less dramatically sited, is also extremely photogenic, set against a background of encircling cliffs. The village was a place of some importance in the eleventh century when its Benedictine abbey controlled much of the surrounding country including the sanctuary at Rocamadour. It showed no particular interest in what was, after all, just another isolated little chapel until the mysterious body discovered on the site gained a reputation for working miracles. Then everyone took notice. Monks from Tulle, who had moved in before the discovery, were thrown out by their counterparts from Marcilhac but returned with the blessing of their abbot to repossess the increasingly famous, and therefore increasingly wealthy shrine. For the next 100 years neither side gave the other any peace; the Bishop of Cahors was asked for a ruling, so were the Archbishop of Bourges and, at last, the Pope but none of them came up with a satisfactory solution. Eventually money talked and Marcilhac agreed to sell its claims to Rocamadour.

The abbey was prosperous enough to become a target for both sides during the Hundred Years' War, recovered slightly after the Reformation but gave up the unequal struggle at the time of the Revolution. All that is left now is ancient history, some lovely old houses and a collection of ruins. The remains of the abbey fall into two categories, one Romanesque and the other Gothic. The former, which is little more than a shell, has a square tower and some stone carvings thought to be anything up to 1,000 years old while the latter still includes a chapel with fifteenth-century frescoes, contemporary woodwork and a path leading to the former chapterhouse. Additional to all this are the remains of the old ramparts, a tower where the abbot's house used to stand and a campsite on the river banks but nothing at all memorable in the way of hotels.

Lovers of stalactites and stalagmites are inclined to deviate slightly in order to visit the **Grotte de Bellevue**, less than 2km (1 mile) from Marcilhac-sur-Célé. However the distance seems to be a bit longer because the road climbs in a series of steep, tightly constructed bends towards Pailhès with an occasional view of the river below. The cave, discovered just 25 years ago, is very colourful and all set about with columns, the largest of which is 4m (13ft) high, measures nearly the same amount round the outside and rejoices in the name of the Colonne d'Hercule. It is about here that the valley starts to widen out sufficiently to provide fertile ground for crops with fields of sunflowers jockeying for position with vineyards, maize and tobacco plants, although the surrounding hills are every bit as rocky as before and seemingly unable to support anything much more ambitious than scrub. The main route, still following the course of the river, calls at **St Sulpice-sur-Célé**, a modest hamlet watched over by a twelfth-century castle rebuilt some 500 years ago. Anyone looking for a bed for the night is liable to be disappointed but owners of tents and caravans will find a pleasant little campsite beside the water with trees, a food shop, a tennis court, canoes and plenty of opportunities for fishing and rambling.

Pressing on upstream, past some apparently affluent farm houses and the village of **Brengues**, where several *gîtes* are available and the campsite has rooms and a restaurant as well as all the other amenities, the next place of interest is **Espagnac-Ste-Eulalie**. It is an enchanting little village that owes its existence to the former priory of Notre-Dame-du-Val-Paradis, founded in the twelfth

century. Almost before it was properly established the priory was converted into a convent and, apart from a lot of trouble in the Hundred Years' War, remained in the hands of the Augustine Order until the Revolution. The main building, which had to be moved from its original position in 1282 because of a tendency to flooding, is now an operational centre for the whole community with furnished accommodation available to visitors. The old church was almost completely rebuilt in the fifteenth century and provided with an unusual brick and timber room perched on the top of the bell tower with a steep octagonal roof covered in limestone tiles. Inside are the tombs of three medieval knights. Beyond Boussac, a hamlet of no particular note, the cliffs give way to wooded hills for the last part of the journey to Figeac.

The last area to be explored lies to the south of Figeac — a slither of country between the river Célé and the Lot where it marks the border with Aveyron. The River Lot rises some 1,219m (4,000ft) up in the Cévennes and trickles down across the moors, through orchards and farmlands, until it reaches Mende. From here onwards the country becomes rougher, wilder and more desolate with little sign of life on Les Grandes Causses apart from flocks of sheep put out to graze in areas that were infested with wolves 200 years ago. The stream has become a modest river by the time it reaches the beautiful high-sided gorges between Estaing and Entraygues, two captivating little waterside villages full of atmosphere and elderly houses. The Lot joins forces with the Truyère before pushing on past a small industrial pocket known as the Black Country towards the Causse de Gramat, skirting chestnut forests to the north, with a winding road following each twist and turn as it makes its way resolutely towards Quercy and on into the sunset.

For all practical purposes the first place of interest in Quercy is **Capdenac-le-Haut**, originally the site of a Gallo-Roman town. In fact some experts maintain that it, and not the Puy d'Issolud near Martel, was the stronghold known as *Uxcellodunum* where Caesar finally conquered Gaul. The narrow streets and medieval wooden houses have hardly changed at all but the ramparts are in tatters, the castle has all but disappeared and a busy railway junction in the valley does not improve the view. Occupying a strategic site on the top of a hill, partly surrounded by the River Lot, the village has been a glutton for punishment since its very early days. It was seized by Pepin the Short at the beginning of the eighth century, fell to Simon de Montfort in 1209 and again in 1214 and was captured by the English during the Hundred Years' War, although the French recovered it somewhat later. Galiot de Genouillac, who built the massive *château* at Assier, took a liking to it, after which it became a Protestant stronghold in the Wars of Religion and the home of the Duke of Sully after Henry IV was assassinated in 1610. Apart from the

formidable stone keep, housing the information office and a small museum, there is an antiquated fountain with a stairway up the face of the cliff to a grotto containing two pools. Nobody seems to know much about them but they are treated with respect. Even Jean-François Champollion, the famous Egyptologist who was not given to flights of fancy, said that they had the atmosphere of a cave occupied by an oracle.

Further to the west, **St Pierre-Toirac** has a fortified church which has remained on site in one form or another for the past 500 years. It is known chiefly for its pillars whose capitals are reputed to be among the most viewable of their kind in Quercy although the workmanship is somewhat crude and occasionally even brutal. Also worth inspecting are the early Gaulish sarcophagi which were discovered there quite recently. **Larroque-Toirac**, more or less next door, vies for attention with its twelfth-century castle, poised for action against the hillside. It is a relatively nondescript kind of fortress, mainly because the large keep was reduced to about a quarter of its original height in 1793. Inside there is a spiral staircase giving access to the main hall and a number of rooms with furniture covering the period from the reign of Louis XIII to the late eighteenth century.

The river continues on its convoluted way, accompanied by a pleasant road, past the ruins of Montbrun castle which, in its younger days, belonged to a brother of Pope John XXII and still has its little terraced village in attendance. Further on is **Cajarc**, an elderly riverside resort which has not yet fully recovered from the fact that President Pompidou had a house there. Its other claims to fame include a ruined *château* and a well maintained campsite, offering its guests all the usual facilities as well as organised tours, events based on local folklore and traditional cooking. From here anyone short of time, or anxious to explore fresh territory, will undoubtedly opt for the main route along the northern bank of the river, past the remains of a twelfth-century chapel and on to Larnagol in the fourth and final section of the *département*. However there is also a bridge across the Lot at Cajarc and a road which doubles back to the Saut de la Mounine, facing Montbrun castle on the opposite bank of the river.

This so-called 'Leap of the Little Monkey' is situated at the top of a high cliff with a view across the valley and a pathetic legend to account for its name. At some time in the distant past the Lord of Montbrun's daughter fell in love with a young man who appears, on the face of it, to have been eminently suitable. However there must have been a problem of some sort because her father was so angry that he ordered her to be thrown over the cliff. A local hermit disapproved of this so much that he dressed up a blind monkey and hurled it over instead. The sight upset her father so much that, on finding the girl alive, he welcomed her back with open arms. The story does not recall her feelings or whether she was reunited with the young man, nor does it show any sympathy for the unfortunate monkey.

LA VALLÉE DU LOT & LE QUERCY BLANC

The fourth and final section of the *département* is La Vallée du Lot and Le Quercy Blanc which accounts for the whole area to the south of the river as well as a strip along the northern bank. It stretches from Lot-et-Garonne in the west and along the border with Tarn-et-Garonne to Aveyron, also part of Midi-Pyrénées. The limestone plateaux that give this part of Quercy its name have been eaten into by a series of small rivers between which are narrow uplands with forests of oak trees, some crops and plenty of grazing for sheep. The valleys are often quite wide and well cultivated, producing cereals and tobacco interspersed with orchards and vineyards, the latter especially to the west of Cahors. The towns and villages are concentrated mainly along the Lot Valley but tend to thin out considerably elsewhere, more particularly in the south.

Cahors is both the main centre from a commercial point of view and a city that should definitely not be missed. Its roots are firmly planted in antiquity when both the Gauls and the Romans worshipped at a spring, now known as the Fontaine des Chartreux, which still produces drinking water for the town. The Romans called it *Divona* and the settlement that grew up round it *Divona*

Cadurcorum, which was abbreviated first to *Cadurca* and then to Cahors. They took such a liking to the place that they built a forum, a theatre, several temples, baths and all the usual villas and protected them with ramparts. The town expanded by leaps and bounds until, in the thirteenth century, it was regarded as one of the most important centres in France. The export of linen, which had sustained it in earlier times, gave way to trade and banking under the expert tuition of businessmen from Lombardy. Before long it had gained an international reputation equivalent to that of its counterparts in Germany and the Low Countries. Kings came crown in hand to borrow money, for which they paid an exorbitant rate of interest, popes took advantage of the facilities and so did a host of other borrowers until, as with Shylock, the name Cahorsin came to be another term for usury.

At the onset of the Hundred Years' War Cahors was the only place of note in Quercy to hold out against the English, and even when it was ceded to them under the Treaty of Brétigny in 1360 the inhabitants refused to take the transfer seriously. At last the French king ordered the keys to be handed over and was promptly informed that it was he who had deserted Cahors and not the other way round. Sad to say, when the English retreated 90 years later they left little of any real value behind. However, the townspeople picked up the pieces and started to knit them all together, only

to become sharply divided amongst themselves during the Wars of Religion. Today Cahors has expanded beyond the encircling loop of the River Lot in a sprawl of typically unattractive suburbs but the old quarter has retained much of its medieval charm and atmosphere.

Mont St Cyr, 7km (4 miles) to the south, is one of the best places to go in order to get an overall impression of the city, especially with the help of the viewing table. It is easy to pick out the Boulevard Gambetta, slicing its way down from the neck of the horseshoe to the Pont Louis Philippe at the far end, thereby cutting off the ancient section from the somewhat newer town. Contrary to expectations the famous **Pont Valentré** is on the opposite side from the old quarter, at the far end of Rue du Président Wilson. It is a magnificent stone structure, heavily fortified when it was built in the early fourteenth century, somewhat changed when restored in 1879 but still, according to many people, the most beautiful bridge in the world. It is hard to believe that it was one of three a little over 100 years ago. Its contemporary was replaced by the Pont Neuf in 1907 after the older and even more spectacular Vieux Pont had been pulled down in 1868 to make way for the Pont Louis Philippe.

According to legend the Devil played an important part in building the Pont Valentré. Apparently the bridge, with its seven arches and three massive towers, took more than 50 years to complete. The architect, who must have been getting a trifle elderly towards the end, became more and more depressed. At last he decided to ask the Devil to help and, as was customary under such circumstances, pledged his soul in exchange. He had second thoughts as the day of reckoning drew near so he ordered the Devil to bring him water in a sieve and, when he failed, declared the contract null and void. The Devil took great exception to this and responded by tearing off the top stone of the watch tower in the centre and then toppled each one that was fixed in its place. When the bridge was restored in the nineteenth century the empty space at the top of the tower was filled with new stone, identified by a tiny carving of an irate Devil trying to push it off. Unfortunately this is almost impossible to locate unless it is pointed out. At the same time the fortified gates at either end of the bridge were removed. This was an unfortunate decision although it does make the approaches much easier for the streams of traffic that cross it.

There are one or two other places of interest on the same side of Boulevard Gambetta, foremost among them being the **Musée Henri-Martin**. It faces the Palais de Justice across the Rue Emile Zola and was once the bishops' palace with a decorative little chapel. Sections are devoted to the paintings of Henri-Martin, the life of Pope John XXII, who was born in the town and founded the University of Cahors in 1332, and the statesman Léon Gambetta. He was the son of a local grocer who studied law in Paris, became a staunch Republican, an uncompromising member of the government and an extremely able Minister for War. He was elected President of the Chamber of Deputies in 1879, retired after serving briefly as Prime Minister and died a year later when he was shot accidentally at his villa near Sèvres in December 1882. The museum also contains an interesting collection of ceramics in the original library and a few archaeological exhibits.

Within walking distance of the museum are the exceedingly sparse remains of the Roman baths, just a trace of the ancient theatre, pieces of ramparts from the Middle Ages and the Lycée Tower that was once part of the Jesuit college.

On the opposite side of Boulevard Gambetta the old world attractions are more concentrated, with pride of place going to the **Cathédrale St-Etienne**. In architectural terms it is an undecided sort of building, started in the eleventh century on the site of a much older church and then repeatedly enlarged and rearranged. The main door, which was moved to the north side 200 years later, is finely carved and shows Christ attended by two jubilant angels, a number of apostles and scenes from the life of St Stephen. Many of the paintings inside date from the same period whereas the cloisters were added in the early sixteenth century. They suffered a great deal of damage at one time and another and have only been partially restored. There is still a certain amount of stone carving and a spiral staircase but the niches lost their statues many years ago. The Chapel of St Gausbert with its fresco of the Last Judgement and its painted ceiling acts as a kind of mini museum with statues and vestments, not to mention the portraits of more than ninety different bishops of Cahors.

Further up-river are a number of old towers. 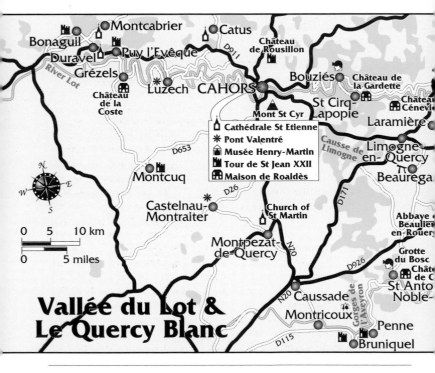 The Tour du Collège Pélegry was a fifteenth-century addition to the original college which opened with thirteen impoverished students in 1368 and was an important centre for the next 400 years. Beyond it, the Tour du Château du Roi was part of a much larger build-ing where the governor had his official residence. Left on its own this royal castle tower was demoted and is now a prison. Almost last, but by no means least, the **Tour de Jean XXII** is left over from a palace that once belonged to the pope's brother, Pierre Duèze. It keeps a watchful eye on the much restored church of St Barthélemy next door, which the pope would be hard put to recognise as the place where he was baptised in the mid-thirteenth century. It even changed its name from St Etienne de Soubiroux, meaning St Stephen of the Upper Quarter, which was where the Catholics and Protestants

Map key:
- Cathédrale St Etienne
- Pont Valentré
- Musée Henry-Martin
- Tour de St Jean XXII
- Maison de Roaldès

Vallée du Lot & Le Quercy Blanc

The Pont Valentré at Cahors

clashed repeatedly and ferociously during the Wars of Religion. It is hardly surprising that the church needed a good deal of attention afterwards or that it recalls its association with John XXII by means of a bust, a marble plaque and scenes from his life on the cover of its modern font.

At the far end of the Rue de la Barre the **Barbacane** and the **Tour St Jean**, also known as the Tower of the Hanged Men, mark the eastern end of the ramparts that once sealed off the whole area. They make a pleasing combination but serve no useful purpose these days because the Barre Gateway that was once attached to the guardhouse has completely disappeared. Further along the line of the ancient ramparts the Porte St Michel provides a fortified entrance to the cemetery and beyond it is St Mary's Tower, built to house the powder magazine.

There are not nearly so many towers on the opposite side of the cathedral but rather more little narrow streets and antiquated mansions. The **Maison de Roaldès**, where Henry IV may possibly have stayed in 1580, is a fine example of medieval architecture and one of the few that are normally open to the public. It is said to be beautifully decorated inside with some interesting furniture but at the moment it is closed although it was fully restored in 1912. The Rue St Urcisse, lined with half-timbered houses, passes a twelfth-century church of the same name and is a good place to start exploring all the little streets which separate it from the Boulevard Gambetta. This busy thoroughfare owes little or nothing to the past but makes up for it with a plethora of shops, restaurants and cafés as well as a comfortable hotel about a block away which has all the usual amenities apart from a diningroom. There are many *logis* and *auberges* both in and around the town, some furnished apartments and a modest campsite for about fifty tents and caravans.

Bicycles are available at the railway station with a choice of cycle paths covering recommended circuits of anything from 50km to 104km (31 miles to 64 miles). Kayaks and canoes can be hired, with or without tuition, for trips either up or down the river and expert advice on fishing is obtainable from the local authorities with details of where and when to go and the types of fish in season. For example, trout may be caught from early March to late September whereas salmon are nearly always a forbidden species. Riding stables will supply horses for short outings or longer excursions with overnight stopping places along bridle paths linking the city with such places as Puy-l'Evêque, Gourdon, Rocamadour and Figeac. For long distance walkers several Grandes Randonnées converge on the capital from Martel and Rocamadour in the north, Bonaguil on the border with Lot-et-Garonne, Villefranche-de-Rouerigue in Aveyron and Figeac on the GR65 from Conques.

The main road from Paris to the south skirts round Cahors, bisecting the River Lot and cutting the area into more or less equal parts. **Catus**, just over the border with Gourdonnais, is a popular if unsophisticated stopping place for local holidaymakers. The village is distinctly short of hotels but it has an excellent campsite, open from Easter to mid-October. Among its other offerings are bungalows, mobile homes and caravans set in a leisure park with a food shop, a restaurant, a bar and takeaway food. The only other attractions are the old chapterhouse, which was once attached to a priory, and a direct link with Mercuès on the banks of the Lot down-river from Cahors. Here the *château*, which once belonged to the bishops of Cahors, has been turned into a splendid luxury hotel. It is a impressive medieval castle with towers, turrets and battlements that started life as a fortress in 1212, fought its way through the Hundred Years' War and the Wars of Religion and was fully restored about 100 years ago. It stands, surrounded by terraces and gardens, on a prime site overlooking the river, has apartments as well as individual rooms and provides both tennis and swimming but it is not a good choice for anyone who needs to economise.

From Mercuès the D145 heads west through orchards and vineyards to rejoin the Lot and meander beside it to **Luzech**. This village, set in the neck of another teardrop of land almost totally surrounded by the river, has its foundations anchored firmly in prehistory. The Impernal Hill was occupied by primitive tribes before the Gauls took it over and built their own stronghold, only to be ousted in turn by the Romans. Richard Coeur de Lion installed himself in the citadel towards the end of the twelfth century but it was back in the hands of the French nobility during the Hundred Years' War, when the English made several fruitless attempts to recover it. Nor were the Protestants any more successful during the Wars of Religion when Luzech remained faithful to the bishops of Cahors. The old quarter still has its fair share of ancient houses and secretive alleyways dominated by the frowning thirteenth-century keep while the pendant shaped area beyond is a patchwork of cultivated fields edged with trees that line the river.

A bridge across the Lot westwards from Luzech leads to the D8 which continues to follow the valley. It passes a number of hamlets like Albas, Anglars and **Bélaye**, attractively sited on a hilltop with a pleasant view from the square, and pauses at the **Château de la Coste** at Grézels. This was originally a feudal stronghold, built by the bishops of Cahors to defend their territory. Predictably it suffered in all the local wars from the Albigensian Crusade onwards and was finally left to its own devices after the Revolution. However, the building was conscientiously restored in 1960 and now contains a museum of wine and folklore of particular interest to gourmets who want to learn more about the history of food and wine in Quercy.

The next port of call is **Puy**

l'**Evêque**, on the opposite bank of the river and reached by means of a suspension bridge which also provides a comprehensive view of the little town. Once again the keep is all that is left of the thirteenth-century bishop's palace but the well fortified church, built a century or so later, is rather more impressive. There are some delightful old houses, some wood and stone carving and a graveyard full of ancient tombs. Although the village is steeped in history there is little evidence of the English occupation of 1346. It has a handful of rather basic hotels and a riverside campsite with swimming, fishing and boating, as well as tennis and mini-golf quite close by.

At **Martignac**, roughly 4km (2 miles) to the north on the D28, the nave of the church is decorated with scenes ranging from St Peter at the gates of heaven to illustrations inspired by the Seven Deadly Sins. These fifteenth-century frescoes are quite amusing and include some original ideas, but the paintings owe more to religious intent than outstanding artistic ability.

By way of contrast **Duravel** has a crypt to be proud of, partly because it claims to have some of the oldest pre-Roman stonework of its kind in France. An additional attraction is a sarcophagus containing the remains of three saints — Hilarion, Poémon and Agathon — brought back from the Holy Land at the time of the crusades. Sceptics, remembering the Shroud of Turin and St Veronica's various handkerchiefs, are inclined to think that these so-called Holy

Cathédrale St-Etienne, Cahors

Opposite: A fifteenth-century doorway at Puy l'Evêque with a coat-of-arms

Bones may have no genuine religious significance. It was the time when merchants in the Middle East were making a fortune out of their apparently inexhaustible supply of Christian souvenirs. However the faithful have no such doubts about them and turn out in force every five years, on 21 October, when the relics are shown with due ceremony to the waiting congregation.

Château de Bonaguil, just across the border in Lot-et-Garonne, is an unforgettable example of military architecture towards the end of the Middle Ages. It was built essentially as a place of refuge, capable of housing several hundred people although it only needed a fraction of their number to defend it successfully. The story began when an extremely unpleasant feudal baron, one Bérenger de Roquefeuil, goaded his vassals to such an extent that they threw caution to the winds and rose in revolt against him. Bérenger immediately retired with his family to what was then a fortified thirteenth-century castle and, over the next 40 years, they converted it into an impregnable stronghold overlooking a ravine. Nothing was forgotten in the interests of security. It had an underground entrance and a double line of defensive walls, a series of tall round towers, one of which is reputed to be among the strongest ever built in France, and gun emplacements slanted so that an enemy would certainly be caught in the cross-fire. Beyond the barbican, where the garrison was quartered, a moat and a drawbridge protected the inner courtyards on either side of the oddly shaped keep. The family lived on one side, close to the well and the armoury, leaving the opposite side clear for all the outbuildings. In addition vaulted tunnels were built to enable the defenders to move about easily and safely to any area where they might be needed. As it turned out the whole operation was a complete waste of time because nobody ever attacked the castle and it took the Revolution to bring it to its knees. Nowadays a conducted tour lasts for well over an hour and includes an energetic climb to the top of the keep and a visit to the small museum filled with odds and ends that either fell or were tossed into the nearest moat.

Not far from Bonaguil, and north of the Lot on the return trip to Cahors, is **Montcabrier**, a French *bastide* founded in 1297 and largely unchanged over the years. Its streets are laid out on the usual grid pattern, giving added protection to the typical old houses that still gaze at each other across the main square. The church, which was updated in the fourteenth century, was once a place of pilgrimage and contains a statue of the saintly King Louis, the patron saint of the village, surrounded by a collection of votive offerings. Somewhat further on **Les Junies** has both a fifteenth-century castle, which is not open to the public, and a large unfriendly looking church. It was part of a Dominican priory about 600 years ago but contains little of interest apart from its seventeenth-century retable.

The whole region to the west of Cahors is saturated with vineyards and cultivated fields, frequently encircled by wooded hills. Some of the *châteaux* have been producing wine for centuries while others are comparative newcomers to the scene. The Château de Cayrou belonged to the Counts of Montpezat before it changed hands some 20 years ago whereas the Couture family, who own the Château Eugenie, have been in residence since 1470. They take great pride in the fact that they supplied table wines to the courts of England, France and Russia and have now extended their horizons to include the United States. A number of these *châteaux* are only too delighted to welcome passers-by and encourage them to taste the wines while others prefer to leave this side of the business to the Wine Growers' Co-operative at **Parnac**.

The area to the south of the Lot and west of the Paris-Toulouse highway is not overburdened with tourist attractions. It is largely agricultural country threaded through with little rivers and a network of minor roads that wander from one limestone plateau to another. However it provides a pleasant outing for those anxious to avoid the more popular routes at the height of the season.

Montcuq is a typical small village dating back to the twelfth century when it was both important and fortified. However it was also in the firing line during the Albigensian Crusade, the Hundred Years' War and the Wars of Religion as a result of which it lost all its landmarks apart from the 800-year-old castle keep. This stands resolutely alone on a rocky mound overlooking both the river and the village where there is a *logis* offering both meals and accommodation. Collectors of small historic churches have several to choose from in the vicinity. **Bovila** weighs in with a carefully restored and attractively uncluttered example from the distant past while **Saux** relies for attention on its baroque retable and seventeenth-century statues.

Castelnau-Montratier, to the south-east, is somewhat larger and younger than Montcuq, having been built as a *bastide* in the thirteenth century to replace Castelnau-de-Vaux, destroyed by Simon de Montfort in 1214. It has an attractive square, a few old houses and covered arcades, a modern church and two *logis*, both of which make provision for any of their guests who may be handicapped. Nearby are three elderly stone windmills, one still in working order, of the type which were a feature of the Quercy countryside not so very long ago. The village also boasts a small, partly shaded campsite, provides holiday-makers with facilities for tennis and swimming and lays on special entertainments for them during the season.

Eastwards from Cahors the outlook is very similar. North of the river, and within easy reach of the capital, is the ruined **Château de Roussillon**, a once-impressive medieval fortress that has managed to retain at least part of its ancient walls and towers. However, Laroque-des-

Arcs, on the banks of the Lot, is even older. It was the site of a Roman viaduct which supplied the citizens of *Divona Cadurcorum* with water from the River Vers about 20km (12 miles) away. For some apparently unknown reason it was pulled down in 1370, leaving little apart from the name to prove that it ever existed at all.

Further upstream, past the twelfth-century pilgrim chapel of Notre-Dame de Vêles, where the river boatmen once paid their respects to Our Lady of the Sails, the road dodges in and out of a series of small tunnels cut through the overhanging rocks. At **Bouziès**, where the cliffs are punctured by prehistoric caves and shelters, there is a little fortified grotto known as the Défilé des Anglais. It consists of a miniature fortress wall, set well back in a crevice above the road and floodlit during the summer months. It is said to have been built by the English during the Hundred Years' War to protect a rabbit warren of interleading passages and tunnels from which they could keep an eye on the river traffic. The village can offer both meals and accommodation at the *logis* as well as trips along the river, swimming, canoeing, fishing, cycling and mini-golf with a special fête at the end of July.

From Bouziès a relatively minor road crosses over to the south bank of the river to **St Cirq-Lapopie**, a captivating hamlet described as the 'first village of France'. Its tumble of old honeycoloured houses cling like limpets to the face of the cliff in the shadow of a ruined castle whose origins are all but lost in antiquity. Legend has it that the village was named after St Cyr, the youth who was martyred in Asia Minor at the end of the second century AD. According to some sources his remains were discovered and brought back by St Amadour, although why he should have left them in such a lonely spot remains a mystery. On the other hand there is no doubt that the Duke of Aquitaine made good use of the fortress in AD8 during his fracas with Pepin the Short or that Richard Coeur de Lion tried and failed to capture it shortly before his death in 1199. The stronghold proved a thorn in the side of the English during the Hundred Years' War but ironically it was the French king, Louis XI, who eventually decided to pull it down. The demolition workers could not have done a particularly good job because the Huguenots fought savagely for possession of the ruins during the Wars of Religion. At last Henry of Navarre, having captured Cahors in 1580, became exasperated and ordered his troops to obliterate it once and for all. They did not miss much and today there is nothing left apart from a useless piece of wall, overgrown with grass and creepers, and a very rewarding view.

The most outstanding building in St Cirq-Lapopie is undoubtedly the fifteenth-century church, but only because it is a great deal larger and more obtrusive than anything else. The Château de la Gardette with its matching turrets has much more in common with all the antiquated lit-

St Cirq-Lapopie in the late evening sunshine

tle houses lining the steep alleyways that clamber up and down the hillside. It is home to both the information office and a small museum containing a rather strange selection of old furniture, not very memorable statues, some African exhibits and a job lot of frescoes and lacquered articles from China. The wood turners who once lived and worked in St Cirq-Lapopie have given way to modern craftsmen who have restored their old houses and filled the newly-created shops with pottery, leather and anything else calculated to catch the eye of passing tourists.

There are one or two rather rustic hotels, as well as *gîtes* and a campsite on the river bank with a good view of the village, a shop, a snack bar and caravans for hire. Swimming, canoeing, riding and fishing are all available with a tennis court a fairly brisk walk away.

The impressive **Château de Cénevières** stands, surrounded by trees, on a rocky outcrop 70m (630ft) above the Lot. It is another thirteenth-century castle built on a site chosen by the Dukes of Aquitaine as an ideal place for a stronghold 600 years before. The *château* was altered considerably in the fifteenth and sixteenth centuries and much restored thereafter, even to the extent that it has now lost its moat. However there is still a trap door in the keep below which are the cellars, the prison and some thoroughly unhealthy looking dungeons. On the floor above the salt room and the kitchen the owners lived in considerable style. The rooms are exceedingly well decorated and attractively furnished, especially the great drawingroom with its painted ceiling, eyecatching tapestries and even spoils of war appropriated by Antoine de Gourdon when he joined forces with Henry of Navarre at the siege of Cahors and was personally responsible for stripping the cathedral. The terrace has a commanding view of the valley which includes the hilltop village of Calvignac. It is less imposing but nevertheless has the remains of yet another fortress and is positioned just inside the demarcation line between Quercy Blanc and Figeacois.

The **Causse de Limogne** south of the Château de Cénevières is short of towns and villages but is liberally sprinkled with dolmens and megaliths as well as truffle oaks and lavender. **Limogne-en-Quercy** is one of the busier agricultural centres with a single *logis*, a large campsite and several dolmens of assorted shapes and sizes in the area round about. The best way to discover them is on foot, either by blazing a fresh trail or following the GR65 south-eastwards to the point where it joins the GR36 and the GR46 before they part company at **Beauregard**. This is a small *bastide*

with an unremarkable church and a covered market where the old grain measures are carved into the stone. The **Borie du Bois** dolmen, considered to be one of the finest in Quercy, is about 3km (2 miles) distant, along a path marked by a sign post that leads off the D55. In the interests of variety **Jamblusse**, a touch further south, contributes an antiquated wash house and an old well half hidden in the grass and brambles.

Laramière, along the D55 in the opposite direction, has the remains of an ancient priory which, from the outside, looks more like an ordinary warehouse. It was founded in the twelfth century, partly destroyed during the Wars of Religion and then moderately restored. A small section is open to visitors including the vaulted chapterhouse and the hall where pilgrims once called in for rest and refreshments on their way to Santiago de Compostela, on the far side of the Pyrénées. Strictly speaking Beauregard and Laramière mark the southern border of Lot but in earlier days Quercy extended into Aveyron, Tarn-et-Garonne and Tarn, and included the Gorges de l'Aveyron below St Antonin-Noble-Val. As a series of attractive little roads and the GR46 all head in that direction it would be a pity not to turn back the clock to take advantage of them.

St Antonin-Noble-Val started life as a Gallo-Roman settlement before the saint in question built an oratory there, to be succeeded by an abbey in AD8. A mineral spring which had acted like a magnet on the Romans also attracted wealthy holidaymakers in the Middle Ages. Their houses still cluster round the former *hôtel de ville*, built in 1125 and described as one of the oldest examples of civil architecture in France. Sadly it was over-restored in the nineteenth century by Viollet-le-Duc who apparently liked the two pillars apportioned to King Solomon and Adam and Eve. The building has now been turned into a museum with a prehistoric section and a lively interest in local folklore.

A scenic road follows the course of the river, crossing and recrossing the gorges in order to find the best views and visit the ancient village of **Penne**. This is an attractive little place consisting of narrow streets, a few half-timbered houses and the ruins of a splendid castle. In spite of the fact that it took the side of the so-called Heretics of Albi against Simon de Montfort in the early thirteenth century, and changed hands repeatedly during the Hundred Years' War, the fortress managed to survive until the 1800s when the greater part of it fell down: A path near the church makes its way up to the world-weary towers, balanced on the top of a limestone peak with very little to support them but still commanding a worthwhile view.

Bruniquel, at the southern end of the gorges, is another hamlet with a bloodthirsty history and an unsavoury legend. It is said to have been the site of a fortress built in the sixth century by Brunhilda, a Visigoth princess and the wife of a local warlord. She was an exceptionally cruel and vindictive woman who died an equally nasty death — tied to the tail of a wild horse. The present castle, parts of which date from the twelfth century, is supposed to incorporate some of the original foundations but Queen Brunhilda could not possibly have created the tower that is named after her. The Knights Hall is at least 700 years old but other parts of the *château* were added as recently as the eighteenth century. **Montricoux**, on the other side of the river and about 6km (4 miles) away, has retained both its old walls and a square keep but has lost all the rest of the castle that once dominated the little houses built on terraces up the side of the valley. It scores over its neighbour with a small, rather basic hotel and a direct link with St Antonin through the Forêt de la Garrigue and along the west side of the gorges.

For those with time to spare there are one or two other places of interest in the surrounding area. The **Grotte du Bosc** was once part of an underground river but now draws attention to its stalactites and a small prehistoric museum. A short drive away to the north-east is the ancient **Abbaye de Beaulieu-en-Rouergue**, founded on the orders of St Bernard in 1144 and transformed into a farm after the Revolution. It was expertly restored in 1960 and is now a centre of contemporary art where concerts and exhibitions are held during the season. The **Château de Cas**, on the D19 to Caylus, is another twelfth-century relic that was constantly altered and restored until today it is open for guided tours which include a number of furnished rooms but nothing of unusual interest.

Alternatively, if time is short a more direct route back to Cahors from Montricoux would be through Caussade, where there is a perfectly acceptable *auberge* with rooms en suite, followed by a short deviation to **Montpezat-de-Quercy** which has an excellent restaurant with rooms attached. The latter is a photogenic little town on the edge of the Causse, brimming over with attractive old houses and some covered arcades. Its most famous landmark is the Collegiate Church of St Martin, built in 1337. It is neither particularly large nor in any way over decorated but it does possess a number of treasures that are worth stopping to see. Foremost among these are the brightly coloured sixteenth-century tapestries, 25m (82ft) long and 2m (7ft) high, that were specially woven to fit the sanctuary. They tell the story of St Martin in a series of episodes including, as one would expect, the famous occasion on which he shared his cloak with a beggar. All the reliquaries, gilded caskets, alabaster panels and two statues of the Virgin are housed in little chapels on either side of the nave. The marble tomb of Cardinal Pierre Des Prés stands on one side of the entrance to the chancel, balanced by the expertly carved figure of his nephew Jean who, at one time, was Bishop of Coïmbre in Portugal and later of Castres, across the border in Tarn. From Montpezat-de-Quercy it is a simple matter to rejoin the N20 for an undemanding run up to Cahors about 30km (19 miles) away.

ADDITIONAL INFORMATION

PLACES TO VISIT

Assier
Château
☎ 65 40 57 31
Open: 10am-12noon and 2.30-6.30pm. Closed Tuesdays. By appointment out of season.

Beaulieu-en-Rouergue
Abbey
☎ 63 67 06 84
Guided tours daily morning and afternoon April to September. Closed Tuesdays.

Bouzies
River trips daily 3pm, 4pm and 5pm early July to early September.
☎ 65 22 19 29

Bruniquel
Castle
Open: for guided tours 11am July and August. Sundays and holidays 11am Easter to late June. Other tours arranged at set hours in the afternoons from Easter to mid-September. Closed Tuesdays.

Cabrerets
Grotte du Pech-Merle
☎ 65 31 26 61 or 65 31 27 05
Caves open: 9.30am-12noon,1.30-5.30pm.Llimited to 700 visitors a day.

Amédée Lemozi Museum
☎ 65 31 23 33
Open: 9.30am-12noon and 1.30-5.30pm Palm Sunday to All Saints Day. Closes at 4.45pm in October.

Cahors
Château de Roussillon
☎ 65 36 87 05
Visits on request throughout the year.

Musée Henri-Martin
Rue Emile Zola
Open: partly mornings and afternoons
July and August during reorganisa-
tion. Thereafter times to be advised.
Closed Mondays. Enquire at the
Office de Tourisme.

Maison de Roaldès
☎ 65 35 04 35
Normally open: 10am-12noon, 2-6pm
Easter to end of April, July-Septem-
ber. Enquire at Office de Tourisme.

Pont Valentré
☎ 65 35 09 56
Towers open: 9am-12noon and 2-7pm

St Barthélemy Church
☎ 65 35 06 80
If closed enquire at the presbytery.

Cathédrale St-Etienne
☎ 65 35 12 30
Treasures can be seen on request
July to September.

Capdenac-le-Haut
Fountain & Museum
In castle keep
☎ 65 34 17 23
Both open: 9.30am-12noon and 3-
6pm July and August. Otherwise by
appointment.

Catus
Chapterhouse
Open: daily.

Caylus
Château de Cas
☎ 63 67 07 40
Open: for guided tours morning and
afternoon Easter to late October.
Closed Mondays.

Cuzals
Quercy Open-Air Museum
☎ 65 22 58 63
Open: 10am-8pm June to September.
Closed Saturday. Also open Easter
Sunday and school holidays.

Espagnac-Ste-Eulalie
Near Brengues
Church
☎ 65 40 00 03
If closed enquire at the town hall.

Figeac
Champollion Museum
Place Champollion
Open: 10am-12noon and 2.30-
6.30pm May to September. Closed
Monday. Also open during the Easter
and Christmas school holidays but
closed Christmas Day.

Mint and Musée du Vieux Figeac
Place Vival
☎ 65 34 06 25
Open: 10am-12noon and 2.30-
6.30pm July and August. Last two
weeks of June and first two weeks of
September 10am-12noon and 2.30-
5.30pm. Closed Sunday and holidays. Otherwise 3-5pm, closed
Sunday and holidays.

Gourdon
Grottes de Cougnac
North of Gourdon
☎ 65 41 18 02
Open: 9am-6pm July-August. 9-11am
and 2-5pm Palm Sunday to June and
September to All Saints Day.

Eglise des Cordeliers
☎ 65 41 06 40
Apply to the Office de Tourisme.

Chapelle Notre-Dame des Neiges
Apply to the Office de Tourisme.

St Pierre Church
Apply to the presbytery.

Gramat
Parc de Vision de Gramat
☎ 65 38 81 22
Open: 9am-8pm April to October.
2pm until nightfall November to
March.

Centre de Formation des Maîtres de Chien de la Gendarmerie
☎ 65 38 71 59
Open: 3.30pm on Thursdays mid-June to mid-September except if it is a public holiday.

Grézels
Château de la Coste
☎ 65 21 34 18
Open: for guided tours 5pm Sundays June to September. Otherwise by appointment only.

Laramière
Priory
Open: daily 10am-12noon and 2-5pm except Tuesday mornings.

Luzech
Museum
Maison des Consuls
☎ 65 20 17 27
Open: 9.30am-12noon and 2.30-7pm June to early September.

Labastide-Murat
Musée Murat
☎ 65 31 11 86
Open: 10am-12noon and 3-7pm July and August. Closed Tuesday.

Larroque-Toirac
Château de Larroque
Guided tours 11am, 12noon, 2pm, 3pm, 4pm, 5pm and 6pm second week in July to first week in September.

Martel
Musée de la Raymondie
Place des Consuls
☎ 65 37 30 03
Open: 10am-12noon and 2-6.30pm July and August.

Padirac
Gouffre de Padirac
☎ 65 33 64 56
Open: 8.30am-12noon and 2-6.30pm July. 8am-7pm August, 9am-12noon and 2-6pm April to June, September to mid-October.

Puy l'Evêque
Château de Bonaguil
☎ 53 71 39 75 or 65 36 57 24
Open: for guided tours 10am, 11am, 2.30pm, 3.30pm, 4.30pm and 5.30pm June, July and August. 10.30am, 2.30pm, 3.30pm and 4.30pm April, May and September.

Church
Open: Sundays in July and August but it is worth enquiring at other times.

Rocamadour
Churches
Guided tours from June to late September. Closed Sundays.

Forêt des Singes
Near L'Hospitalet
☎ 65 33 62 72 and 65 33 63 28
Open: 9am-7pm July and August, 10am-12noon and 2-6pm Palm Sunday to June and September to mid-November.

Francis Poulenc Treasure Museum
☎ 65 33 63 29
Open: 9am-12noon and 2-6pm Palm Sunday to All Saints Day.

Grotte des Merveilles
L'Hospitalet
☎ 65 33 67 92
Open: 9am-12noon and 1.30-7pm July and August. 10am-12noon, 2-6pm Palm Sunday to All Saints Day.

Hôtel de Ville
☎ 65 33 62 59
Open: 8am-12noon and 3-8pm July and August. 8am-12noon and 3-7pm Easter to mid-November. Closed Wednesday.

Jardin des Papillons
Near L'Hospitalet
Open: 9am-7pm July and August. 10am-12noon and 2-6pm April to June and September and October.

Moulin de Cougnaguet
☎ 65 38 73 56
Open: 9am-12noon and 2-7pm July and August. Palm Sunday to June and during September.

Ramparts
☎ 65 33 63 29
Open: 9am-7pm July and August. 9am-12noon and 1.30-6pm Easter to June and September to All Saints Day.

Rocher des Aigles
☎ 65 33 65 45
Open: 10am-12noon and 2-7pm Palm Sunday to mid-November.

Roland le Preux Museum
☎ 65 33 66 83
Open: 8am-8pm Easter to September.

Rudelle
Church
Open: all day in summer but only on winter afternoons.

St Antonin-Noble-Val
Grotte du Bosc
☎ 63 56 03 12
Guided tours morning and afternoon July and August. Sunday and holiday afternoons only June and September.

Museum
☎ 63 30 63 47
Open: afternoons only July and August. Closed on Tuesdays. 3-4pm April to June and September and October, Saturday, Sunday and holidays. Otherwise 3-4pm Saturdays. Closed 1 May.

St Céré
Château de Montal
☎ 65 38 13 72
Open: 9.30-12noon and 2.30-6pm July. 3-7pm August. 9.30am-12noon and 2.30-6pm Palm Sunday to June and September to All Saints Day.

Grotte de Presque
Near Château de Montal on the road to Gramat
☎ 65 38 07 44
Open: 9am-12noon and 2-7pm July and August. 9am-12noon and 2-6pm April to June, September and October.

Jean Lurçat Museum
In the St Laurent Towers
☎ 65 38 28 21 or 65 30 05 01
Open: 9.30am-12noon and 2.30-6.30pm mid-July to end of September. Also Palm Sunday and the Sunday after Easter.

St Cirq-Lapopie
Château de Cénevières
☎ 65 31 27 33
Open: 10am-12noon and 2-6pm. Easter to All Saints Day.

Museum
Château de la Gardette
☎ 65 31 23 22
Open: 10am-12noon and 2-6pm April to October. Closed Tuesdays except in July and August.St Pierre-Toirac

St Pierre-Toirac
Church
Open: Easter to the end of October.

Turenne
Caesar's Tower & Clock Tower
Open: mornings and afternoons early April to late September. Otherwise Sunday and holiday afternoons only.

FACTS FOR VISITORS

Accommodation & Eating Out

* = inexpensive   ** = moderate
*** = expensive   **** = luxury

Alvignac
Palladium Hôtel**
Route de St Céré
☎ 65 33 60 23 Fax 65 33 67 83
Swimming pool.

Annesse-et-Beaulieu
2km from Périgueux
Château de Lalande Hôtel***
☎ 53 54 52 30 Fax 53 07 46 67

Antonne
Near Périgueux
Hostellerie de l'Ecluse***
☎ 53 06 00 04 Fax 53 06 06 39

Beaulieu-sur-Dordogne
Central Hotel Fournié*
☎ 55 91 01 34 Fax 55 91 23 57

Belvès
Le Belvédère de Belvès** (logi)
Avenue Paul-Crampel
☎ 53 29 90 50 Fax 53 29 90 74

Hôtel-Restaurant Le Home*
Place de la Croix-des-Frères
☎ 53 29 01 65 Fax 53 59 46 99

Bergerac
Hôtel de Cyrano** (logi)
2 Boulevard Montaigne
☎ 53 57 02 76 Fax 53 57 78 15
Good restaurant.

Hôtel de Bordeaux*** (logi)
Place Gambetta
☎ 53 57 12 83 Fax 53 57 72 14

Hôtel du Commerce***
Place Gambetta
☎ 53 27 30 50 Fax 53 58 23 82

Beynac-et-Cazenac
Hôtel Bonnet**
☎ 53 29 50 01 Fax 53 29 83 74

Hostellerie Maleville**
☎ 53 29 50 06 Fax 53 28 28 52
Overlooking the river.

Bourboule, La
Hôtel Pavillon**
Ave d'Angleterre (near Fenêstre Park)
☎ 73 65 50 18 Fax 73 81 00 93

Hôtel International**
Ave d'Angleterre (near Fenêstre Park)
☎ 73 81 05 52

Auberge Tournebride
2km (1mile) to the north on the D88
☎ 73 81 01 91
A restaurant with a few rooms.

Bourdeilles
Châteaux de la Côte***
☎ 53 03 70 11 Fax 53 03 42 84
Atmospheric hôtel-restaurant.

Hôtel Griffons**
☎ 53 03 75 61 Fax 53 04 64 45

Bouzies
Les Falaises*
☎ 65 31 26 83 Fax 65 30 23 87

Brantôme
Hôtel Moulin de l'Abbaye****
☎ 53 05 80 22 Fax 53 05 75 27
Excellent restaurant.

Hôtel Moulin du Roc****
6km (4 miles) northeast off the D78
☎ 53 54 80 36 Fax 53 54 21 31
Tennis and swimming.

Chabrol Hôtel-Restaurant***
57 Rue Gambetta
☎ 53 05 70 15 Fax 53 05 71 85

Hostellerie du Périgord Vert** (logi)
Avenue de Thiviers
☎ 53 05 70 58
Restaurant and a few rooms on the
ground floor.

Bugue, Le
Hôtel Royal Vézère***
Place Hôtel de Ville
☎ 53 07 20 01 Fax 53 03 51 80

Domaine de la Barde***
☎ 53 07 16 54 Fax 53 54 76 19
In attractive gardens, no restaurant.

Hôtel Le Cygne** (logi)
☎ 53 07 17 77 Fax 53 03 93 74
Regional cooking.

Cabrerets
La Pescalerie
On outskirts of town.
☎ 65 31 22 55

Auberge de la Sagne* (logi)
☎ 65 31 26 62
On road to Pech Merle. Swimming pool.

Hôtel des Grottes*
☎ 65 31 27 02
Swimming pool

Cahors
Château de Mercués****
9km on road to Brive at Mercués
☎ 65 20 00 01
Fax 65 20 05 72
Tennis and swimming.

Hôtel France***
252 Avenue Jean-Jaurès
☎ 65 35 16 76
Fax 65 22 01 08
No restaurant, but try *Le Balandre*, a
couple of blocks up the road on the
same side, beyond the station.

Hôtel Terminus**
Avenue Ch de Freycinet 5
☎ 65 35 24 50
Fax 65 22 06 40
Next to Le Balandre Restaurant.

Carennac
Auberge Vieux Quercy*
☎ 65 10 96 59 Fax 65 38 42 38
Swimming pool.

Hostellerie Fénelon*
☎ 65 10 96 46 Fax 65 10 94 86
Swimming pool.

Caussade
Hôtel Dupont*
Rue des Recollets
☎ 63 65 05 00 Fax 63 65 12 62

Collonges-la-Rouge
Relais St Jacques de Compostelle*
☎ 55 25 41 02 Fax 55 84 08 51

Chancelade
Châteaux des Reynats****
☎ 53 03 53 59 Fax 53 03 44 84

Domme
Hôtel Esplanade**
☎ 53 28 31 41 Fax 53 28 49 92
Excellent restaurant.

Eyzies-de-Tayac, Les
Hôtel du Centenaire***
☎ 53 06 97 18 Fax 53 06 92 41
Excellent food, swimming pool.

Hôtel Cro-Magnon***
☎ 53 06 97 06 Fax 53 06 95 45
Excellent food, collection of archaeological finds, swimming pool.

Hôtel-Restaurant des Roches** (logis)
☎ 53 06 96 59 Fax 53 06 95 54

Moulin de la Beune**
☎ 53 06 94 33 Fax 53 06 98 06

Figeac
Hôtel des Carmes***
Avenue des Carmes
☎ 65 34 20 78 Fax 65 34 22 39
Tennis and swimming.

Gourdon
Hôtel Domaine du Berthiol**
1km along the D704
☎ 65 41 33 33 Fax 65 41 14 52
Swimming, tennis, disabled facilities.

Bissonnier et Bonne Auberge*
Boulevard des Martyrs
☎ 65 41 02 48 Fax 65 41 44 67
Caters for non-smokers.

Terminus
Avenue de la Gare
☎ 65 41 03 29 Fax 65 41 29 49
Restaurant with a few rooms.

Gramat
Hôtel Lion d'Or***
Place de la République
☎ 65 38 73 18 Fax 65 38 84 50

Château de Roumégouse***
5km (3 miles) along the road to Brive
☎ 65 33 63 81 Fax 65 33 71 18
Swimming pool.

Relais des Gourmands**
Avenue de la Gare
☎ 65 38 83 92 Fax 65 38 70 99
Provision for non-smokers.

Hôtel Centre*
Place de la République
☎ 65 38 73 37 Fax 65 38 73 66

Hospitalet, L' (near Rocamadour)
Hôtel Belvédère*
☎ 65 33 63 25 Fax 65 33 69 25

Panoramic*
☎ 65 33 63 06 Fax 65 33 69 26
Swimming pool.

Lacave
Château de la Treyne***
3km along the D43
☎ 65 32 66 66 Fax 65 37 06 57
Tennis and swimming.

Le Pont de l'Ouysee
☎ 65 37 87 04
Restaurant with rooms, excellent
food, swimming pool.

Lalinde
Hôtel-Restaurant du Châteaux*** (logi)
☎ 53 61 01 82
Swimming pool.

Hôtel-Restaurant La Forge** (logi)
Place Victor Hugo
☎ 53 24 92 24 Fax 53 68 68 51

Hôtel-Restaurant La Périgord** (logi)
Place du 14-Juillet
☎ 53 61 19 86 Fax 53 61 27 49
These three *logis* serve local dishes
and wines at reasonable prices.

Martel
Hôtel Falaises*
☎ 65 37 33 59

Mont-Dore, Le
Hôtel Panorama**
Avenue de la Libération
☎ 73 65 11 12 Fax 73 65 20 80
In easy reach of Office de Tourisme.

Hôtel Oise**
Avenue de la Libération
☎ 73 65 04 68

Hôtel Castelet**
Avenue Michel Bertrand
☎ 73 65 05 29 Fax 73 65 27 95
Covered swimming pool.

Montignac
Château de Puy Robert***
1km along D65, near Grottes de Lascaux
☎ 53 51 92 13 Fax 53 51 80 11

Relais du Soleil d'Or****
Rue du 4-Septembre
☎ 53 51 80 22 Fax 53 50 27 54
Swimming pool, provision for disabled.

Hôtel la Roseraie***
Place d'Armes
☎ 53 50 53 92 Fax 53 51 02 23
Swimming pool, no private parking.

Auberge Le Lascaux*
109 Avenue Jean-Jaurès
☎ 53 51 82 81

Hôtel de la Grotte*
Rue du 4-Septembre
☎ 53 51 80 18 Fax 53 51 05 96

Nontron
Grande Hôtel Pélisson** (logi)
Place Alfred Agard
☎ 53 56 11 22 Fax 53 56 59 94
Swimming pool.

Padirac
Padirac*
Gouffre de Padirac
☎ 65 33 64 23 Fax 65 33 72 03

Périgueux
Hôtel Talleyrand-Périgord***
Place Francheville 21
☎ 53 54 37 70 Fax 53 54 37 99

Hôtel Bristol***
Rue Antoine-Gadaud 37
☎ 53 08 75 90 Fax 53 07 00 49
No restaurant.

Hôtel-Restaurant du Périgord** (logi)
74 rue Victor Hugo
☎ 53 53 33 63

Hôtel-Restaurant l'Univers** (logi)
18 Cours Montaigne
3 rue Eguillerie
☎ 53 53 34 79

Puy l'Evêque
Bellevue*
Place de la Tuffière
☎ 65 21 30 70 Fax 65 21 37 76
Swimming pool.

Rocamadour
Hôtel Beau Site et Notre Dame***
☎ 65 33 63 08 Fax 65 33 65 23

Hôtel du Château***
1km (½ mile) along Route du Château
☎ 65 33 62 22 Fax 65 33 69 00
Facilites for disabled, tennis court
and swimming pool.

Lion d'Or*
☎ 65 33 62 01 Fax 65 33 72 54
Restaurant and parking.

Ste-Marie*
☎ 65 33 63 07 Fax 65 33 69 08
Restaurant and parking.

Roque-Gageac, La
Hôtel-Restaurant La Belle Étoile** (logi)
☎ 53 29 51 44 Fax 53 29 45 63

Hôtel-Restaurant Gardette**
☎ 53 29 51 58

Hôtel-Restaurant Le Périgord** (logi)
☎ 53 28 36 55 Fax 53 28 38 73
Swimming pool and tennis court.

Sarlat-la-Canéda
Hôtel de Selves***
Avenue de Selves 93
☎ 53 31 50 00 Fax 53 31 23 52
Covered swimming pool, facilities for the disabled, but no restaurant.

Relais de Moussidière***
3km (2 miles) from the town on the D46 towards Domme.
☎ 53 28 28 74 Fax 53 28 25 11
Restaurant, swimming pool. Tennis, golf and riding nearby.

Hôtel de Compostelle**
Avenue de Selves 64 & 66
☎ 53 59 08 53 Fax 53 30 31 65
Provision for non-smokers.

Restaurant Marcel
Avenue de Selves 8
A few inexpensive rooms for guests.
☎ 53 59 21 98

Siorac-en-Périgord
Hôtel L' Escale** (logi)
☎ 53 31 60 23 Fax 53 28 54 42
Menu includes wine.

Sorges
Auberge de la Truffe** (logi)
☎ 53 05 02 05 Fax 53 05 39 27
Swimming pool, facilities for disabled.

Souillac
Vieille Auberge**
Place Minoterie
☎ 65 32 79 43 Fax 65 32 65 19
Restaurant, swimming pool and garage, but no lift.

Belle Vue*
68 Avenue Jean Jaurès
☎ 65 32 78 23 Fax 65 37 03 89
Tennis court, swimming pool and lift, but no restaurant.

Puy d'Alon**
☎ 65 37 89 79 Fax 65 32 69 10
Small with few facilities, but special provision for non-smokers.

St Céré
Trois Soleils de Montal***
2km along the D673 towards Gramat
☎ 65 38 20 61 Fax 65 38 30 66
Swimming, tennis, disabled facilities.

France**
Avenue de Maynard
☎ 65 38 02 16 Fax 65 38 02 98

Le Coq Arlequin**
Boulevard Dr Roux
☎ 65 38 02 13 Fax 65 38 37 27

Auberge du Touring*
Place de la République
☎ 65 38 30 08 Fax 65 38 18 67
No restaurant.

St Cirq-Lapopie
La Pelissaria*
☎ 65 31 25 14 Fax 65 30 25 52

Auberge du Sombral
Restaurant with rooms.
☎ 65 31 26 08 Fax 65 30 26 37

St Cyprien
Hôtel L'Abbaye***
Rue de L'Abbaye des Augustins
☎ 53 29 20 48 Fax 53 29 15 85

Hôtel-Restaurant de la Terrasse** (logi)
☎ 53 29 21 69 Fax 53 29 60 88
Less expensive. Meals on terrace; no swimming pool.

Ste Foy-la-Grande
Grand Hôtel**
Rue de la République
☎ 57 46 00 08 Fax 57 46 50 70
Meals on the terrace, garage.

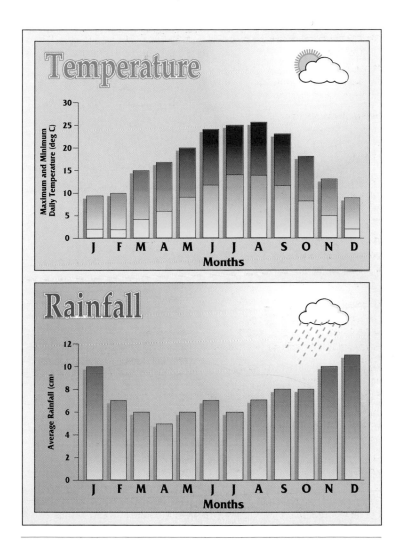

St-Julien-de-Crempse
Manoir du Grand Vignoble***
☎ 53 24 23 18 Fax 53 24 20 89
Swimming pool and tennis court.

St-Yrieix-la-Perch
Moulin de la Gorce***
12km (8 miles) northwest on the D17
☎ 55 00 70 66 Fax 55 00 76 57
Fine restaurant.

Hostellerie Tour Blanche
Boulevard Hôtel de Ville
☎ 55 75 18 17 Fax 55 08 23 11
Restaurant with rooms.

Thonac
Hôtel-Restaurant Archambeau** (logi)
☎ 53 50 73 78 Fax 53 50 78 88

Touzac
8km from Puy l'Evêque on D8
Moulin de la Source Bleue**
☎ 65 36 52 01 Fax 65 24 65 69
Facilities for disabled.

Trémolat
Vieux Logis***
☎ 53 22 80 06 Fax 53 22 84 89
In pleasant gardens, excellent restaurant, garage, facilities for disabled.

Hostellerie Le Panoramic**
Le Cingle
☎ 53 22 80 42 Fax 53 22 47 86

Turenne
Maison des Chanoines
☎ 55 85 93 43
Small restaurant with a few rooms for guests.

Vézac
Near Beynac-et-Cazenac on the D57 to Sarlat
Hôtel Oustal de Vézac***
☎ 53 29 54 21 Fax 53 29 45 65

Swimming pool.

Hôtel-Restaurant Le Relais des 5 Châteaux**
☎ 53 30 30 72 Fax 53 31 19 39
Good food.

Vieux-Mareuil
Auberge de l'Etang Bleu*** (logi)
2km (1 mile) from the village
☎ 53 60 92 63 Fax 53 56 33 20

Châteaux de Vieux Mareuil***
1km (½ mile) southeast on the D939
☎ 53 60 77 15 Fax 53 56 49 33
Swimming pool, facilities for disabled.

Villefranche-du-Périgord
Auberge La Cle des Champs**
Mazeyrolles
☎ 53 29 95 94 Fax 53 28 42 96

La Petite Auberge**
☎ 53 29 91 01

CLIMATE

The weather is fairly uniform over the whole region, but it is no more predictable than it is in Britain. On the whole the spring and autumn are warm and invigorating, the summers can be hot and the winters severe, particularly on the high ground. Occasionally the storms can be quite spectacular with thunder, lightning, hail and heavy rain but even a threatening sky may clear surprisingly quickly to reveal a glorious sunset. Snow is not unknown in March or even April but it melts without causing much trouble although patches are inclined to linger on the mountain peaks of the Massif Central.

Currency & Credit Cards

Visitors may take unlimited currency into France and only bank notes to the value of 50,000FF or more need be declared if they are likely to be re-exported. When shopping around for favourable exchange rates, take into account any commission charges that may be added. The French *franc* (abbreviated F or FF) is divided into 100 *centimes*. Current coins include 5, 10, 20 and 50 *centime* pieces as well as 1, 2, 5 and 10 *franc* pieces. Bank notes come in denominations of 20, 50, 100, 200 and 500 francs.

When changing travellers' cheques banks usually give the best rate of exchange. Travellers' cheques in French francs cost more than Sterling ones initially, but may offset a poor rate of exchange and high commission charges for changing your cheques in France. Do not let anyone charge you for changing franc travellers' cheques — ask in advance, and try another bank if they do.

Most major credit cards, such as Access (Mastercard), American Express and Visa (Carte Bleue in France), are accepted by the majority of large hotels, restaurants, and some shops and garages. However there are exceptions, so if no logo is displayed it is as well to enquire. Eurocheques and travellers' cheques may also be accepted but in out-of-the-way places it would be wise to have adequate French *francs* as well.

Customs Regulations

In the normal course of events, customs regulations no longer apply between member countries of the European Union. However this does not apply to visitors from other countries, who should enquire about the prevailing rules and regulations before leaving home.

Disabled

France is becoming increasingly aware of the needs of disabled visitors. Several towns reserve parking bays for drivers who display disabled discs and some hotels have rooms on the ground floor, but contrary to expectations, not all motels provide easy access for people in wheelchairs. The French Government Tourist Office issue a special information sheet for disabled visitors to France. This is available on application with a stamped addressed envelope.

The Liaison Committee for the Transport of Disabled Persons (Comitée de Liaison pour le Transport des Personnes Handicapées) 34 Avenue Marceau, Paris 8e, and the Ministry of Equipment, Housing, Transport and the Sea (Ministère de l'Equipment, du Logement, des Transports et de la Mer) 92055 Paris, La Defense, Cédex 04, publish a transport guide for the disabled.

The French National Committee of Liaison for the Re-Education of the Disabled (Comité National Français de Liaison pour la Réadaptation des Handicapées), 38 Bld Raspail, Paris 7e, sells two guides for the use of those people with a handicap: *Paris-Guide to Cinemas, Theatres, Concerts* and *Paris — Museums, Libraries, Cultural Centres and Workshops*.

A list of *gîtes* with accommodation for disabled travellers and regional numbers of the APF (Association des Paralyses de France) can be obtained from the central office at:

17 Boulevard Auguste-Blanqui
75013 Paris
☎ 140 78 69 00

Other useful addresses for information are:

Croix Rouge Paris (Red Cross)
1 Place Henri Dunant
75384 Paris
☎ 1 44 43 11 00

Royal Association for Disability and Rehabilitation
25 Mortimer Street
London
W1N 8AB
☎ 0171 637 5400

ELECTRICITY

220 volt AC electricity is available almost everywhere and plugs are two-pin or very occasionally three-pin, which are also round. The supply in some small areas is still at 110 volt. Adaptors will be needed by those people who do not use continental two-pin plugs at home.

PASSPORTS

British nationals only need an ordinary valid passport. With a few minor exceptions in Europe the nationals of every country other than those in the European Union also need a visa.

HEALTH CARE

British travellers have a right to claim health services in France by virtue of EU regulations. Form E111 — available from Post Offices — should be obtained to avoid complications.

American and Canadian visitors will need to check the validity of their personal health insurances to guarantee they are adequately covered. For emergency assistance, dial 19 in all towns. In country areas it may be necessary to phone the local police (*gendarmerie*). Pharmacies, clearly marked with a green cross, can usually deal with minor ailments or advise people where to go if additional help is needed.

MARKETS

Open-air markets are held in towns and villages throughout the region, usually on one, or sometimes two, days a week. They are busy, colourful and interesting quite apart from the fact that nearly everything one needs is instantly available. The farm produce is seasonal and fresh. Everything is on sale from clothes and shoes to flowers and kitchenware, at very competitive prices.

Metric Measurements

1 kilo (1,000 grams) = 2.2lb
1 litre = 1¾ pints
4.54 litres = 1 gallon
8km = 5 miles

Motoring

The speed limits currently applied to French roads are:

Autoroutes	130kph (81mph)
	110kph (68mph)
National (N) roads	110kph (68mph)
	90kph (56mph)
Other roads	90kph (56mph)
	80kph (50mph)
In towns	60kph (37mph)
	60kph (37mph)

The speeds in italics are for wet conditions.

Although all the rules of the road must be observed there are a few which are particularly important. Drinking and driving is one of them. Motorists can be stopped for a breath test anywhere, at any time. Heavy fines are imposed for being over the limit and they have to be paid in cash on the spot. There are also spot fines for speeding, drivers must be over 18 and hold a valid licence, not a provisional one, no children under 10 years old are allowed on the front seat and safety belts are compulsory. Every car must have spare bulbs, especially for the headlights, and, although red triangles are not obligatory for vehicles equipped with hazard warning lights, it is as well to have them in case of an electrical failure or to give plenty of warning to oncoming traffic if their vision is obscured. Dipped headlights must be used in all built-up areas between dusk and daybreak and hooting is forbidden except in an emergency. Stop signs mean exactly what they say and it is an offence to edge slowly up to the line and then move off, even if there is nothing coming in either direction.

Generally speaking French roads are extremely well maintained. Fuel is available almost everywhere, although it is advisable to have a full tank before wandering off into the more sparsely populated areas, especially if you are hoping to pay with a credit card. Cars can be hired in the larger cities and the CSNCRA, 6 Rue Leonardo-de-Vinci, Paris, publishes a list of members who can supply most, if not all, the popular makes. Taxis can only be picked up from a rank or ordered by telephone. They all have meters but the price for an out-of-town trip should be agreed with the driver at the start of the journey to avoid unnecessary arguments later. Expect to tip the driver about 15 per cent of the fare.

When time is of no particular consequence it is often a good idea to plan an individual itinerary, using both major and minor roads to visit some of the outstanding attractions along the way. It may take a trifle longer than using the highways, and mean spending an extra night on the road, but in most cases this adds to rather than detracts from the holiday. It is also much less tiring for a driver who is not used to travelling on the Continent and far less boring for any young children in the party.

Once in the Dordogne area the choice is almost endless because even the byways are usually in a good state of repair and very few of them peter out unexpectedly. They may not always be the quickest or the most satisfactory shortcut from one point to another but most of them are scenically attractive, provide opportunities for pulling off the road to stretch one's legs or have a picnic and carry less traffic than their larger counterparts.

Special Routes

The main tourist offices in both *départements* have devised a series of different itineraries for holiday-makers who are not particularly keen on joining conducted tours but would like to visit as many places of interest as possible. Périgord has suggestions for pre-arranged trips of one to four days which include hotel bookings where necessary. One example is a three-day outing to prehistoric caves and shelters in the Vézère Valley followed by visits to Sarlat and a number of historic *châteaux* such as Beynac, Castelnaud and Les Milandes. Lot has specialised trips of 50km to 150km (31 miles to 93 miles). The Circuit du Vin from Cahors accounts for 120km (74 miles) whereas a round trip along the valleys of the Lot and the Célé involves an additional 40km (25 miles). The Circuit Merveilles, based on Gramat, is another case in point. It includes Rocamadour, the Gouffre de Padirac, St Cère and Castelnau-Bretenoux but only covers about 75km (46 miles) in all.

Other Methods of Transport

There are several other ways of exploring the countryside. Bicycles can be hired in a dozen or more different centres with recommended cycle tracks of varying lengths plus overnight stops where necessary. Riding stables provide horses and ponies for short outings or longer expeditions using bridle paths which also call in at convenient *logis* and *auberges*.

Horse-drawn caravans are available for those with a taste for the gipsy life. Little rustic carriages can be hired for the day and there are even some places where walkers may find a donkey to carry all their extra bits and pieces. Kayaks and canoes are available on all the main rivers, either for an hour or two or for longer trips, in which case there are waterside hamlets and campsites offering food and accommodation. The Grandes Randonnées and the shorter blazed footpaths cater for long distance hikers and enthusiastic ramblers as well as people who only want to do a small part of the journey on foot. The conditions vary from moderately demanding to very easy and can be chosen to suit one's own inclination and ability.

MOTOR INSURANCE

The Green Card is no longer obligatory but full comprehensive cover is advisable. It is as well to check with the motoring organisations.

Opening Hours

Banks are open on weekdays from 9am-12noon and 2-4pm but they are closed all day on either Saturdays or Mondays. They also close early on the day before a bank holiday.

Generally speaking post offices open from 8am to 7pm from Monday to Friday but have half a day off from 12noon on Saturdays. However it is possible that a small country post office may also take time off for lunch. It is useful to know that stamps (*timbres*) are on sale in most news agents and some of the hotels.

Shopping hours also tend to vary somewhat but the usual practice is to open at 9am, close for lunch at 12noon, reopen at 2pm and remain open until 6.30pm or 7.30pm. Large shops in the cities may stay open throughout the lunch hours and supermarkets sometimes do not close before 9pm or 10pm at night. However a great many shops of all descriptions are closed on Mondays, either in the morning or for the whole of the day. Some food shops, especially bakers, open on Sunday mornings for a few hours and there is an occasional Sunday market but they are few and far between.

Check on opening times of privately-owned *châteaux* and small museums as times usually alter according to the season and may well vary from year to year. Most national museums are closed on Tuesdays whereas municipal museums prefer to close on Monday. Entrance fees may be reduced on certain days or for people under 18 or over 65.

Some attractions set out the precise times of guided tours while at others it may be necessary to wait until a guide is available or until a few more people arrive. The most rigid rules apply in the case of prehistoric grottoes filled with cave paintings. Many of them restrict the number of visitors allowed in at the same time and, in some cases, on the same day. Where this applies it is essential to arrive early in the morning to buy a ticket for a tour, particularly in the summer as queues can be long.

Most museums and places of interest, as well as some nature reserves, close for lunch from 12 noon until 2pm although there is a growing tendency to stay open all day in July and August. Churches in general are open both morning and afternoon while others will show people round on request and expect a small contribution towards the upkeep of the building in return. If a quantity of treasure is kept under lock and key it is usually treated as a museum with an entrance fee and specified opening and closing times.

Public Holidays

There are eleven public holidays in France when all the banks, administrative offices and most museums are closed although an occasional shop and several restaurants may be open. They are:
New Year's Day
Easter Monday
Labour Day (1 May)

Ascension Day (6 weeks after Easter)
VE Day (8 May)
Whit Monday (10 days after Ascension Day)
Bastille Day (14 July)
Assumption Day (15 August)
All Saints' Day (1 November)
Armistice Day (11 November)
Christmas Day

SOUVENIRS

Périgord and Lot have all the usual run-of-the-mill souvenirs, with whole shops devoted to them in the main tourist centres. Alternatively it is possible to find attractive or tasty examples, especially in less frequented areas. *Foie gras* and truffles can be bought to take home and so can walnut or plum brandies and bottles of fruit preserved in spirits. Where craftsmen have moved into villages there are attractive and often useful articles made from wood or metal. Weaving and traditional pottery may be worth considering and, very occasionally, something unusual such as the mounted butterflies from the Jardin des Papillons near L'Hospitalet.

TELEPHONES

Telephoning France from the UK, you start with the international access code (00 33). There are no French area codes. For Paris city and Greater Paris dial 00 331 plus eight digits. For rest of country dial 00 33 plus eight digits.

Telephoning the UK from France, you dial 19, wait until the continuous tone recurs, then dial 44 followed by your STD code minus the first 0, and then your number, eg 19-44-21-345-2850. To phone the USA from France 19-1, Canada 19-1, Australia 19-61 followed by the telephone number.

Cheap rates give you 50 per cent extra time: on weekdays between 10.30pm and 8am, and at weekends starting 2pm on Saturdays.

Phonecards, called *télécarte*, operate in most booths. You can buy them from post offices, tobacconists, newsagents, and where advertised on telephone booths. Buy them in the UK from Voyages Vacances Int, 34 Savile Row, London W1X 1AG ☎ 0171 287 3171.

Incoming calls can be received at phone boxes with a blue bell sign.

Emergency Numbers

Fire 18; Police 17; Operator 13; Directory Enquiries 12.

TIPPING

Tips (*pourboires*) or service charges are included in the bill but no-one will object if you leave a little extra to show appreciation for good service or for any other reason. This applies to hotels, restaurants, cafés, bars etc. However guides, cinema attendants, church caretakers and other people doing similar jobs do expect to be given a tip.

Tourist Offices

French Government Tourist Offices

Great Britain

178 Piccadilly
London
WIV OAL
☎ 071 491 7622

USA

610 Fifth Avenue Suite 222
New York
NY 10020-2452
☎ 212 757 1683

Canada

1981 Avenue McGill College
Tour Esso Suite 490
Montreal
Quebec
H3A 2W9
☎ 514 288 4264

Regional Tourist Offices in France

Office Départemental du Tourisme
  de la Dordogne
16 Rue du President Wilson
24009 Périgueux Cedex
☎ 53 53 44 35

Comité Départemental du Tourisme
  du Lot
Chambre de Commerce
BP 79
46002 Cahors Cedex
☎ 65 35 07 09

Local Tourist Information Offices

These are known as either Syndicat
d'Initiative or Office de Tourisme.

Beaulieu-sur-Dordogne
Place Marbot
☎ 55 91 09 94
Open: July to September

Bort-les-Orgues
Place Marmontel
☎ 55 96 02 49

Bourboule, La
Place Hôtel de Ville
☎ 73 81 07 99

Bretenoux
☎ 65 38 40 23

Carennac
☎ 65 38 48 36

Castillon-la-Bataille
Hôtel de Ville
☎ 57 40 00 06

Libourne
Place Abel-Surchamp
☎ 57 51 15 04

Le Mont-Dore
Avenue Général Leclerc
☎ 73 65 20 21

Souillac
Boulevard Malvy
☎ 65 37 81 56

St Emilion
Place des Créneaux
☎ 57 24 72 03

Brantôme
Hôtel de Ville
☎ 53 05 80 52 or 53 05 70 21

Nontron
Rue Verdun
☎ 53 56 00 53 or 53 56 25 50
Open: mid-June to mid-September.

Thiviers
Place Maréchal Foch
☎ 53 55 12 50 or 53 55 19 00

Arnac-Pompadour
At the château entrance.
Closed in November.

St-Yrieix-la-Perche
6 Rue Plaisances
☎ 55 08 14 95
Open: July and August.

Uzerche
Place Lunade
☎ 55 73 15 71
Open: April to September.

Mussidan
9 Rue Libération
☎ 53 81 04 77
Closed February.

Périgueux
1 Avenue Aquitaine
☎ 53 53 10 63

Sorges
Maison de la Truffe
☎ 53 05 90 11
Closed in the morning except during
July and August.

Bergerac
97 Rue Neuve d'Argenson
☎ 53 57 03 11
Closed in the morning out of season.

Beaumont du Périgord
☎ 53 22 39 12
Open: July and August.

Villafranche-du-Périgord
Rue Notre-Dame
☎ 53 29 91 48
Open: June to September.

Domme
Place Halle
☎ 53 28 37 09

Les Eyzies-de-Tayac
Place Mairie
☎ 53 06 97 05
Open: mid-March to October.

Montignac
Place Bertran de Born
☎ 53 51 82 60

Sarlat-la-Canéda
Place Liberté
☎ 53 59 27 67
Avenue Général de Gaulle
☎ 53 59 18 87
Open: July and August.

Gramat
Place Republique
☎ 65 38 73 60
Open: June to mid-September.

Martel
At the Mairie
☎ 65 37 30 03

Rocamadour
Hôtel de Ville
☎ 65 33 62 59
Open: Palm Sunday, Easter and
May to September.

St Céré
Place Republique
☎ 65 38 11 85
Closed mornings out of season.

Gourdon
Allées Republique
☎ 65 41 06 40
Closed afternoons out of season.

Figeac
Place Vival
☎ 65 34 06 25

Cahors
Place Aristide-Briand
☎ 65 35 09 56

Catus
In the Mairie
☎ 65 22 70 31

Luzech
In the Mairie
☎ 65 30 72 32

St Cirq-Lapopie
In the Château de la Gardette
☎ 65 31 23 22

TRAVEL

Nothing could be more simple than getting to the Dordogne, no matter how you intend to travel. There are plenty of alternatives, none of which take a great deal of time, and even the slowest methods have a great deal to recommend them. The choice is just as wide when it comes to moving about locally. As the region is not too extensive it is possible to visit all the main attractions within a week or two but obviously it takes much longer to explore all the highways and byways of both Lot and Périgord.

Air

There are no international flights into either *département* so it is necessary to fly to Paris and then transfer to a domestic airline such as Air Inter for the remainder of the journey. Périgueux, Bergerac, Cahors and Figeac all have their own airports, used primarily by charter companies and light aircraft. Alternatively it is possible to fly to Bordeaux or Toulouse and then hire a car or catch a train. Details are available from travel agents or from the French Government Tourist Offices in London or New York.

Buses and Coaches

France does not provide anything worth mentioning in the way of long-distance coaches but local bus services operate in many of the larger towns and between some country villages. Details of local times and fares can be obtained from the various bus stations and from the information offices. However special tours and excursions are commonplace during the season. They may cover a reasonably wide area or be designed for passengers who have a specific interest such as prehistoric caves, fortified towns, river courses, wine or truffles. Périgueux also offers special lecture tours of the city's Gallo-Roman remains or the old medieval quarter. Several towns in both *départements* lay on guided tours which may be confined to their own attractions or venture much further afield. It is wise to book for these in advance and to find out if the price takes care of all the necessary entrance fees. It is extremely unlikely that the cost of lunch will be included for day-long trips so it is always as well to have enough francs and a little over for such things as postcards and souvenirs. Once again local information offices are the places to find out all the details, although some hotels will also have them at their finger tips.

Rail

Air France and French Railways operate a comined ticket for a flight to Paris and the subsequent train journey, at a competitive, inclusive price. For drivers bringing their own cars Motorail services are available from Paris and the Channel ports to both Brive-la-Gaillarde and Bordeaux, details of which can be obtained from French Railways, 179 Piccadilly, London WIV 0BA ☎ 0171 409 3518 from British Rail and from ABTA travel agents. Motorcycle transport is arranged in the same way as cars while bicycles have their own service to Brive-la-Gaillarde and Bordeaux from Boulogne, except during the winter.

The train journey from Paris to Périgueux lasts about 4 hours, from Toulouse 3 hours and roughly 1¼ hours from Bordeaux. Trains from Paris to Toulouse pass through Cahors and other main stations such as Gourdon, Gramat and Figeac and take only slightly longer.

It is important to remember that rail tickes bought in France must be stamped in the automatic, orange-coloured date stamping machines at the entrance to platforms. Anyone who forgets will be charged 20 per cent extra with a minimum, currently, of 52 francs. It is possible to travel by rail within the two *départements* and some local tours include trains as well as coaches.

Road

The majority of holidaymakers find that motoring is the best way of exploring Périgord and Lot. Driving in France is no more difficult than it is in Britain, provided the basic rules and regulations are observed; remember to keep to the right-hand side of the road. This may need a conscious effort to start with at roundabouts and T-junctions or after using a one-way street. Traffic coming in from the right has priority except on roundabouts or on roads which have automatic right of way and are signposted accordingly — a diamond shape with yellow in the centre surrounded by a white border.

Apart from main roads and *autoroutes* it is not always clear which way signs are pointing, as they are often at an angle, as well as being right on a junction, not before it.

On *autoroutes* a toll is payable. On entry take a ticket, and at the exit hand over the ticket at a kiosk, where you will be charged for the distance travelled.

There are many different ways of getting to Périgord and Lot by road. The quickest, but by no means the most interesting, starts off along the *autoroutes* linking the Channel Ports via Paris, with Orléans, Tours, Poitiers and Bordeaux. Major roads branch off at more or less regular intervals, such as the N147 from Poitiers to Limoges where the N21 heads for Périgueux while the N20 carries on through Brive-la-Gaillarde to Cahors. Both capitals are about the same distance from Paris, 500km (310 miles) in the case of Périgueux and roughly 560-590km (347-366 miles) to Cahors, depending on the route.

Index

Visitor's Guides

Itinerary based guides for independent travellers

MPC

America:
American South West
California
Florida
Massachusetts, Rhode
Island & Connecticut
Orlando & C Florida
USA
Vermont, New Hampshire & Maine

Austria:
Austria
Austria: Tyrol &
Vorarlberg

Britain:
Cornwall & Isles of
Scilly
Cotswolds
Devon
East Anglia
Hampshire & Isle of
Wight
Kent
Lake District
Scotland
Somerset, Dorset &
Wiltshire
N Wales & Snowdonia
North York Moors,
York & Coast
Northern Ireland
Peak District
Treasure Houses of
England
Yorkshire Dales &
North Pennines

Bruges
Canada
Cuba
Czech & Slovak
Republics

Denmark
Egypt

France:
Champagne &
Alsace-Lorraine
France
Alps & Jura
Brittany
Burgundy &
Beaujolais
Dordogne
Gascony & Midi
Pyrenees
Loire
Massif Central
Normandy
Normandy Landing
Beaches
Provence & Côte d'Azur
Vendee & Poitou-
Charentes

Germany:
Bavaria
Black Forest
Northern Germany
Rhine & Mosel
Southern Germany

Greece:
Greece (mainland)
Athens &
Peloponnese

Holland
Hungary
Iceland & Greenland

India:
Delhi, Agra & Rajasthan
Goa

Islands:
Corsica
Crete
Cyprus
Gran Canaria
Guernsey, Alderney &
Sark
Jamaica
Jersey
Madeira
Mallorca, Menorca,
Ibiza & Formentera
Malta & Gozo
Mauritius, Rodrigues
& Reunion
Rhodes
Sardinia
Seychelles
Sri Lanka
Tenerife
Windward Islands

Italy:
Florence & Tuscany
Italian Lakes
Northern Italy
Southern Italy

New Zealand
Norway
Portugal

Spain:
Costa Brava
& Costa Blanca
Northern & Central
Spain
Southern Spain
& Costa del Sol

South Africa
Sweden
Switzerland
Thailand
Turkey

MPC Visitor's Guides are available through all good bookshops. In case of local difficulty, you may order direct (quoting Visa/Access number) from Grantham Book Services on ☎ 01476 67421. Ask for the cash sales department. There is a small charge for postage and packing.